REJECTED F.C. Of Scotland

Volume 1: Edinburgh and The South

Histories of the ex-Scottish League Clubs

ISBN 0 9513321 9 8

By Dave Twydell

Published by:
Yore Publications,
12, The Furrows, Harefield,
Middlesex. UB9 6AT.

© D.A.Twydell 1992

British Library Cataloguing–in–Publication Data
A catalogue record for this book is available from the British Library.

ISBN 0 9513321 9 8

Printed by:
BPCC Wheatons Ltd.

Acknowledgements:

As in the past my grateful thanks are given to many people (almost Worldwide!). The list of people and
organisations below represents the major sources of help that I received in producing this book; there are many
others who have helped with the occasional fact or statistic, who have not been named, but to whom I collectively
offer my gratitude.

The staff of, and facilities provided at, the following:
The National Library of Scotland including the Map Library.
The Scottish Record Office.
(Documents reproduced are with the permission of the Keeper of the Records of Scotland)
The Public Libraries at: Annan, Armadale, Bathgate, Broxburn, Dumfries, Lockerbie & Peebles.
The Scottish Football League.
The British Library including the Newspaper Library and the Map Library.

The following individuals, particularly Bill Gibbs, plus (in random order):
Chris Ambler, Stuart Borrowman, Davy Clark, David Thomson, John Litster, R.B. Boyes, George Campbell, John
Weir, Peter Cogle, David Nivison, Mark Grabowski, Stewart Davidson.

Principle sources of reference:
'A Record of Scottish League Football' (The Association of Football Statisticians)
'The Dale. A History of Armadale Football Club from 1879' (Stuart Borrowman)
'Historic Saints of Edinburgh' (George Campbell)
'Edinburgh City Football Club. City on a downward slide' (George Campbell)
'Scottish non–League Review' (Stewart Davidson)
'The First Hundred Years. The Scottish Football League' (Bob Crampsey)
'Scottish Football League Review 1990–91'
'Non–League' (Bob Barton)
'Marshall Cavendish Book Of Football'
'The Footballer' (magazine)
'The Association of Football Statisticians' reports
Sports Dispatch (Edinburgh), Edinburgh Evening News, (Edinburgh) Evening Dispatch, West Lothian Courier,
Lothians Express, Dumphries and Galloway Standard, Annandale Observer and Advertiser, Peebles Advertiser.

Contents:

Introduction

Readers of my earlier books – 'Rejected F.C. Volumes 1 and 2' (now out of print but re-formatted editions to be available later) will be aware of my approach to the subject of former Football (in this case Scottish) League Clubs. The histories of these Clubs, as related here, cannot be considered as the final definitive answers but are far more detailed than any previous individual Club publications (with a very few exceptions), and certainly more complete than any earlier collective works. My aim has been to give a detailed written history of each Club – prior to each clubs' entry into the Scottish League, whilst in the League, and the subsequent history in the post–League days. In addition reasonably detailed statistics have been assembled on each Club. A good selection of illustrative material has been included, but in respect of many of these clubs – either due to their relatively minor nature and short length of League status or in view of an individual club's short and early life – such items are not easily obtained, despite detailed searches in various directions.

'Rejected F.C.' is a simple phrase used to refer to Football (Scottish, here) League Clubs that were at one time members, but were eventually 'rejected', i.e. voted out. This interpretation is only a loose one, for in some cases the Club in question resigned from the League or folded during the season. Essentially the clubs were members at one time, and are now no longer in the Scottish League.

The following clubs have not been considered for these reasons:
'Ayr' and 'Ayr Parkhouse' – the two combined to become the current 'Ayr United'. 'Dundee Wanderers' – although not directly related, their Ground became that of the current 'Dundee United', and in view of their short existence (and only one season in the League), I consider that they are more readily accepted as part of the United's history. 'Dundee Hibernian' have not been considered here as they were the straight forerunners of 'Dundee United. Conversely 'Clydebank' do have a place as they are not in any way related to the later Scottish League Club of the same name. On this basis there are 33 relevant Scottish Clubs, which have been roughly equally split to form three volumes of Club histories,and based on a broad geographical basis.

In England, the 'rejected' Clubs were almost always a straightforward case of a team being voted out of the Football League, normally following a period of several years when that Club had to apply for re-election on more than one occasion. Similarly that is the case with the majority of the relevant Scottish teams. However, there are a significant number that were 'rejected', due to the dissolving of the Scottish League Division 3, in the mid–1920's – following three struggling seasons – and this explains the relatively high number of 'failed' clubs, as compared to their counterparts in England, where the numbers are well under thirty. Another dissimilarity is the falling along the wayside of the teams in the original Scottish League, where there are only five clubs remaining – of the original ten – whereas in England, of the initial twelve, it was only Accrington F.C. who floundered. Prior to the introduction of automatic relegation and promotion (the

'Pyramid') in England, there were the occasional 'rejected' teams – e.g. Barrow, Southport, Workington, etc., and this process continued into the 1970's. In Scotland there is far more of a 'closed shop' (principally due to wider geographical considerations and the far fewer population concentrations North of the border), and consequently in the last fifty years there have only been three such failures.

Under the *'Major honours and achievements'* heading in the statistical sections, is each team's notable progressions in the Scottish Cup. An explanation of the working of this competition would not be out of place here for readers other than those in Scotland itself – and I suspect a for few of these readers too! In England, subject to various requirements, any Club may enter for the English F.A.Cup (including *amateur* teams from the pre–1974 period). Several hundred hopefuls set out on the way to Wembley in September, and on a very locally regionalised basis the numbers are whittled down, in a straight knock–out manner, until they join the Third and Fourth Division clubs in the first round proper.

In Scotland the structure of football is somewhat different. All Scottish League Clubs are members of the Scottish F.A., together with a number of other 'senior' – but non–Scottish Football League – clubs (by virtue of their current or earlier stature). These teams are the only ones allowed entry into the Scottish Cup. Below this 'senior' level, are clubs that although often part–professional, are known as – rather confusingly – 'Junior clubs', and who compete in their own 'Junior Cup', a rough equivalent to the English F.A.Trophy

competition. The non–League Scottish F.A. member clubs compete in early rounds on a knock–out basis, which are currently regionalised into South and North sections. These two tournaments are played through to the finals, and the two winners become the 'Qualifying Cup Winners' (in earlier years there have been periods when there was only one Qualifying Cup, i.e. not regionalised, and also for a time three geographical regions). Currently the four semi–finalists of each region (eight clubs in total), then join the Scottish League clubs in the first round proper. Between 1907 and 1914 a 'Consolation Cup' was run, which was a knock–out competition for those teams that failed to qualify for the Scottish Cup. This competition for the 'also rans' was not very well supported and hence it was soon abandoned.

The amount of text devoted to each Club varies, and is due to a number of considerations and factors. Obviously a club that lasted for a long period, e.g. Leith Athletic, deserves greater coverage than say Edinburgh City's fairly brief (albeit relatively recent) life. However the likes of, say, Solway Star (a name that is unfamiliar to many) deserves, in my view, comparatively more extensive coverage than the likes of Leith Athletic, simply due to little – if anything – having been written on such a Club in the past. Unfortunately the remote location of some clubs – notably Nithsdale Wanderers (who operated from Sanquhar which was little more than a village) – makes extensive coverage impossible, since they were rarely featured in either National or Local (because there wasn't any!) newspapers. Consequently illustrative items have often been either difficult to come by, or in the case of the big 'City' teams of the last seventy years or so, there is a plethora of material which has had to be reduced to provide a reasonable balance in these books.

Many readers will be aware of my near obsession with the actual Football Grounds, and they will be pleased (or otherwise!), with the attention that I have given to this particular heading. It is my firm opinion that 'The Ground' is the one unchanging (except for the actual change of the home Ground itself) factor that remains constant with respect to a club; the status, the management and even the supporters themselves all change, but the Ground doesn't. The Ground is an important part of any club's history. In addition there is very often no Club left now, but pinpointing the home venue(s) can often be rewarding, with traces (or the actual Ground itself) being left. For the inquisitive these Grounds (or only sites) can be visited today, and with a little imagination the glories (or failures) of yesteryear can be more readily re-enacted in the mind. Armed with this book, if you are passing through Bathgate or Annan, etc., you can always make a slight detour and – on the spot – wallow in a little nostalgia!

In common with my earlier 'Rejected' books, the 'people' (with notable exceptions) have been ignored. I cannot claim to be an authority on all, or any, of these Clubs, and although the research has been detailed it is inevitable that if 'names' were included, there would be inevitable omissions – or some included where the local expert (should one exist) would consider them unjustified!

Finally, spare a thought to the memories of the men (and women) behind these clubs. The 'never–say–die' spirit that kept the name of Leith Athletic alive for so many years despite the overwhelming obstacles, the enthusiasm that ensured the continuance of Edinburgh City (despite their complete lack of success), and the brief glory for the likes of Nithsdale Wanderers, who – for a short period – carved their name on the tree of Scottish Football history.

****

Providing sales of this Volume are successful, then the remaining Clubs will be covered in Volumes 2 & 3 (Therefore if you are pleased with what you read please encourage your friends to buy a copy!)

****

'YORE PUBLICATIONS'
Was established in May 1991 with the intention of publishing (and to a lesser degree selling titles by other Publishers) Football Books, generally with a historic theme, including single Club histories. Previous titles include: 'Rejected F.C. Volumes 1 & 2' (ex–Football League Club histories), 'Grounds For A Change' (former Grounds of Football League Clubs), 'Official History of Cardiff City F.C.', 'The Ironsides' ('Who's Who' of Newport County) etc. If you are not on our mailing list, then the details of such books (by Dave Twydell and other Authors) can be obtained by sending a S.A.E. to:

Yore Publications
Yore Publications **12 The Furrows, Harefield,** **Middx. UB9 6AT.**

The Clubs - and Their locations

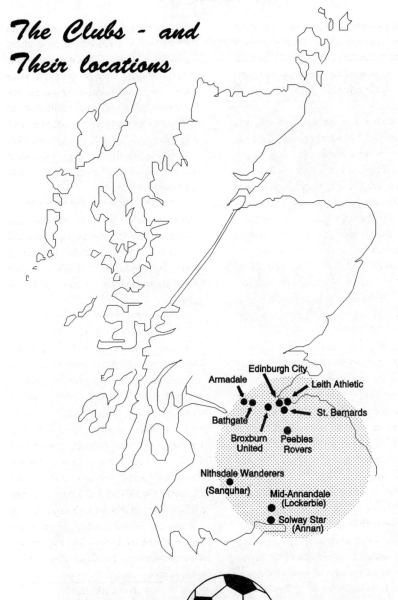

Edinburgh City

Armadale

Leith Athletic

Bathgate

St. Bernards

Broxburn United

Peebles Rovers

Nithsdale Wanderers (Sanquhar)

Mid-Annandale (Lockerbie)

Solway Star (Annan)

Volume 1: Edinburgh & The South

THE SOUTH

(Un–named) **Nithsdale Wanderers**
c. 1902 Team Group (Not taken in Sanquhar)

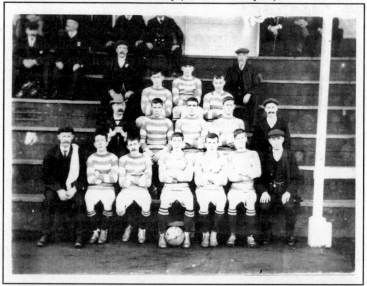

Solway Star 1921/22 Season – Players believed to be '1 –11' order (but not in photo order):
Dalrymple, D.Alexander, McHallum, Martin, Duncan, Harvey, Knox,
Mitchell, Dick, Mitchell, W.Alexander, Wallace (Trainer), Kempsall (Sponsor)

The South.

WINNERS OF QUALIFYING CUP.

Photo by]   *[Hood, Moffat and Lockerbie.*

MID-ANNANDALE TEAM.

Standing—F. Paterson, J. Stewart, L. Lennox, J. M'Alpine, T. Wilson, J. B. Richardson, G. Frew
Sitting—F. Wilson, W. Davis, A. D ickson, C. Dawson, and W. Stewart.
J. Stewart took part in earlier rounds but did not play in the final.

Team Group of the 1926/27 season.

The South.

MID-ANNANDALE

Founded 1910.
Defunct 1935.

League Career

1910 – 1914	Friendly and Cup Matches
1914/15 –	Southern District League.
1915/16 – 1917/18	Inactive.
1918/19 – 1920/21	Friendly and Cup Matches.
1921/22 – 1922/23	Southern Counties League.
1923/24 – 1925/26	**Scottish League Division 3.**
1926/27 –	Alliance League – Southern Division.
1927/28 –	Provincial League.
1928/29 –	South of Scotland League.
1929/30 – 1930/31	Friendly and Cup Matches.
1931/32 – 1932/33	South of Scotland League.
1933/34 – 1935/36	Friendly and Cup Matches.

....

Ground:
Kintail Park.

Record Attendance:
(Probable) 2,100 versus Queen of the South
(Scottish League 1923/24 season)

Colours:
Black and Gold.

Members of Scottish F.A.
1910 – 1936 (Resigned 2nd July)

Major honours and achievements:

Scottish Cup: Third Round (last 16) – 1926/27.
                Second Round – 1920/21.
Qualifying Cup: Winners 1926/27.
Southern Counties Consolation Cup Winners: 1919/20. 1922/23.

Scottish League (Division 3) – Complete Record.

1923/24 season:

August	18	(Away)	2–1	Peebles Rovers.
	25	(Home)	4–3	Helensburgh.
September	8	(Away)	0–2	East Stirling.
	22	(Home)	4–1	Royal Albert.
October	6	(Home)	0–1	East Stirling.
	27	(Away)	0–2	Montrose.
November	3	(Home)	1–3	Queen of the South.
	10	(Away)	2–3	Arthurlie.
	17	(Home)	6–1	Clackmannon.
	24	(Home)	2–0	Nithsdale Wanderers.
December	1	(Home)	4–1	Galston.
	8	(Home)	2–1	Dumbarton Harp.
	15	(Away)	1–2	Beith.
January	1	(Home)	3–3	Helensburgh.
	2	(Away)	3–2	Peebles Rovers.
	5	(Away)	2–3	Brechin City.
February	2	(Away)	2–3	Dykehead.
	16	(Home)	0–0	Dumbarton Harp.
	23	(Away)	0–1	Clackmannon.
March	1	(Home)	2–1	Arthurlie.
	8	(Home)	0–2	Nithsdale Wanderers.
	15	(Home)	2–3	Beith.
	20	(Away)	0–3	Queen of the South.
	22	(Away)	1–1	Royal Albert.
	29	(Home)	0–1	Solway Star.
April	5	(Away)	1–3	Solway Star.
	12	(Home)	1–0	Dykehead.
	19	(Home)	1–1	Montrose.
	22	(Away)	4–1	Galston.
	26	(Home)	6–1	Brechin City.

Played	W	D	L	F	A	Points	Position
30	13	5	12	59	48	31	8th

1924/25 season:

August	23	(Home)	2–2	Montrose.
	30	(Away)	0–4	Peebles Rovers.
September	13	(Home)	4–4	Helensburgh.
	27	(Home)	1–2	Lochgelly.
October	4	(Away)	3–8	Beith.
	11	(Home)	1–1	Dykehead.
	18	(Away)	1–3	Dumbarton Harp. *
	25	(Home)	2–3	Vale of Leven.
November	1	(Away)	1–1	Queen of the South.
	8	(Home)	1–1	Clackmannon.
	15	(Away)	1–2	Solway Star.
	22	(Away)	0–5	Brechin City.
	29	(Home)	1–2	Queen of the South.
December	6	(Home)	4–2	Nithsdale Wanderers.
	13	(Away)	1–4	Vale of Leven.
	20	(Home)	1–0	Leith Athletic.
January	1	(Away)	1–2	Helensburgh.
	3	(Home)	3–2	Peebles Rovers.
	10	(Away)	1–3	Clackmannon.
	17	(Away)	1–1	Dykehead.
	31	(Home)	3–1	Brechin City.
February	7	(Home)	2–2	Galston.
	21	(Away)	2–3	Galston.
	28	(Away)	1–3	Nithsdale Wanderers.
March	7	(Away)	1–2	Montrose.
	14	(Home)	4–1	Royal Albert.
	21	(Away)	0–2	Lochgelly.
	28	(Home)	2–1	Beith.
April	4	(Home)	0–2	Solway Star.
	11	(Away)	0–2	Leith Athletic.
	18	(Away)	3–2	Royal Albert.

* Dumbarton Harp – games not completed (Record Expunged)

Played	W	D	L	F	A	Points	Position
30	7	7	16	47	70	21	15

1925/26 season:

August	15	(Away)	2–4	Brechin.
	22	(Home)	1–3	Solway Star.
	29	(Away)	0–3	Royal Albert.
September	12	(Home)	0–3	Lochgelly.
October	10	(Away)	1–3	Forfar.
	17	(Home)	4–1	Dykehead.
	24	(Away)	1–1	Johnstone.
	31	(Home)	4–0	Beith.
November	14	(Home)	1–0	Montrose.
	21	(Away)	4–2	Peebles Rovers.
	28	(Away)	2–3	Clackmannan.
December	5	(Home)	3–1	Vale of Leven.
	19	(Home)	2–1	Forfar.
	12	(Away)	0–2	Galston. *
	26	(Home)	3–1	Peebles Rovers.
January	1	(Home)	1–0	Helensburgh.
	2	(Away)	1–0	Solway Star.
	9	(Away)	1–2	Dykehead.
	30	(Away)	0–4	Montrose.
February	6	(Home)	5–2	Clackmannon.
	13	(Away)	0–2	Helensburgh.
	27	(Home)	3–1	Leith Athletic.
March	6	(Away)	1–0	Lochgelly.
	13	(Home)	2–0	Royal Albert.
	20	(Home)	1–1	Brechin.
	27	(Away)	0–2	Beith.
April	3	(Away)	2–2	Vale of Leven.
	10	(Away)	2–6	Leith Athletic.
	24	(Away)	1–1	Johnstone.

* Galston did not complete fixtures, but record allowed to stand.

Played	W	D	L	F	A	Points	Position
29	14	3	12	50	54	31	6th

SOLWAY STAR
Founded 1911. Defunct 1946.

League Career:

1911 – 1914	Friendly and Cup Matches
1914/15 –	Southern District League.
1915/16 – 1917/18	Inactive.
1918/19 – 1920/21	Friendly and Cup Matches.
1921/22 –	Southern Counties League.
1922/23 –	Western League.
1923/24 – 1925/26	**Scottish league Division 3.**
1926/27 –	Alliance League – Southern Division.
1927/28 –	Provincial League.
1928/29 –	South of Scotland League.
1929/30 –	Friendly and Cup Matches.
1930/31 – 1932/33	South of Scotland League. †
1933/34 – 1938/39	Friendly and Cup Matches.
1939/40 – 1944/45	Inactive.
1945/46 –	Friendly and Cup Matches.
1946/47 –	South of Scotland League.

† Resigned during 1931/32 season.

....

Ground:
1911 – 1921: Greenlea Park (Also known as Mafeking Park?)
1921 – 1947: Kimmeter Park Green
Record Attendance: 2,000+ Versus Vale of Leven
         (Scottish Cup 2nd Round replay 1924/25)
Colours:
Black and Gold.
Members of Scottish F.A.
1912 – 1916 (Expelled – non payment of subscription)
1919 – 1940 (Resigned)
Major honours and achievements:
Scottish Cup: Third Round (last 16) – 1924/25.
        Second Round – 1920/21. 1936/37.
Southern Counties – Consolation Cup Winners: 1913/14
Southern Counties Cup Winners: 1912/13
Charity Cup Winners: 1913/14   Potts Cup Winners: 1912/13.

....

Scottish League (Division 3) – Complete Record.

1923/24 season:

August	18	(Away)	0–2	Galston.
	25	(Home)	2–1	Peebles Rovers.
September	8	(Home)	2–3	Royal Albert.
	22	(Away)	1–3	Dumbarton Harp.
	6	(Away)	2–3	Arthurlie.
October	13	(Home)	1–0	Beith.
	20	(Away)	1–2	Nithsdale Wanderers.
	27	(Home)	1–1	Clackmannon.
November	10	(Home)	0–0	Dumbarton Harp.
	17	(Home)	3–3	East Stirling.
	24	(Away)	1–5	Montrose.
December	1	(Home)	2–1	Helensburgh.
	8	(Away)	2–0	Brechin
	15	(Home)	2–0	Arthurlie.
	29	(Home)	1–1	Brechin.
January	1	(Away)	2–2	Peebles Rovers.
	2	(Home)	4–1	Galston.
	5	(Away)	1–1	Queen of the South.
	12	(Home)	3–1	Montrose.
February	2	(Away)	1–1	Helensburgh.
	16	(Away)	1–1	East Stirling.
	23	(Home)	0–1	Nithsdale Wanderers.
March	1	(Away)	0–1	Dykehead.
	8	(Away)	3–3	Royal Albert.
	22	(Home)	3–0	Dykehead.
	29	(Away)	1–0	Mid–Annandale.
April	5	(Home)	1–3	Mid–Annadale.
	12	(Home)	0–2	Queens of the South.
	19	(Away)	1–2	Clackmannon.
	21	(Away)	0–4	Beith.

Played	W	D	L	F	A	Pts.	Pos.
30	9	9	12	42	50	27	11th

1924/25 season:

August	16	(Home)	4–1	Brechin.
	23	(Away)	3–2	Beith.
	30	(Home)	1–0	Leith Athletic.
September	13	(Home)	1–0	Montrose.
	20	(Away)	2–0	Brechin.
	27	(Away)	2–0	Clackmannon.
October	11	(Home)	1–1	Queen of the South.
	18	(Home)	2–1	Helensburgh.
	25	(Away)	1–1	Dykehead
November	1	(Home)	3–2	Galston.
	8	(Away)	0–3	Nithsdale Wanderers.
	15	(Home)	2–1	Mid–Annandale.
	29	(Away)	0–2	Royal Albert.
December	6	(Away)	0–1	Galston.
	13	(Home)	0–0	Nithsdale Wanderers.
	20	(Away)	0–4	Queen of the South.
	22	(Home)	7–1	Dumbarton Harp. †
	27	(Home)	2–1	Peebles Rovers.
January	3	(Home)	5–0	Beith.
	10	(Away)	0–0	Helensburgh.
	17	(Away)	2–1	Montrose.
	31	(Away)	0–0	Vale of Leven.
February	14	(Away)	1–2	Lochgelly.
	28	(Away)	3–2	Leith Athletic.
March	7	(Home)	0–0	Vale of Leven.
	14	(Away)	1–1	Peebles Rovers.
	21	(Home)	0–0	Clackmannon.
	28	(Home)	1–0	Lochgelly.
April	4	(Away)	2–0	Mid–Annandale.
	11	(Home)	1–1	Dykehead.
	13	(Home)	1–0	Royal Albert.

† Dumbarton Harp – games not completed (Record Expunged)

Played	W	D	L	F	A	Pts.	Pos.
30	15	10	5	14	28	40	3rd.

1925/26 season:

August	15	(Home)	1–6	Vale of Leven.
	22	(Away)	3–1	Mid–Annandale.
	29	(Home)	2–1	Forfar.
September	5	(Home)	1–2	Montrose.
	12	(Away)	5–2	Beith.
	26	(Away)	1–1	Helensburgh.
October	10	(Home)	2–1	Galston.
	17	(Away)	0–5	Peebles Rovers.
	24	(Home)	5–2	Royal Albert.
November	21	(Away)	2–4	Montrose.
	28	(Home)	0–0	Leith Athletic.
December	12	(Home)	0–2	Helensburgh.
	26	(Home)	0–0	Clackmannon.
January	1	(Away)	3–4	Clackmannon.
	2	(Home)	0–1	Mid–Annandale.
	9	(Away)	1–4	Forfar.
	16	(Away)	1–4	Royal Albert.
	30	(Home)	0–3	Brechin.
February	13	(Home)	1–1	Lochgelly.
	20	(Away)	2–3	Johnstone.
	27	(Away)	2–1	Vale of Leven.
March	6	(Home)	7–1	Peebles Rovers.
	13	(Home)	2–1	Dykehead.
	20	(Home)	2–1	Beith.
	27	(Away)	0–2	Leith Athletic.
April	3	(Home)	2–3	Johnstone.
	10	(Away)	2–2	Dykehead.
	17	(Away)	2–3	Brechin.
	24	(Away)	1–1	Lochgelly.

Played	W	D	L	F	A	Pts.	Pos.
29	9	6	14	50	62	24	11th

NITHSDALE WANDERERS

Founded (probable) 1897. Defunct 1964.

League Career:

1897 – 1908	Friendly and Cup Matches
1908/09 – 1910/11	Football Combination. †
1911/12 – 1914/15	Scottish Union. †
1915/16 – 1918/19	Inactive.
1919/20 – 1921/22	Friendly and Cup Matches.
1922/23 –	Western League.
1923/24 – 1924/25	**Scottish League Division 3.**
1925/26 – 1926/27	**Scottish League Division 2.**
1927/28 –	Provincial League.
1928/29 – 1929/30	Scottish Alliance.
1930/31 – 1931/32	Friendly and Cup Matches.
1932/33 –	South of Scotland League.
1933/34 – 1934/35	Friendly and Cup Matches.
1935/36 – 1937/38	Football Combination.
1938/39 –	Friendly and Cup Matches.
1939/40 – 1945/46	Inactive.
1946/47 – 1949/50	South of Scotland.
1950/51 – 1962/63	Western League (Ayrshire Region)
1963/64 –	Inactive.

† Fixtures not completed in 1910/11 and 1914/15 seasons.

....

Ground:

1896 – 1920: Castleholm.

1920 – 1963: Crowick Holm.

Record Attendance: (Probable)4,200 (£199 receipts)

Versus Queen of the South. (Scottish Cup 1924/25)

Colours: Blue and White.

Members of Scottish F.A.

1897 – 1963.

Major Honours and Achievements:

Scottish League Division 3: Champions 1924/25.

Scottish Cup: Third Round (last 16) – 1920/21 1922/23

Second Round – 1902/03 1910/11 1913/14 1927/28 1929/30 1937/38 1947/48

Football Combination: (Joint) Champions 1909/10.

Southern Counties: Cup Winners: 1903/04 1906/07 1910/11 1911/12

1913/14 1919/20 1921/22 1922/23.

Charity Cup Winners: 1910/11 1912/13.

Potts Cup Winners: 1908/09 1909/10 1913/14 1919/20 1922/23.

Scottish League (Division 3) – Complete Record.

1923/24 season

August	18	(Away)	3–1	Clackmannon.
	25	(Home)	5–0	Brechin
September	8	(Away)	3–2	Galston.
	22	(Home)	1–1	Queen of the South.
	29	(Away)	1–2	Royal Albert.
October	6	(Home)	3–1	Royal Albert.
	13	(Away)	1–2	Montrose.
	20	(Home)	2–1	Solway Star.
	27	(Away)	0–0	Helensburgh.
November	3	(Home)	3–2	Peebles Rovers.
	10	(Away)	0–4	East Stirling.
	24	(Away)	0–2	Mid–Annandale.
December	1	(Home)	3–0	Montrose.
	8	(Away)	1–2	Arthurlie.
	15	(Home)	2–0	Helensburgh.
	22	(Away)	0–1	Dumbarton Harp.
January	1	(Away)	3–3	Brechin.
	5	(Away)	0–0	Peebles Rovers.
	12	(Home)	0–0	East Stirling.
	19	(Home)	0–1	Arthurlie
February	2	(Away)	0–3	Beith.
	9	(Home)	1–0	Dykehead.
	16	(Away)	0–0	Queen of the South.
	23	(Away)	1–0	Solway Star.
March	1	(Home)	1–1	Clackmannon.
	8	(Home)	2–0	Mid–Annandale.
	15	(Away)	0–2	Dykehead.
	22	(Home)	0–4	Dumbarton Harp
April	5	(Home)	4–0	Galston.
	19	(Home)	2–0	Beith

Played	W	D	L	F	A	Pts.	Pos.
30	13	7	10	42	35	33	6th

1924/25 season

August	16	(Home)	3–2	Leith Athletic.
	23	(Away)	4–1	Dumbarton Harp. †
	30	(Home)	1–1	Lochgelly.
September	13	(Away)	1–1	Brechin.
	20	(Home)	4–0	Dykehead.
	27	(Home)	0–0	Dumbarton Harp. †
October	2	(Away)	1–2	Queen of the South.
	11	(Home)	4–3	Helensburgh.
	25	(Away)	2–0	Montrose.
November	8	(Home)	3–0	Solway Star.
	15	(Away)	2–0	Lochgelly.
	22	(Home)	4–0	Galston.
	29	(Away)	0–0	Leith Athletic.
December	6	(Away)	2–4	Mid–Annandale.
	13	(Away)	0–0	Solway Star.
	20	(Home)	3–1	Beith.
	27	(Away)	1–1	Dykehead.
January	1	(Home)	3–1	Clackmannon.
	3	(Away)	1–1	Galston.
	10	(Home)	7–1	Peebles Rovers.
	17	(Home)	5–3	Brechin.
	31	(Home)	6–2	Royal Albert.
February	7	(Home)	2–0	Queen of the South.
	14	(Away)	2–2	Vale of Leven.
	21	(Home)	6–1	Vale of Leven.
	28	(Home)	3–1	Mid–Annandale.
March	7	(Away)	4–1	Royal Albert.
	21	(Away)	2–3	Peebles Rovers.
	28	(Away)	0–4	Helensburgh.
April	4	(Away)	1–0	Clackmannon.
	11	(Away)	0–3	Beith.
	18	(Home)	8–0	Montrose.

† Dumbarton Harp – games not completed (Record Expunged)

Played	W	D	L	F	A	Pts.	Pos.
30	18	7	5	81	40	43	1st

1925/26 season – Second Division:

August	15	(Away)	1–4	Dunfermline.
	22	(Home)	3–1	East Stirling.
	29	(Away)	4–2	Armadale.
September	5	(Home)	5–1	Dumbarton.
	12	(Away)	4–2	Alloa Athletic.
	19	(Home)	3–2	Queen of the South.
	26	(Away)	0–3	Stenhousemuir.
October	3	(Home)	3–0	Albion Rovers.
	10	(Away)	2–0	Broxburn United.
	17	(Home)	1–0	Third Lanark.
	24	(Away)	1–1	Bathgate.
	31	(Home)	0–0	Bo'ness.
	14	(Home)	3–3	East Fife.
November	7	(Away)	0–2	Clyde.
	21	(Away)	2–2	Kings Park.
	28	(Away)	1–6	Ayr United.
	5	(Home)	2–1	St. Bernards.
December	12	(Home)	3–1	Arthurlie.
	23	(Away)	1–4	Arbroath.
	26	(Home)	4–0	Broxburn United.
January	1	(Away)	3–0	Queen of the South.
	4	(Away)	2–2	Dumbarton.
	2	(Home)	4–2	Armadale.
	9	(Home)	2–1	Bathgate.
	16	(Away)	1–4	Bo'ness.
	30	(Home)	2–5	Kings Park.
February	6	(Home)	1–3	Ayr United.
	13	(Away)	6–6	Arthurlie.
	17	(Away)	0–3	Albion Rovers.
	20	(Home)	0–3	Alloa Athletic.
	27	(Home)	2–3	Arbroath.
March	6	(Away)	2–3	East Stirling.
	13	(Home)	0–1	Dunfermline.
	20	(Home)	5–1	Stenhousemuir.
	27	(Away)	1–1	St. Bernards.
April	3	(Home)	0–2	Clyde.
	9	(Away)	2–3	Third Lanark.
	24	(Away)	2–4	East Fife.

Played	W	D	L	F	A	Pts.	Pos.
38	15	7	16	78	102	37	12th

1926/27 season – Second Division:

August	14	(Home)	2–1	Third Lanark.
	21	(Home)	1–1	Queen of the South.
	28	(Home)	2–2	Armadale.
September	4	(Away)	2–7	East Stirling.
	11	(Home)	2–2	Stenhousemuir.
	18	(Away)	0–1	Raith Rovers.
	25	(Home)	3–0	Dumbarton.
October	2	(Away)	0–2	Forfar Athletic.
	9	(Home)	2–2	Ayr United.
	16	(Away)	2–5	Alloa Athletic.
	23	(Away)	0–1	St. Bernards.
	30	(Home)	3–3	Kings Park.
November	6	(Home)	3–1	East Fife.
	13	(Away)	1–7	Arthurlie.
	20	(Home)	2–2	Albion Rovers.
	27	(Away)	0–3	Bo'ness.
December	4	(Home)	4–0	Bathgate.
	11	(Away)	0–2	Arbroath.
	18	(Away)	1–4	Clydebank.
	25	(Away)	0–1	Third Lanark.
January	1	(Away)	1–2	Queen of the South.
	3	(Away)	1–5	Armadale.
	8	(Home)	2–1	East Stirling.
	15	(Away)	4–3	Stenhousemuir.
	29	(Home)	2–4	Raith Rovers.
February	12	(Home)	2–0	Forfar Athletic.
	16	(Away)	2–6	Dumbarton.
	19	(Away)	0–4	Ayr United.
	26	(Home)	0–3	Alloa Athletic.
March	5	(Home)	2–3	St. Bernards.
	12	(Away)	2–2	Kings Park.
	19	(Away)	3–5	East Fife.
	26	(Home)	3–1	Arthurlie.
April	2	(Away)	2–2	Albion Rovers.
	9	(Home)	1–1	Bo'ness.
	16	(Away)	0–3	Bathgate.
	23	(Home)	2–3	Arbroath.
	30	(Home)	3–4	Clydebank.

Played	W	D	L	F	A	Pts.	Pos.
38	7	9	22	59	100	23	20th

Wandering 'Stars' of the South.

The South of Scotland, despite the large area that it covers, has never been a football stronghold. This is principally due to the dearth of towns in the region. The only concentration of population, of any consequence, is Dumfries where of course there is current Scottish League representation in the shape of Queen Of The South. With a population of less than 35,000, this is hardly sufficient to sustain a top Club.

Stranraer, a nightmare journey – in respect of distance – for all opponents, is situated at the extreme Western tip of the area, but with its population of around 10,000 the chances of the big time are remote to say the least. Yet against this background, a wilderness from a football point of view, there emerged – albeit for only a short period – three more football teams that rose to Scottish League status. Rather like the representatives from Dumfries, they all chose to have names that did not include the town from whence they came, a trait that is repeated a number of times elsewhere in Scotland, yet is very rare for their contemporaries from South of the Border. The quaint titles help to provide an almost romantic quality about these teams. Of the trio to be dealt with here, the representatives from Annan, viz. 'Solway Star' provide the biggest catchment area, with a population of over 8,000.

Whilst it must be appreciated that there is the potential of a vastly larger area than the town itself it must be remembered that habitation–wise this is a fairly barren part of the British Isles, and travel between centres, particularly pre–1940, was not easily accomplished. Indeed it is a tribute to the football enthusiasts that they were ever able to raise professional teams and play on equal (or perhaps unequal) terms with their urban brothers.

'Mid–Annandale' who hailed from Lockerbie, in size barely qualifies as a town, for even now the population is under 4,000. But 'Nithsdale Wanderers' who were based at Sanquhar must surely be regarded with the most respect. Barely on a main route – the little town is located around 20 miles off of the main Carlisle to Glasgow road – they not only achieved Scottish League status, but were actually promoted, and for one season even held their own with the big city Clubs of the Second Division, which at this time included the likes of Dunfermline, Clyde, Ayr and Third Lanark.

Nithsdale Wanderers come on the Scene:

The Scottish League first appeared in the 1890/91 season, although of course football had been played for many years before. No doubt it was also played in the South of Scotland, but this was at such a minor level that such contests rarely got a mention in the local Press. To properly identify the origins of the Nithsdale Wanderers club of Sanquhar is very difficult since Nithsdale refers to a large general area, and teams with similar names that were mentioned could well have been based as far South as Dumfries. Indeed one of the earlier references of a football team during the 1895/96 season, referred to Nithsdale and Nithsdale Swifts (conceivably the first and reserve elevens of the same Club), who played at Kingholm Park – in Dumfries. Upper Nithsdale Wanderers who competed for the Southern Counties Cup that season also received rare mentions. In view of the similarity of the later Scottish League team's name, and the fact that Sanquhar is located in the upper (i.e. Northern) reaches of Nithsdale, then it is a reasonable assumption that the two were one of the same. A magazine published in the 1940's refers to the Club celebrating it's Jubilee (presumably diamond) in 1949, therefore this would give the founding year as 1899. But since the Club were first admitted into the Scottish Football Association in 1897, it would appear that, c.1895 is the more correct date. Whatever the correct one, it was to be only a few years before the Club achieved some notable honours!

In the 1902/03 season, the Wanderers won the Annandale Cup by beating Maxwelltown Volunteers 3–2 in the final. The match was played at High Croft Park in Annan (Maxwelltown's Ground was at Palmerston Park, a Ground that was destined to become the home of Queen Of The South from their formation in 1919), but following a protest by the Volunteers, the match was replayed at Alexandra Park, also in Annan. Before a crowd of 500, the Wanderers repeated their victory, this time with a 2–1 scoreline. The final of the Dumfries and Galloway Cup was also reached, after beating Annan United by three unopposed goals at Alexandra Park before 300 spectators. Yet again there was a protest, this time regarding the eligibility of Galacher. On this occasion the protest was overruled, but Nithsdale lost in the final when they played the Maxwelltown team again. But without doubt the Club's finest achievement was their run in the Scottish Cup. They fought through to the first round proper, at which stage they beat Orion – after two postponements due to the bad weather – by the only goal of the match, at home.

By reaching the second round, the Club were down to the last sixteen, but they were then in opposition to the might of Dundee. The Club accepted the offer of £50 to 'reverse' the tie and play at Dundee – a figure that was thought by many to be too low. The result was no shock as the homesters demolished the non-Leaguers by 7-0! In the Southern Counties Charity Cup, the Wanderers easily deposed of Vale of Dryfe (at Palmerston Park) in the semi-finals, but in a third Cup meeting with Maxwelltown, they lost in the Final. The Wanderers completed a very successful season, for the first defeat (other than the Scottish Cup match) did not come until one of the last games when they were easily beaten in a Friendly at Thornhill, with a 0-4 scoreline. A bad tempered game, was frequented with bad language and two missed penalties by the visitors in the second half.

Nithsdale's Ground at this time was at Castleholm, to the South of the town, behind the old Castle ruins. It is notable that only Cup matches and Friendly encounters were played then, and for some years afterwards. With the limited opposition and relatively long distance travelling required for all but a few matches, a suitable League competition was not practical. And so there was a succession of games against the same Clubs.

The Club had another good run in the Scottish Cup during the 1903/04 season when they were only eliminated at the 1st round stage. Kilmarnock were the victors, but only by a 2-1 scoreline, and this after two drawn games. In the Scottish Qualifying Cup Competition, the 5th round was reached. Douglas Wanderers were beaten in the 3rd round at Castleholm before a 'large turnout of spectators', and the 4th round match was won in a home replay. In terrible weather, and before only a few spectators the 6th GRV (a military team) were beaten 3-0. The run came to an end at Ayr with a 0-3 result. Although drawn at home, the Wanderers were happy to reverse the tie for £30 and half the gate, over £50.

The Club had by now become one of the leading outfits in the area. In the 1905/06 season, the Wanderers once again reached the 1st round of the Scottish Cup, but on this occasion they lost to the Heart Of Midlothian team. In 1909, the Club were able to at last enter a suitable League, the Scottish Combination. This League had been founded in 1896, and catered for the Reserve teams of the Scottish League and the leading non-League teams in the large, but broadly Southern, area of the country. The Club's first season in League competition came to an exciting end as they challenged strongly for the Championship.

After many Cup matches, there was a fixture build-up, and the match at the Ground of the 5th King's Own Scottish Borderers (from Maxwelltown) was played as a 'double-header' (i.e. the one scoreline determined the results of both the home and the away matches). The 3-1 victory was enough to ensure a play-off with the other League leaders, Girvan. But it appears that this decider never took place and so the Championship was shared! The excitement was reserved not only for League matches, since a good run in the Scottish Consolation Cup ensued.

In the 4th round, and aided by 250 enthusiastic Sanquharians in a crowd of 2,000 at Lanemark, the homesters were beaten, in a match marred by the rough tactics of the losers. The next round saw the East Stirlingshire team beaten at Castleholm before a large gate that produced receipts of £13.20p. This took the Wanderers through to the semi-final stage, at which point they entertained Arthurlie. The prospect of the match produced great excitement in the little town of Sanquhar, and attracted a probable record attendance of 1,500 with match receipts of nearly £30. But an appearance in the Final was not to be, as the visitors - together with 350 noisy supporters - won the game by 3-2.

The Club's experience of Combination football was destined to be shortlived, for with a membership of only seven teams in both their first and second seasons, the matches for the 1910/11 season were never completed! But at least the Club were able to maintain a fairly full fixture list with the inevitable Cup Competitions. They reached the 2nd round proper of the Scottish Cup after several notable victories. In the 2nd qualifying round, Hurlford were beaten at Castleholm by four unopposed goals before a good attendance of around 700, and they then triumphed in the next round at the Ground of Wishaw Thistle. This game produced a record attendance for the home team of around 4,000 (with 250 from Nithsdale) and match receipts of over £68.

A new record crowd for Nithsdale was present, 2,000, for the visit and victory over Johnstone in the 4th qualifying round when the town was invaded by 600 away fans. After a 3-1 home win over Inverness Caledonians, the Wanderers finally narrowly lost by the only goal (in a replay) in the game at Motherwell. For the sum of £65 plus travelling expenses the Wanderers agreed to play the first match in Motherwell, on February the 11th. The non-Leaguers nearly caused a sensation for although the result was a scoreless draw, many of the 5,000 present considered that the minnows were unlucky not to have won. The replay, at the same venue, finished with a scrambled 1-0 win to the Scottish

League team. Two years later another good run took them to the first round, when Kilmarnock were the victors.

In the run–up to the First World War, the team turned their attention to the Scottish Union for league competition. This competition was a successor to the Scottish Alliance, a League which was to appear and disappear on several occasions from 1891 until 1940. Once again it was difficult to find sufficient suitable competing Clubs, and the Wanderers had no real success in this League before the Union folded during the 1914/15 season. The Club were the holders of the Southern Counties Charity Cup (and also won it in 1911) and reached the Final in the 1913/14 season, when they lost by 1–4 (the heaviest defeat of the season) to Solway Star, the new and rapidly rising Club from Annan. But by capturing the Southern Counties Cup, they recorded their 5th success in only eleven years.

The Annan team were well beaten one year later when the Wanderers scored six goals without reply, in the Scottish Qualifying Cup Competition, and they carried on to the second round yet again. This time they were defeated at Partick Thistle. But with the war in Europe, football began to take on only a minor importance, and the Club rapidly wound down (they scratched from the Southern Counties Cup) for the inevitable period of inactivity.

The Rising Star of Solway:

There is no doubt that Annan had football representation at a reasonable level prior to, and around, the turn of the century. The town frequently hosted the finals of several local (South of Scotland) Cup Competitions, at both High Croft Park and Alexandra Park, the latter being known as Mill Park until 1901. But it was not until the formation of Solway Star in 1911 that any serious attempt was made to promote a Senior status Club. Annan United existed in the late 1890's, and Annan F.C. at the turn of the century – and at this time there were definitely two separate Clubs in the town) – Annan Athletic around 1908 (who played in the Carlisle and District League) and Annan Juniors as recently as the 1910/11 season – when the latter entered for the Scottish Junior Cup. But all four faded away without any real impression being made. Just before the emergence of the new Mid–Annan Club, the only team in the town was 'Our Boys F.C.'. Although not related, there was also a 'Star (Annan)' – in 1895 – and an Annan Wanderers in the 1911/12 season!

But in August 1911, it was decided by a large and enthusiastic gathering that it was time that there should be a team of sufficient status to fully represent the town. Jack Higgins was elected as Secretary, and several 'first class' Players were signed on. It was decided that there was no suitable League that the Club could apply for entry into, and so, at least for the first season, Friendly matches would be relied upon for fixtures, plus attempts to win the Southern Counties and Annandale Challenge Cups. Greenlea Park, in the town centre (which had previously been used for football matches) was chosen as a home Ground. There appears to have been an abundance of suitable venues for apart from those previously mentioned, there was also Caledonian Park which was used by Annan Juniors. A large and enthusiastic gathering of spectators was present for the first game by the new Club on the 31st of August. In ideal weather, the Dumfries Amateurs team were the visitors, with the homesters line-up consisting of:

Burns, Sharkey, Connor, F.Crombie, Richardson, Kenny,
Cheeney, Saunderson, Henderson, J.Crombie and Rae.

In the 26th minute, J.Crombie became the first ever Solway Star goalscorer, and Saunderson made it 2-0 from the penalty spot, before half-time. During the second half, Cheeney retired with a knee injury, but this did not stop the new team by winning with a 5-2 scoreline.

On the 14th of September, another large crowd was present to see a scoreless draw with Thornhill, and one week later the Club's first Cup match was played. The prestigious team from Maxwelltown, the 5th K.O.S.B., were the visitors to Greenlea Park, and the Annan Town Band provided the half-time entertainment. The fans, who paid 4d. (2p) at the entrance gate, were well pleased with the homesters surprising 2-1 victory. In the next round after a draw at Mid-Annandale (which attracted a large attendance), the replay also ended up undecided. An exciting game finished at 2-2, when much interest was generated from the special train load of 200 visiting supporters. The final decider was won by Solway by 4-3 after a single goal half-time lead. Stranraer scratched from the 3rd round match, which put Solway into the final. Although this game was lost to Nithsdale Wanderers, to have reached thus far was a great achievement by the newcomers.

In the Annandale Junior Cup, the Star surprisingly lost to the 'Our Boys' team with a 4-2 scoreline, which was played at yet another football venue in Annan, the Cricket Field.

Despite the apparent abundance of pitches, Greenlea Park was probably the best equipped. It was no doubt enclosed, and had dressing Rooms on the Ground. There was also a Pavilion, which was enlarged during the season, and a cinder path was laid around the pitch. The Club's early successes came up to the founder's expectations, and in November 1912, they were honoured when their application to join the Scottish Football Association was accepted. However a small town team were always going to have a financial struggle, but a Benefit Concert for Club Funds raised the encouraging sum of over £12. By the end of the 1913/14 season the Club had established themselves as a formidable outfit. When they beat Nithsdale Wanderers 4-1 in the final of the Southern Counties Charity Cup, and they received their fourth trophy in just two seasons. The game was played at Eastfield Park, Dumfries, and produced gate receipts of £29. That season also saw the Star fight through to the 4th round of the Scottish Consolation Cup. Mid-Annandale were first easily overcome by 6-2 at Greenlea Park, and this was followed with an 8-2 thrashing of Stranraer. The end came at the hands of Johnstone, but only after a replay. The first match, in Annan, was played on the 14th of February, and attracted a full house of 2,000 (aided by two trainloads of visiting fans), to easily create a new record attendance at the Ground. Six goals were shared, but the Annan team lost the replay with a 1-4 scoreline. Further success came when the Club won the Southern Counties Consolation Cup and their progress included another win over Mid-Annandale.

The Club still depended on Friendly matches for fixtures, but their reputation was tarnished in the game versus the 5th K.O.S.B. from Campbelltown. The anticipated sporting encounter developed into a free-for-all, in which both players and spectators took part, although the Solway Club eventually came out well on top (in the footballing sense), with an 8-2 victory. The 1914/15 season saw the crowds dwindling as many players and fans were lost to the impending War. Ironically this campaign saw the Club enter their first League, the Southern District, but with only eight teams this was insufficient to provide a full fixture list. In the home match versus Dumfries, Colonel Irving made an appeal for men to volunteer for the War effort, and by the season's end there was little option but for the Club to close down until hostilities had ended.

The men from Lockerbie:

The history of football in Lockerbie dates back to the late 1870's. Before this era, Rugby was the dominant winter field sport, but following a visit by the renowned Queens Park team, in 1877, the first *Mid-Annandale* Club was formed. Other teams quickly sprang up in the area, but the Mid–Annandale outfit soon became the major force, and eventually entered for the Scottish Cup. Their most notable achievement was in the 1891/92 season when they were drawn to play Orion (the forerunners of the current Aberdeen Club) at the granite City's Ground. This was a very long journey, but when their hosts refused to guarantee a gate share that would pay the fares for fifteen Mids. players and officials, a compromise was reached when both Clubs agreed to meet 'halfway' – and stage the game in Falkirk! This match was a disaster as it was abandoned after only ten minutes. The Mids. eventually agreed to play in Aberdeen, and romped away with a six (two disputed) goals to two victory. The Lockerbie team were unceremoniously dumped out of the Cup in the second round when they lost by 11–2 to Cowlairs.

In their early years, it was rumoured that Blackburn Rovers got to hear of a good Mid–Annandale full–back, and arranged to play a Christmas fixture with the border team. The Mids. were supposedly informed of the Rovers intentions, and not wishing to lose their star, on the day they used a 'substitute' player – with the same name. Unknowing of this deception, the Rovers were duly impressed with 'their' man, and promptly signed him on as a professional; supposedly the Blackburn Club did not find out the true situation for twenty years! But poaching of players by the rich professional Clubs in England was not uncommon and for some years the Mids. were at a low ebb as they continually lost promising players. It would appear that by the mid 1890's the Club had disappeared, but the remnants of the earlier team reappeared under a different guise.

In November 1896, a meeting was held, at which it was decided that a new Junior Football Club would be formed, by the name of 'Vale of Dryfe'. William Gardiner was chosen as Captain and the Secretary and Treasurer was James Jardine. It was hoped that Dr. Baird of Broomhouses would be able to provide a suitable field as a home Ground. However, before a ball was kicked, a number of Clerks in the town also decided to form a Club in Lockerbie, and M.C.Nutt was made the Captain with J.G.Carruthers as Secretary. A,J, Baird, the Laird of Broomhouses, agreed to act as Treasurer, and granted the new team the use of a suitable field on his land! After an initial practise match attended by twenty members, on the 17th of December, the first match was played, when The Clerks met Vale of Dryfe at the Mill Field, Broomhouses! However, their was no suggestion of any acrimony between the two teams. The Vale won substantially with an 8–2 scoreline.

The Vale of Dryfe Club became the long term survivors, and after playing at Broomhouses Park, they moved, around 1902, to Kintail Park. Mid-Annandale were created from the original Vale of Dryfe in c.1909, and continued to use the same venue for home matches. In the 1909/10 season references were made to a 'Mid-Annandale Amateurs' team (which could well have been one and the same as the newly named organisation).

On the 27th of August 1910 the 'Mid-Annandale Club' played their first match of the season when they shared two goals with Dumfries Amateurs. A few weeks later they played in the Scottish Cup, when they lost away in the 1st qualifying round to the 5th Kings Own Scottish Borderers Club by 0-8. The Club attracted one of the biggest crowds for years at Kintail Park when they entertained Solway Star in the Scottish Consolation Cup. To add to the *names* confusion, during the 1911/12 season references were made to the Amateur team once again and also to 'Mid-Annandale' (with the 'Amateurs' omitted). It is perhaps reasonable to assume that these 'two' Mid-Annandale Clubs were one and the same, since the future professional Club almost certainly used unpaid players unpaid at that time. To cap this highly confusing situation, the Mid-Annandale Wanderers won the Southern Counties Consolation Cup in 1910!

One thing that can be certain is that there were no very successful Clubs in Lockerbie until after the First World War, as there were no winners of any Senior Competitions. In the 1913/14 season Mid-Annandale entered for the Scottish Consolation Cup and also the Southern Counties Cup, losing on both occasions to Solway Star with 2-6 and 2-5 scorelines respectively.

The next season, like their near neighbours Solway Star, they tried their luck in the their first league competition, the Southern District League, in which only eight teams competed. Also like their neighbours, they ceased playing until after the Great War

The three Clubs re-emerge after the War:

Nithsdale Wanderers re-appeared after the great War at the start of the 1919/20 season, as a newly constituted team. With the lack of sufficient competition they were destined to play only Friendly and Cup matches for three years.

But the first game since pre-war days was a significant one, for they visited the newly founded Queen of the South from Dumfries, who were of course later to become an established Club in the Scottish Football League. The match was played at Palmerston Park (which had previously been used for football by other Clubs) on the 16th of August. After losing by 2-1 at half-time, the homesters scored another goal in the second half to record a 2-2 draw in their first competitive match.

The Sanquhar team re-established themselves at Castle Holm where their home games continued. The team soon proved themselves as a football force in the South of Scotland, for they won both the Potts Cup (for the fourth time in their history) and also the Southern Counties Cup. In addition to these two trophy wins, they also reached the first round proper of the Scottish Cup, but were easily beaten at Heart of Midlothian with a 1-5 scoreline. The next season was significant as the Club moved to a new Ground at Crawick Holm, which was situated on the other side of the town, out on the northern outskirts, and this venue was to become the Club's final headquarters. Along with Queen of the South, the Club were invited to join the Western League, which had been initially formed during the War to provide fixtures principally for suitable Scottish League Clubs, who were not admitted to the League's wartime competition. Although the prospect of regular opposition must have been tempting, both Clubs declined the offer since, due to their relative remoteness, the gate guarantees for visiting Clubs (£15 plus half the receipts over £30) were considered too high.

The first match at the new enclosure was versus Solway Star, who sent a somewhat weak team, for they were thrashed 7-0, on the 27th of August 1920. Once again the Wanderers reached the final rounds of the Scottish Cup, and after a bye in the first round they were entertained at Palmerston Park in the next tie. Queen of the South were beginning to establish themselves as a major Club in the area, and on the day of the Cup match a new record attendance of 5,000 (paying £202 match receipts) was present. The game produced great interest in both towns – even a telegram was sent to the Wanderers from Canada from 'exiled' Sanquharians – and the visitors were well supported in Dumfries. Nithsdale claimed a well earned 3-1 victory and so progressed on to the third round when they had to visit Dumbarton. The non-Leaguers met their match, for despite good support once again, they put on a poor display and lost the game by five unopposed goals. The attendance was also a disappointment, for it only numbered 4,000, the lowest of the round.

An un-named team Nithsdale Wanderers team group at Crawick Holm c.1920.

No major trophies were won in the various local Cup competitions, but the Dumfries Club were met once again, this time in the Final of the Potts Cup. The match was played at Palmerston Park, and another 5,000 crowd was present with receipts totalling £212 on this occasion. The visitors should have won the match, but had to be satisfied with four goals shared between the two teams. After being offered an attractive gate guarantee, the Wanderers agreed to play the replay at Palmerston Park again, but for this second encounter there were only 3,000 present. The visitors lost the match by 1-2, and the Wanderers fans, incensed by some of the decisions of the Officials, invaded the pitch at the final whistle; during the ensuing melee, the Referee was punched!

Solway Star were once again the visitors for the first match at Crawick Holm in the 1921/22 season, and like one year earlier were easily beaten by a 0-7 scoreline. For the third year, it was to be another of only Friendlies and Cup games, but once again the Club showed their potential in the latter. For the first time in their history, the Club fought through to the final of the Scottish Qualifying Cup Competition, after a long string of victories in the early rounds. Newton Stewart were easily disposed of in the 1st round, when the visiting Wanderers team thrashed them by 10-2. The next round required a visit to Dalbeatie Star, when the home team were once again comfortably overcome, this time with a three-nil score. Helensburgh provided stiffer opposition in the 4th round, and after a close match at Crawick Holm, the Wanderers won with the only goal of the game.

Dykehead were the next visitors to Sanquhar, and a record crowd producing gate receipts of £65 was present. In probably the most impressive game in the Club's history, the visiting Clachnacuddin team were cast aside, with a 6–1 scoreline after being three goals in arrears after 45 minutes. Montrose provided the opposition in the Final, which was played at Ibrox. Although 900 Wanderers supporters made the journey, the total attendance of 5,000 was most disappointing. Six goals were shared, and so a replay was necessary. The second encounter was played at Tynecastle, and a 7,000 crowd (receipts of £227) watched a scoreless draw. This result required a second replay, which was held back at Ibrox, but only 400 supporters could afford the third long trip in such a short period. The attendance was no more than 3,000, and the Wanderers lost by the odd goal in three.

For the third consecutive season the Club reached the first round of the Scottish Cup, but there was no joy for them as they lost by 1–3 at Queen's Park. The rest of the season was taken up by friendly games – including a 10–0 crushing of St. Cuthbert's Wanderers – and more local Cup ties. Queen of the South were met yet again in the Pott's Cup, this time before only 1,500 spectators, when a goal from the penalty spot took the Wanderers through to the final, where they lost to Douglas Wanderers. But success did come in the Southern Counties Cup, their seventh win in this competition.

On the 4th of November 1921, the Club became a Limited Company, and 1,000 shares at £1 each were made available. Eight Directors ran the Club, each of whom had a nominal five shares, and each man was connected to the Sanquhar Colliery.

Notable amongst the directors was the miner David Nivison. Nivison was a former player, and had been one of the driving forces behind the Club and was to make a notable contribution to the game in Scotland. He first became a member of the South of Scotland Football Association, and became Vice–Chairman in 1908. In 1927 he was elected as the Chairman and filled this role for many years. In the pre–second World War days he was a selector for the Scottish International team.

D. Nivison, Nithsdale Wanderers.

(Photo. taken in April 1939)

By the end of January 1922, over 600 shares had been taken up, and eighteen months later they had all been allocated. Crawick Holm was purchased by the Club in April 1922 at a cost of £325, and £125 was spent on enclosing the field with a further £50 allocated to provide huts.

The second invitation to join the Western League was taken up for the 1922/23 season, and it was obvious that the post–war years had shown that the Club were worthy of this competition. Queen of the South also entered the League, and when they visited Crawick Holm they were heading the table. The match receipts produced over £62 plus another £11 from the seated Stand. But the season's highlights centred on the Scottish Cup where an excellent run took the Wanderers through to the third round. The first round produced an easy 4–0 home victory over Second Division Arbroath, but this was not altogether surprising since the Scottish League members had a miserable season.

In the second round the Club had to travel again, this time to the Ground of Dundee Hibernians. Before a crowd of nearly 6,000 (receipts of £218), a narrow single goal victory was obtained, and the station at Sanquhar was packed with several hundred fans to welcome home their heroes. One hundred and fifty supporters accompanied the team to Bo'ness for the third round tie, but with heavy rain and a gate of only 3,000, the Wanderers could not maintain their good Cup form and lost the tie by two goals to nil. However there was no disputing that the Sanquhar team had shown their ability over the past three years, and it was obvious that they were worthy founder–members of the proposed Third Division of the Scottish League for the 1923/24 season.

Down in Annan, football in the town followed very similar lines to those in Sanquhar. Solway Star also reformed in 1919, and for two seasons were content with Friendly and Cup fixtures, albeit without so much success as Nithsdale Wanderers. The Club once again used Greenlea Park for the 1919/20 season, and after a successful sports day at this venue, their first match was at home to the Wanderers from Sanquhar. The game, on the 6th of September, was the first in the Scottish Qualifying Cup, but there was no celebratory return to football for the homesters as they lost 1–4. It was obvious that the Star were not going to emulate their pre–war successes, as no major trophies were won during the season.

The next campaign was very much the same as the first, as the team consolidated rather than picked up honours, although the highlight of the season was the Club's run in the Scottish Cup when they reached the final rounds for the first time. After a bye in the first, East Stirling were entertained in the next round, and a record attendance of nearly 1,000 was present. But there was to be no further progress as the homesters crashed out with a 1–5 scoreline. At the Club's A.G.M. during the summer of 1921, some doubts were expressed as to the Club's continued existence, as the team were not as successful during the previous year as had been hoped for. Of 23 games played only 8 were lost, but the opposition had been very variable due to the Club's relative isolation.

The Club did reach the final of the Southern Counties Cup, after a semi–final victory over Mid–Annandale, but the home crowd of 500 reflected the difficulty the Club had in attracting sufficient support. Even so the season had shown a financial credit with £10 surplus after the total expenditure of £662 on the season. The Club had been using the Summergate Park Ground, which was owned by Sir John Rutherford and let out to the Club at £36 per annum.

Although it may have been possible to find a cheaper venue, including the Cricket Field which had been considered, the expense of moving the Pavilion would probably have cancelled out any small savings made. But in the final event a move was eventually made before the start of the 1921/22 campaign to Kimmeter Park Green, the move that proved to be the last for the Club. A good attendance was present for the first match, when Mid–Annadale were beaten in a 8–5 thriller for a Friendly game on the 20th of August. The Star at least were able to enjoy regular fixtures when they joined the newly re–introduced Southern Counties League. The first League match was not played until the 5th of November, since there were only six Clubs in the competition, and before an encouraging attendance of 600, St.Cuthbert's Wanderers were easily beaten by six unopposed goals. In the Scottish Qualifying Cup competition, the Star enjoyed a good run.

In the first round, Thornhill were narrowly defeated by the odd goal in three before a 500 Kimmeter Park crowd, and other victories took the team through to the fourth round. At this stage Arthurlie entertained the Annan team, and a good crowd of close on 1,000 was present for the scoreless draw. The Star were induced to waive home advantage for the replay and were happy to receive £60 or a half share of the match receipts. The second game at the same venue produced a much increased crowd of 3,000, but a defeat for the visitors. Once again the first round of the Scottish Cup was reached, but the Star were well beaten with a 2–7 scoreline at St.Mirren. The best home gathering saw around 1,500 present for a visit from Blackburn Rovers Reserves.

The 1922/23 season saw Solway Star accepted into the Western League. The Club made a good start in the new competition and remained undefeated at home until the 30th of December, when they lost to Royal Albert. Although no honours were won in the League, the Club held their own, and the last League match was played on the 31st of March 1923, when a scoreless draw with Queens Park Victoria was watched by 400 at Kimmeter Park.

The Club qualified for the later rounds of the Scottish Cup, and a notable victory was achieved over Arbroath by four unopposed goals. The match in Annan attracted a new record attendance of 1,500 which produced match receipts of £55.

At the end of the season, a meeting was held at Albert Hall, and was attended by around forty members. Although the post war years had been quite successful on the pitch, financially it had become a struggle, with attendances rarely exceeding 500 at home games. The best (non-Cup) crowd of the season was present for the match versus Queen of the South, when an exceptional attendance of close on 1,500 (aided considerably by 800 travelling supporters) was present. In February, with the Club in debt by over £200, it was only a two day Bazaar that raised a considerable sum of money for Club funds that kept their heads above water. Once again talk centred on whether the Club could carry on! But after some difficulty in finding volunteers a new Committee was voted in and the membership voted to try and make a go of it.

It was agreed that the Club should try and operate on a more professional basis, and with this in mind a Secretary was appointed at a salary of £10 per annum, plus a Trainer and Groundsman. Expenditure had shot up during the just completed season to a new high of £1,500, and it was obvious that the wages bill had to be reduced. Instead of paying Players by the week, a decision was taken to reward them per match, and based on performances alone! The final proof of the Club's forward thinking was their intention to immediately register with, and become members of the Scottish Football Association. Before the start of the historic 1923/24 season, a new Grandstand was built with a capacity in excess of 300. The work was substantially undertaken by volunteers from the Chochrane boiler making factory, the major employer in the town at this time.

Football started after the War a year earlier in Lockerbie. But matches were of a fairly minor key and probably limited to Friendly encounters only.

A team entitled 'Lockerbie', was probably the nucleus of the Mid-Annandale side, for they played at Kintail Park. The next season the 'Lockerbie' team were not referred to, whereas the Mids. name was prominent once again. For the Mids., as for their other South of Scotland neighbours, competition was limited at first to Friendly and Cup matches only. The first game of the 1919/20 season brought a new Club to Kintail Park, Carstairs United, and they were beaten by 2-1 before a good gate which realised £8. The new look Mid-Annandale proudly wore their new black and gold jerseys, and the goals had received a facelift with new nets.

For a Charity cup-tie the players whilst travelling in the Club Charabanc passed by a Mids. fan. Anxious to bring the team good luck he threw his lucky horseshoe, which was decorated with the team colours, into the vehicle. The horseshoe did prove to be lucky, for it narrowly avoided a possible serious injury when it hit a player's bowler hat, and completely ripped off the brim! The one major triumph of the season was the Club's winning of the Southern Counties Consolation Cup, their first success in this competition. The season finished with an emphatic home victory over Eskdale Juniors on the 21st of April, with a 5-1 scoreline.

Earlier the Annual Spring Fair match was played when Lochmaben was entertained. Shannon, who was injured in a cup match was given a testimonial, and the game brought in £13-25p from a crowd of 500. At the Club's A.G.M. in June there was a large attendance at the Kintail Hall, and it was decided at the meeting that the Club should be representative of all classes and walks of life. With this aim in mind a new Committee was elected, but since they would be liable for any financial deficiencies, it was not an easy task to find sufficient volunteers! A number of new players were signed on for the next season, including former Queen of the South, Albion Rovers and Vale of Leven men.

The Club continued to rely on friendly and Cup matches for the 1920/21 season, and the campaign was noted for the success of the Club in the Scottish Cup. The Mids. made their first entry into the competition (apart from their predecessors of the 1890's), and reached the first round when they received a bye. A visit to Albion Rovers in the second produced an excellent attendance of 11,000 (including 50 visiting supporters) who saw their favourites lose to the home team by 1-3. But this defeat was softened by the share of the £200 match receipts.

During the season a concert was held to raise funds which would enable the Club to enlarge the pavilion and so provide a dressing room for visiting teams – until then they had changed outside the Ground! At the A.G.M., in May, it was recorded that of the 19 games played, only seven of these were lost (and one drawn). In all the team had travelled 734 miles to away matches, and the total income had amounted to £618, from which a very healthy credit balance of £159 was left. This compared with £21 surplus a year earlier, although if it had not been for a share of the Albion Rovers Cup game, then the position would not have been so healthy. £100 was allocated to the Pavilion fund, and overall the season was seen as a successful one, particularly on the money front even though for many weeks it was not possible to arrange suitable games.

Along with five other teams, the Mids. entered the Southern Counties League for the following season, and of course continued in the various Cup competitions. When nearby Queen of the South came to Lockerbie in a Southern Counties Cup match, the crowd totalled over 2,000, an almost unheard of number for the small town.

Mid-Annandale Qualifying Cup Finalists 1922/23 season

But the 1922/23 season was to see the Club establish itself as one of the top outfits in the area. Although the team were content to remain in the Southern Counties League, it was to the Cup competitions that most eyes were turned – ironically in League matches it was a wretched season with the Mids. holding bottom place for much of the season! The first round of the Scottish Cup was again reached – following an appearance in the final of the Qualifying Cup (a 1–4 defeat to Royal Albert) – when only a goal scored from a penalty separated the non–Leaguers from Aidrieonians in a 1–2 defeat.

The Club won the Southern Counties Consolation Cup following an easy 4–0 semi–final victory over Newton Stewart and the beating of Stranraer in the final which was played at Castle Douglas. The final stage of the Southern Charity Cup was also reached when Nithsdale Wanderers were beaten after extra time at Dumfries.

This produced a crowd of 2,600 and receipts of £81. In a thrilling final against Queen of the South, which was held at the Dumfries Ground, a record attendance for the competition of 5,000 was present. The last game of the season, and as a non–league Club (for three years) produced a comfortable 5–1 victory over Eskdale Juniors.

There was a large attendance at the Club's A.G.M. in early June, when, despite the poor League record, the 24 matches played in total showed a balance in favour of wins against defeats. £353 had been raised for Charities, but it was recognised that it was important for more spectators to be attracted to Kintail Park for league games. From a total income of £1,034, £404 had been raised by Charity Concerts and Dances, etc., with most of the remainder coming from Cup games. It was calculated that £65 per match was required, a tall order since this represented around 2,000 spectators, and with the aim of raising more money a Supporters Club was formed. The Club's determination to attract more support was shown when a Stand was erected – at a cost of under £13!

The introduction of the Third Division:

Emulating their counterparts in England, a Third Division was created in Scotland for the 1923/24 season. A meeting had been held in Glasgow on the 30th of May when sixteen invited teams were invited to form the new Division. The bulk of the membership was to be from the Western League, from where eleven of the competing Clubs joined the new venture; Arthurlie, Beith, Dykehead, Galston, Helensburgh,

Nithsdale Wanderers, Peebles Rovers, Queen of the South, Royal Albert, Solway Star plus Dumbarton Harp (members in the 1921/22 season); Hurlford and Queen's Park Victoria X1 were the two that were not included. Brechin, Clackmannan, East Stirling, Mid–Annandale, and Montrose made up the final five teams. It was agreed that two Clubs would automatically be promoted at the season's end (if only twelve Clubs had joined then only one would have been promoted), and 'away' teams would get gate guarantees of £15 plus half the receipts over £40. Long distance travel had to be anticipated since these sixteen teams were drawn from a wide area.

In several cases the teams were representative of small to very small towns, a situation which however great the enthusiasm, could never attract large attendances for those concerned. All of the newcomers were also new to the Scottish League, and it is significant that only three of these have kept their membership of the Scottish League to adte – East Stirling (eventual runners–up), final third placed Queen of the South, and tailenders Brechin. Apart from Queen of the South, the three others from the South of Scotland were – Mid–Annandale, Nithsdale Wanderers and Solway Star.

After the earlier hesitancy regarding the continuance of Solway Star, the members and fans made great efforts to ensure their team's hoped for success. A Supporters Club was formed for the Solway Star team, and with weekly subs. from the initial 200 members, £50 was raised in the first seven weeks of the season. In addition other money–raising events were planned, including the holding of regular dances. Basically the same team from the previous campaign signed on for the Club, with the notable addition of David Robinson from Mid–Annandale, a Player that had been watched by a number of both Scottish and English League Clubs. With an expenditure of £1,500 over the previous season, cost cutting was necessary (despite the elevation in status), and it was decided that players would continue to be paid on the basis of results rather than a regular weekly wage.

On August the 18th, the Star kicked off the season with a match at Galston.
Little, Robinson, Fergusson, Patrick, Duncan,
Davidson, Logan, Alexander, Carey, Thom and MacDonald
represented the Club, but a disappointing display resulted in a two goal defeat for the visitors. One week later the team made it's home debut on a miserable day with frequent showers of rain during the match.

Peebles Rovers were the visitors, and the local supporters were cheered up when Devlin (one of three team changes from the earlier match) scored to give the homesters a one goal interval lead. The team had noticeably improved, Brown the ex–Portsmouth man had also been included, and they ran out final 2–1 victors.

Nithsdale, probably had the strongest team of the trio from the South (excluding the Queen of the South), and they proved this with their final League placing. Their season got off to an excellent start with a 3–1 victory at Clackmannan. McConnel opened the scoring for the Wanderers, which equalised the earlier lead taken by the homesters from the penalty spot. By half–time the visitors had built up a lead that was to be the final result after 90 minutes. Heavy rain fell throughout the match and no doubt contributed to the gate which only raised £24 in total. The Nithsdale team consisted of;

Armour, McHallum, Borthwick, Crate, Bankes, Turnbull,
Shankly, Anderson, McConnel, McMillan and Keegans.

Anderson the ex–Third Lanark player was the Captain. In the Club's debut home game on the 25th of August, Brechin were thrashed by five unopposed goals, with McConnel scoring all three, and a large attendance produced match receipts of £37. This resulted in the Wanderers heading the table after these two initial games.

Mid–Annandale had virtually reformed during the close season, with the most significant changes being a new Committee, and the surprise transfer of Willie Tennant from Motherwell. Motherwell Reserves sent a team down to play the Mids. in a Friendly 'opener', in which the homesters finally lost by 5–8, and before only 300 spectators. But the team made an excellent start to their League campaign.

They travelled across country to the Ground of Peebles Rovers and recorded a 2–1 victory after MacLaine had given the Mids. a single goal half–time lead.

The match consisted of 'end to end' football, and despite the periods of pressure from the homesters, a second goal from the earlier scorer ensured the visitor's victory. The match was played in heavy rain throughout, and it was agreed by both teams to change round immediately after 45 minutes and forego the customary break. Large numbers of fans travelled to the match – by bus, car, and motorcycle – but there was only a total attendance of 800.

For the Mids.;
> *Smith, Murray, Alexander, Noble, McSorland,*
> *Henderson, Moffat, Robb, MacLaine, Grove and Simpson*
> were the eleven team members.

Mid-Annandale Football Team

["Standard" Photo.

Above we reproduce a photograph of the Mid-Annandale Football Club's new team. The players from left to right are:

Standing—D. Henderson, R. Noble, "Lammie" Smith, A. M'Sorland, and T. Simpson.

Sitting—Willie Groves, Willie Robb, J. Murray, E. MacLaine, A. P. Moffat, and Archie Alexander.

Helensburgh were the first League visitors to Kintail Park, seven days later. There was a crowd of close on 1,000 (receipts of £35), and an exciting and closely fought match produced a win for the homesters with the odd goal in seven. The Mids. opened the scoring from a fortunate 'own Goal'. The Club President, James McLure had presented the Club with a new match ball, which was inscribed: *"Good Luck 1923/24"*. These two victories ensured a second place in the table for the Club.

An Encouraging First Season in the Third Division:

On the 8th of September 1923, Mid–Annandale lost 0–2 to the strong East Stirling team, but made amends two weeks later when they recorded an excellent home victory (4–1) over Royal Albert in front of a reasonable crowd of 800. The return match with East Stirling on October the 6th resulted in a single goal victory by the visitors, but before an excellent attendance of 1,800. In early November the eagerly awaited visit of Queen of the South drew a crowd of 2,100 to Kintail Park, of which 1,000 had travelled from Dumfries. On a bitterly cold day, the Mids. suffered another defeat (1–3), and began to slip down the table after their encouraging start. There was a gathering of 1,500 at Arthurlie for the 10th of November game which ended as a 3–2 home victory which left the Lockerbie team in the fifth from bottom slot in the League. After several team changes they bounced backed and recorded a 6–1 home victory over Clackmannan on the 17th of November. At the end of the year, a moderate recovery saw the team in 8th place with 14 points from 13 matches, and a similar second half of the season saw them maintain this placing. Wooden–spoonists Brechin provided the last opponents in Lockerbie, and they suffered a 6–1 beating.

Nithsdale's third match, at the Portland Park Ground of Galston, resulted in a 3–2 victory and ensured that the Wanderers maintained their top placing. There was a large crowd at the game, and support for the visitors came from 100 enthusiastic travelling fans. The first point was dropped when the Club entertained Queen of the South, in front of a good attendance of 1,500 (match receipts of £70), on the 22nd of September. But seven days later the team lost by the odd goal in three at Royal Albert. Another defeat came at Montrose, where the gate produced only £47, a lowly figure due to the high unemployment in the Tayside town.

Although the Club managed to maintain a high place in the table, the results then began to go against them. In early November they were well beaten by 0–4 at leaders East Stirling, and by mid–December, when Helensburgh were the visitors, the home support had dropped, to a gate producing only £20, which with the required split of the proceeds left the homesters with £5! Yet if this figure looked black, pity the poorest supported Dumbarton Harp F.C. When Nithsdale made their pre–Christmas visit to the Strathclyde Club, a pathetic attendance produced a gate of 150, and receipts of £5, leaving the homesters with minus £10!

It was surely something of a miracle that not only did this hapless Club survive the first season of the Third Division, but actually finished in a moderately respectable 10th place. The Wanderers last game of the year, versus Mid-Annandale, was postponed when five inches of snow lay on the Kintail Park pitch, but with 4th place in the table, 6 points behind the leaders East Stirling, the Club at least had something to be happy about. The general good form was not fully maintained during the second half of the season, but a final place in the table of 6th represented a good start to the Club's Scottish Football League career.

For Solway Star the season became something of a struggle throughout. Although there were no real disasters in the League matches (0-4 at Beith and 1-5 at Montrose being the worst results), they never really looked like achieving anything. A moderate home record (four defeats) but a poor set of results on their travels ensured a poor final place in the table of 11th. But fortunately for the Club the encouragement and support given in Annan ensure the continued existence of the Club. Although the home gate receipts amounted to only £555, the total income came to £1,633, the vast difference being made up by many donations (one of £100), the Supporters Club contributions and the regular fund-raising schemes.

At the A.G.M. in May it was announced that there was a loss on the season of £145, less than many had feared. But this was virtually wiped off with the fee received from Glasgow Rangers on the transfer of Dick, the Star's top goalscorer with 15 successes of the total of 45. At the Ground the main improvement had been the building of the Grandstand, which with voluntary labour had incurred little expenditure. The plans had been drawn up by a local Architect, Gladstone, and the structure also provided accommodation for dressing rooms and baths, etc.

With eleven players retained for the 1924/25 season, Solway Star looked forward to the 1924/25 season with optimism, as of course did their two neighbouring Clubs.

The 1923/24 season produced no real shocks in the various Cup Competitions. None of the trio reached the final rounds of the Scottish Cup, nor were any of the major local trophies won by them. Solway Star soon parted from the Qualifying Cup when they lost 0-4 at Queen of the South. Mid-Annandale had no success, and Nithsdale Wanderers did little better. After an easy win over Dalbeattie Star (5-2 scoreline), the Wanderers met the Dumfries Club in the next round.

The home tie produced tremendous enthusiasm in both towns, and a new record attendance of 4,200 was present at Crawick Holm for the game which amassed gate receipts of £199. Nearly half of the support had come from Queen of the South, and a typical cup-tie went against the homesters when they recorded their first defeat of the season with a 2-3 reversal.

Triumph for Nithsdale, encouragement for Solway but gloom for Mid-Annan:

The first home match of the 1924/25 season for Mid-Annandale, when a crowd of 700 turned out to see the locals play Montrose, was evidence of the struggles that lay ahead; although a point was obtained in the 2-2 draw, the visitors enjoyed most of the play. The four goal thrashing at Peebles, one week later on the 30th of August emphasised the warning. Another crowd of 700 were in attendance for the eight goals that were shared with Helensburgh, but this number was reduced by 100 when relegated Lochgelly came to Lockerbie and took away both points. Even table topping Vale of Leven barely stirred any interest in the South of Scotland town and only 800 bothered to come and watch a close 2-3 defeat for the home Club. The earlier thrashing at Beith (by 3-8) and the later 0-5 defeat at Brechin, led to a grim situation with the Mids. propping up the table after twelve matches; five draws and no victories was the dismal record. By the year end the Club had risen just one place, and by then had achieved two victories and two more draws. One of those victories was a home success over the high-flying Nithsdale eleven. After such a bad start, the Club never recovered, and although there were no more heavy defeats, the final position found the team at the bottom of the Division. Dumbarton Harp had withdrawn from the League after only seventeen games, but their record to that time, if continued, would probably have ensured a higher placing than the hapless Lockerbie team.

Things looked a lot brighter for Solway Star. They made an excellent start to the campaign, and after eight games were undefeated with six victories to their credit, and second place in the League table. But despite having a winning team, it was difficult to encourage extra support, and for the near local derby with Mid-Annandale on November the 15th, there were barely 900 present. As the season wore on, the Club faltered, and after 26 games they had slipped to 4th place.

The scoreless home draw with Clackmannan on March the 21st attracted a crowd of only 700, around the Mid-Annandale's moderate average.

The last League game of the season produced a single goal victory over Royal Albert, and ensured the Club of a very good third in the table. It was only an inferior goal average to their neighbours Queen of the South, that prevented the Annan team from being promoted in preference to the Dumfries Club. If further victories had ensued at home – although undefeated they only won nine Kimmeter Green encounters – then promotion would have been easily attained.

THE STALWARTS OF THE SOLWAY STAR.

[By the courtesy of the "Sunday Mail."

The Solway Star share the distinction with other three teams in Scottish football which have an undefeated League record this season. The other teams are Peebles Rovers in Division III., Celtic in the First Division, and Dundee United in the Second. Above is a photograph of the members of the Solway Star team. Back row (left to right), W. Mitchell, D. Robinson, J. Muir, J. M'Hallam, S. Alexander, and D. Duncan. Front row (left to right), A. Baxter, W. Alexander, G. Higgins, J. Knox, and A. Smith.

Pride of place went to Nithsdale Wanderers, for the team, from off the beaten track, caused some surprise in the Scottish Football World when they comfortably finished the campaign as Champions. It was a notable achievement for a Club that had probably the smallest population of all of the Scottish teams from which to command support. The team was strengthened during the close season, and amongst the new signings was Joseph Mounteney, a forward from the reserves of the highly successful Airdrie F.C.

The season started well on the 16th of August when Leith were beaten 3–1 before a very good attendance. This win was followed with another, next week, at Dumbarton, but all to no avail as the Harp's record was deleted at the final count.

The next home match produced another good crowd of around 1,000, and the Crawick Holm team were unlucky to have to only share the two goals with Lochgelly. By the end of the year, the Wanderers held third place in the table, and set about improving their record in the second part of the season. Some notable home victories ensued, including 7–1 versus Peebles on the 10th of January, 6–2 over Royal Albert later that month, 6–1 over the Vale of Leven team in February and the final 'icing on the cake' when they thrashed Montrose by eight unopposed goals in the last game of the season on the 18th of April. The Wanderers finished three points clear at the top of the table, with an almost 100% home record (only the early draw with Lochgelly preventing a faultless record).

Once again for two of the Clubs, little impression was made in any of the major Cup Competitions, but for Solway Star – as consolation for their near promotion sortie – a run through to the third round of the Scottish Cup was achieved. After beating Second Division Stenhousemuir at home, the Star embarked on a marathon with Vale of Leven. A draw away was followed by a six goals shared thriller at Kimmeter Park before an excellent, and all-time record attendance (in midweek) of over 2,000. The tie was finally settled at Cathkin Park before 6,000 spectators (match receipts of £206), when a 2–1 half–time lead remained the same after 90 minutes. The third round took the Star to their biggest ever match, to face the mighty Celtic at Parkhead. Despite loosing by 0–2, the team played well, and the five figure crowd (with 160 from Annan) ensured a cash bonanza from their share of the £312 gate.

The end of the 1924/25 season saw the trio of Clubs in vastly different situations. Nithsdale Wanderers could look forward to life in a higher division, Solway Star could only hope that they could build upon their season which had so nearly been a great success, while poor Mid–Annandale could only hope!

Nithsdale consolidate; for Mid–Annandale and Solway Star, Scottish League football comes to an abrupt end.

It is somewhat ironic that in the greatest moment of glory for Nithsdale Wanderers – promotion to the Second Division – the sparse coverage of the team in the local newspapers came to a virtual end. Sanquhar being such a small town never had independent coverage, and the nearest centres where such newspapers were based, e.g. Dumfries, Kilmarnock and Ayr, were too far away for them to bother about the little provincial town. Therefore the following points with regard to the Club's final two seasons can only be really assessed from their League results. The Wanderers started their Second Division campaign on the 15th of August when they lost by 1–4 to Dunfermline. They made up for this disappointment one week later when they beat East Sirling by 3–1 at Crawick Holm. After that initial set back they got off to a winning run with further victories at home to Dumbarton – by 5–1 – and in the local derby game versus Queen of the South; between times a second away victory came at Alloa.

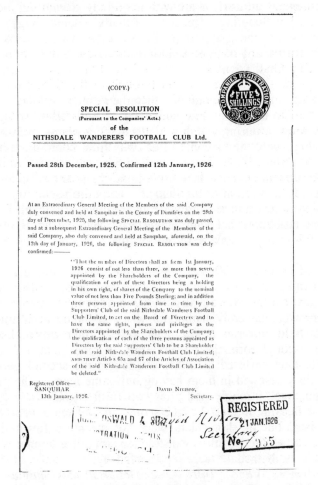

Changes made to the Nithsdale Wanderers constitution in 1926
(SRO Ref no. BT2/11928)

After six games, the Wanderers had confounded the critics with their top position in the League. Although a good ratio of victories was maintained for a few weeks, as the year drew to an end they started a gradual slide down the table. The second half of the season saw more defeats than wins – plus an incredible 6–6 draw at Arthurlie in February – and by the season's end they finished 12th of 20, a reasonable position, but somewhat disappointing after such a good start. On the 12th of January 1926 a special resolution was passed whereby it was agreed that three of the Directors of a total of between six and ten would be elected from the Supporters Club. Such a move was quite radical, since the general attitude of professional Clubs around this period was that while welcoming (indeed virtually demanding) financial contributions by the Supporters Clubs, there was invariably great resistance against any of those fund–raisers having a hand in running the respective Football Club!

If the past season was encouraging, then the next, the 1926/27, was little short of disastrous! The campaign started with three straight home games in August, during which a moderate four points from two draws and a victory, were the outcome. But away from home the start was far from good. After a 2–7 thrashing at East Stirling, defeats on the team's travels continued, and by the turn of the year, the Wanderers were entrenched at the bottom of the League, one point below Arbroath, with only four victories and six draws from the twenty–one games played. The Club's last Scottish League game was played at home on the 30th of April, when Clydebank were the visitors.

A crowd of around 1,000 was present (the average home attendance), and an exciting match unfolded. The visitors took the lead after only five minutes, but this was equalised by 'Junior' (an unnamed player). The Wanderers were severely hampered when goalkeeper Armour had to leave the field through injury, and were further demoralised when Clydebank scored form the penalty spot, to give them a 2–1 interval lead. Nithsdale suffered a further setback in the second period when another injury resulted in them having only nine men on the pitch. But they fought back strongly and after two further goals (one from each side), Cree became the last League scorer for Nithsdale when he scored the equaliser, but the homesters were not meant to finish their brief Scottish League career with any distinction, for a late winner was scored by the visitors. Nithsdale were represented by:

Armour, Vance, Tully, Cree, McLaren, McGonagle,
McCosh, Ballantyne, 'Junior', Allan and Houston.

Although the Wanderers had maintained a reasonable record in Sanquhar (six victories, six defeats and seven drawn games), the away results were terrible. Only one victory, at Stenhousemuir, plus two drawn encounters gave the Club a total of only 23 points. This tally was few enough to guarantee the Club the wooden spoon position, with their nearest rivals a clear nine points above them. Financially things had been a real struggle. Never able to command good attendances the Club had found their outgoings in keeping pace with the higher division Clubs outweighed their income, and at the end of the season they resigned from the League.

There was no opportunity to slip down into the Third Division since this competition had been abandoned a year earlier! There was no option but to drop down into non–League football or fold completely. They chose the former option and joined the Scottish Provincial League, a competition which contained only nine teams.

Further South things were just as bleak for both Mid–Annandale and Solway Star. At the end of the 1925/26 season, the two Clubs virtually reversed their respective positions of a year earlier, with the Mids finishing 6th from top and the Star in a lowly 11th place.

A breakdown of Solway Star's financial affairs showed that they were getting by, but only just. Over the 1924/25 season the total expenditure exceeded the £2,705 income by £39. £940 had been taken at home gates with another sixty pounds from season tickets. The wages bill totalled a near four figures and Ground improvements took another £47. Although £150 had been received for the transfer of Dick, a substantial sum had been donated by the supporters Club – to which the Club Chairman complained saying that more was required!

The Annan team's final position in the League in April 1926 would hardly have seemed possible after their disastrous start, when they lost at home to Vale of Leven by 1–6 in front of a crowd of about 1,000. This prompted the Club to look into the transfer market where they were fortunate to pick up the services of Archie Campbell from Albion Rovers. A fee of £250 was originally asked for, but the Star were fortunate to eventually sign him for nothing. The team strengthening paid dividends for after another home defeat, two victories away from home and an improved record at Kimmeter Park saw the team gradually improve their position in the table to 5th after seven games.

The attention was drawn towards the qualifying competition of the Scottish Cup where some notable victories were gained. Stranraer were first beaten by four unopposed goals, followed by victory at home to Vale of Leven before an attendance of 1,100. In the quarter-final the 200 plus fans represented a third of the crowd at Shawfield Park where Thornhill were easily overcome with another four-nil scoreline. For the first time the Star were in the semi-final, but they went one better when they defeated Buckie Thistle by the only goal of the game.

But this was the limit of the Club's achievements for in the final they lost out to Leith Athletic. Meanwhile steady progress in the League led to a satisfactory 7th by the year end. The worrying aspect was the home gates, which despite the exciting cup matches had slumped to around 600. The second half of the season was a great disappointment as they gradually slid down the table to finish in a lowly position.

The financial situation over in Lockerbie was slightly better, although Mid-Annandale got by with less wages and lower gates. The previous season of 1924/25, had brought in only £366 at the gate, and a total income of £1163, including the extra money from letting out the Bowling Green that was adjacent to the Football Ground. But with only a low wages bill, and a modest £36 spent on the Grandstand, the Club had managed to keep in credit with a £68 surplus.

The 1925/26 season started disastrously with an initial 2-5 reversal at Brechin, followed by four more consecutive defeats. The first home game drew around 1,000 to Kintail Park, but Solway Star stole a 3-1 victory, a game in which Bannister missed a penalty for the Mids. After seven matches only one victory had been achieved and the team were on the bottom rung of the table.

Then a transformation came about following three successive wins that lifted the team into a mid-table position. The first away victory came at Peebles, in dense fog and in front of only 500 spectators. By the end of the year 6th place in the League had been attained, but it was a hard financial struggle as the Club strived to survive, despite the modest requirement of only £35 per week.

On New Year's Day, table-topping Helensburgh were beaten in Lockerbie before a crowd of 800, which for the Mids. represented a good crowd. Without doubt the Club had the most improved record in the division, although there had been complaints about the barracking that took place at home matches.

As the local newsman so politely stated:

> *"The Referee and Players have quite sufficient in hand to keep the game free from blemish, and it ill behoves any professed supporter to cause an irritation which might have an undesired effect."*

The Club's good run continued, particularly at home, where, the 2–0 defeat of Royal Albert was the 11th consecutive victory at Kintail Park. Near the season's end the Club held a remarkable third place, but fell away right at the close. The last Scottish League game was played on the 10th of April at Leith Athletic, and an uncharacteristic four goal defeat was the outcome. The team consisted of:

> *Varrie, Wilson, Dickson, Jardine, Frew, Richardson, Huddart, Stewart, Lennox, Dawson and McLaughlin.*

At the final count the Club finished 6th in the table, and it can only be left to conjecture on whether this could have been improved upon if the Third Division had continued operating. Once again there was no major successes in the principal Cup Competitions. Although the Club's expenditure had risen considerably, so had the gate takings due to their excellent recovery after the bad start, and at the final count the Club were left £150 in credit. But this created something of a false impression since it was only the sale of Frank Wilson to Motherwell for a fee of £500 that had left the Club financially stable. The top goalscorer for the Club was Lennox with 21.

The third, and final, season of the Third Division ended in chaos. All Clubs were feeling the pinch in respect of the bad economic situation as a whole in Britain, and the consequent high unemployment. This was most noticeable for the lower League teams, and Galston folded after playing only 15 games. Champions, Helensburgh were the only Club able to complete all thirty League fixtures.

As well as many unplayed games caused by the premature departure of Galston, several other fixtures were not completed; the rest of the Clubs fulfilled between 25 and 29 games. With Vale of Leven £800 in debt, Johnstone folding (but reforming again), and several other Clubs in a poor financial state, there were several indications that the 1926/27 season would be operating with far fewer Clubs, but the final reality showed that the Third Division was doomed.

The end of the Division.

A meeting of the remaining Clubs was held on the 2nd of June 1926, when the possibility of operating two regionalised Third Divisions was suggested. But even with the introduction of additional Clubs the numbers would be too few, and in any event such an idea was unlikely to be approved by the Scottish League. In the final event the formation of the 'Scottish Alliance' was agreed for a one year trial period, and all but three of the former League teams agreed to join. Yet Mid-Annandale were originally left out in the 'cold', doubtless due to the long travelling that most teams would have to make down to Lockerbie. This isolation led to loud protests by the Mids. supporters and the Club Officials, and eventually the noise was loud enough for the new League to admit the Lockerbie team.

In hindsight it can be seen that the formation of a Scottish Third Division was ill-conceived, at least as far as timing was concerned. There was undoubtably a genuine need for such a competition, since there was certainly a number of Clubs desirous as well as capable of competing in such a higher competition. But two major factors were inevitably going to work against this opportunity that was given to these lesser Clubs. Support could never conceivably be at a high level due to the locations of the new teams that were either based in small towns within sparsely populated areas, or the more urban Clubs that were local to bigger and more established teams. Since the new division was in effect a countrywide competition the greatly increased travelling costs could not be recovered at the gate.

Perhaps more importantly, and arising from a situation that may not have been apparent at the time, the economic situation in Britain was heading for a recession. For those Clubs based in Industrial areas, the slump inevitably drastically cut their incomes. For the likes of Nithsdale, Solway and Mid-Annandale this downturn may not have had such a direct drastic effect since they were based in far more rural surroundings. But coming from small towns, this factor inevitably going to work against these teams, regardless of the economic situation as a whole, since there could never be the support for success at a high level. Based as they were it was impossible to attract high gates from such low populated areas. In fact when related to the per capita, it is quite amazing that the likes of Nithsdale Wanderers could on occasions attract four figure gates, which would have been the equivalent of over 50% of the population of Sanquhar!

Back to non-League football for all three:

Mid–Annadale intended to balance the books by only employing fifteen professional Players for the 1926/27 season, but they still found the money to build a hut which was to serve as improved dressing–rooms. Solway Star also played in the new Alliance League, although after a disappointing 1925/26 season their troubles went from bad to worse. The biggest surprise from the three Clubs in the South, was that from Nithsdale Wanderers, who after being relegated from the Second Division – one year after the folding of the Third Division – chose to opt for inactivity insofar as a League competition was concerned. After their brief moments of relative glory, the trio were to never regain the status which had taken them all into the Scottish Football League. For Mid–Annandale, the route to oblivion was the shortest!

Mid–Annadale soon fade and die.

Along with Royal Albert, Helensburgh, Vale of Leven, Queens Park Strollers, Solway Star, Beith, the reformed Johnstone and several reserve teams of Scottish League Clubs, the Club joined the new Scottish Alliance – Southern Division. On the 28th of August the team suffered a 1–3 defeat at Helensburgh, and by Christmas, although having played less games than most of their opponents, they lay just below the middle of the League table. No honours were won in this competition, but one notable victory was the early success at Kintail Park with the fully deserved 6–1 thrashing of the Queen of the South reserve team. The next season the team continue in the Alliance, during which time there were only nine teams, before moving over to the newly reformed South of Scotland League for the 1928/29 campaign. For the next few seasons this competition was dominated by Dalbeattie Star, but for the Mids. the situation became ever worse.

In October 1929, the Club announced that they would not be able to compete in a League during this campaign. It was hoped that they would be able play in the South of Scotland competition, but eventually decided to remain dormant for one year. However the Mids. did not entirely disappear from the scene during this single season, since they played in the final of the Southern Counties Charity Cup final, albeit in strange circumstances. Having been inactive all season, a team was raised to represent Lockerbie in this competition, but was hardly the true Mid–Annandale since most of the team was composed of Hamilton Academical players!

The match was played at Palmerston Park, Dumfries, and a very good crowd which numbered 3,344 (receipts of £150), saw the 'foreigners' win the trophy as *Mid–Annandale*, with a 2–1 victory. During this same season the Mids. also played in the Scottish Cup, and actually reached the first round proper where they were comfortably beaten at Ayr United by five unopposed goals.

During the Club's post–Scottish League days, the first round of the Senior Cup was also reached two years earlier (a 3–7 defeat at Morton), and in the next – the 1930/31 – campaign when a narrow defeat by two goals was suffered at Montrose. Apart from these achievements, the Club lost out on all other Senior Cup honours. The Club did not appear in a League during the 1930/31 season either, but one year later a re–entry was made in the South of Scotland League. However, this venture lasted for only two unremarkable seasons before they fell back on Friendly matches and occasional Cup games but only for a further two years.

By 1934, the Club's fortunes had reached a very low ebb, and it is quite amazing that the Officials still had the enthusiasm and stamina to attempt a comeback since it was apparent that by now the Club were all but defunct. During the last two seasons of the Club, only very rare appearances were made, and the last two games (perhaps more) played under the Mid–Annandale 'banner' were a farce. The annual Southern Charity Cup was held with the important matches taking place as usual in Dumfries.

After beating Dalbeattie Star by 3–1 in the semi–final – with a team of unknown composition – the Mids. won the final versus Queen of the South. This repeated their success of a year earlier, but it is unlikely that this was achieved by a true Mid–Annandale team. For what appears to have been praiseworthy achievements – Dalbeattie had become a power in non–League football and the Queens were members of the Scottish League First Division – was far removed from the truth. The Mid–Annandale team was composed completely of Hamilton Academical players, and the Dumfries team, who were on a tour of France at the time, consisted of eleven Greenock Morton men! The Mid–Annandale ('substitute') team consisted of:

> *Morgan, Wallace, Bulloch, Cox, McStay, Thomson,*
> *Douglas, McLaren, Wilson, Harrison and King.*

The Final produced a poor crowd (by the standards of the day) of 2,300 which produced gate receipts of £99.

The Mids. took an early lead and followed up with two more before half-time, with Harrison scoring the last. In the second half the Queen's representatives pulled one back to give a final score of 3-1. This is believed to be the last game of Mid-Annandale Football Club.

The current amateur Mid-Annandale Club, who play at King Edward Park (but retain the Mids. old colours of Amber and Black), are not related to the former team.

....

Solway Star's sparkle is finally extinguished.

Solway Star managed to struggle on for a dozen or so years longer than their fellow ex-League neighbours. The first post-Scottish League season for the Club turned out to be something of a nightmare as the team had one of the worst seasons ever when they finished fourth from bottom of the Alliance League; the last League match was played when Helensburgh were entertained and were beaten 3-2. One season was then spent in the newly created Provincial League which contained only nine teams. The Star was still operating at a fairly senior level, but during the summer of 1928, all of the past season players, bar three, returned to the Junior ranks. But it would appear that the Club lowered their own sights somewhat, for amongst the intake of new men, were several locals who showed up well in the trial games and were signed on.

For the 1928/29 season the Club returned to the resurrected South of Scotland League. In opposition there were only seven other teams, amongst them Stranraer (who were yet to make it into the Scottish League), neighbours Mid-Annandale and Newton Stewart. The move proved to be no more successful than a year earlier, and an uneventful season – apart from an appearance in the first round of the Scottish Cup when the Club were well beaten by five unopposed goals at Aberdeen – ended with the Club in financial difficulties. A start in the League was intended for the next season, but it is doubtful if any matches were played.

Crowds had by now dropped to a very low level over the past few years, and money was lost even when Cup matches were played at Kimmeter Park. In the Scottish Qualifying Cup, the Star was drawn to play Montrose at home, but barely able to raise a team they were happy to reverse the tie for a £35 guarantee – as far as the Club was concerned the match was already lost anyway!

The Club's prediction was fulfilled for they crashed out of the competition with a 0–8 scoreline, but the composition of the Solway Star team was strange to say the least. Rather than try to raise a full team, coupled with the expenses to make the journey, most of the Annan team were made up of players who had, probably somewhat tenuous, connections with the Club, but who all lived in the Glasgow area! The attendance of 1,500 drew a gate of £60. This match was only the third played by the Club, and it is doubtful if they re–appeared again that season.

The Ground meanwhile was let out to two local amateur sides. Solway Rovers who withdrew from the letting at mid–season (having only paid half the agreed usage fee), and Watchill Rovers who played in the Annandale League who also never fully fulfilled their obligation.

At the Star's A.G.M., in the summer of 1930, there was a surprisingly good attendance of around sixty members, who, after some debate agreed to commit themselves into reforming the Club. But at this time they reverted to amateur status, and were admitted to the Southern Counties League once more.

The new campaign started out disastrously when the team lost 2–4, at home to the Queen of the South reserve eleven, despite the visitors losing their goalkeeper through injury just before half–time. In the second qualifying round of the Scottish Cup they were drawn against Mid–Annandale. A scoreless draw resulted, but at least the attendance of between four and five hundred was above the norm; they lost by two goals in the replay. A similar number of spectators was present when the Star were hosts to Nithsdale Wanderers who had also, by now, returned to this League. The season was at least completed, which was better than a year later!

Against the odds the Club doggedly fought on, but as far as the League was concerned they gave up at mid–season. The last league game on the 23rd of January 1932 was, ironically, a good match. By the second half they were trailing to the Dumfries Club's reserve eleven, but fought back to take a 4–3 lead, only to lose it again and finish up on the wrong end of a 4–6 scoreline. With no Star team at Kimmeter Park, Solway Rovers came back on the scene. But the Club just would not be beaten, and at the next A.G.M. the members decided to carry on again, at least for one more season, and they were fortunate to be admitted back into the South of Scotland League once more.

The past year had been a financial disaster, for despite expenses that totalled only a modest £130, there was still a shortfall of £8. At least the months ahead provided the Club with a good run in the Qualifying Cup Competition, which culminated in reasonable crowd numbers being attracted back to Kimmeter Park. In the first match they easily beat the Sanquhar team by 3–0, but before only 400 fans. When Mid–Annandale were the visitors in the following round, 700 spectators were attracted to the home venue, and the visitors were narrowly defeated by 2–1.

A new enthusiasm was apparent in the town, and the Supporters Club was reformed in October. The latter cup victory ensured a place in the semi-final, when Beith were drawn to play at Annan. By far the best crowd of the season, and for some time, totalled 800 for the visit of Beith, but the final was not reached since the homesters lost by the odd goal in five. Yet again no honours were won in the League, but in the Scottish Cup the team played in the first round, and lost by 0–3 at Heart of Midlothian.

Although the season had been relatively successful at least by Solway Star's somewhat depleted standards, they appeared to have disappeared off of the scene again during the 1933/34 season. But the scant references to the Club in the local Press continued once again during the 1934/35 campaign, and on the 29th of September they managed to defeat Stranraer in a Qualifying Cup match, despite the use of a somewhat scratch team of former players and local hopefuls.

In spite of the Club's apparent difficulty in playing regular football, they managed another first round appearance in the Scottish Cup, but were completely outclassed when they lost at Hearts, again, this time by seven unopposed goals.

The difference between the level at which the Club were playing by now, and the Scottish League was demonstrated most forcibly again two years later. After beating Larbert Amateurs in the first round of the principal Cup Competition they were required to visit Cowdenbeath for their next tie. Despite the homesters only occupying a middle of the table placing in the Scottish League Second Division, the Star were overwhelmed with a 1–9 defeat!

The 1930's continued with only the occasional references to the Solway Star team, and it is reasonable to assume that during this time it was only Friendly and Cup matches that were played – and even then on an irregular basis.

This assumption can be illustrated from the remarks made by the local Press during the 1938/39 season:

> *"The Solway team has only been in action on a few occasions this season, and this is principally due to the Manager, R.Scott, who has kept the flag flying since Senior football in the provincial towns became almost doomed."*

That season the Club won a major trophy, the first for many years, when they were successful in their Southern Counties Cup quest. But the apathy that by now had descended in Annan can be seen from the fact that only four matches were played throughout the season! The Club lost by 1–7 in the first qualifying round of the Scottish Cup before a large crowd at St.Mary's Park, the home of St. Cuthbert's Wanderers. Surprisingly they returned there two weeks later and recorded a 5–4 victory in the Southern Counties Cup. They defeated Nithsdale Wanderers in the next round – the semi-final – by a surprising 8–2 scoreline, but before no more than 300 Kimmeter Park spectators. The last game of the season produced a successful conclusion in this competition. At Palmerston Park, Dumfries, Stranraer was overcome in an exciting match with a full time score of 5–5, and an extra time result of 8–5. For a team that by now so rarely played matches, such meritorious victories are hard to explain, unless of course the use of 'guest' players had been made!

The Club struggled on in this 'hit and miss' manner during the 1939/40 season, before all activity ceased due to the Second World War. The uplift in spectator interest after the hostilities it was hoped would bring a new interest in Solway Star. After Friendly and local Cup matches during the 1945/46 season, a re-entry was made into the South of Scotland League one year later. The last home match of the season was played versus Nithsdale Wanderers on the 29th of March in the first leg match for the Pott's Cup. But the team were hopelessly outclassed, and lost the game by 2–6. In the second leg, on the 19th of April despite an improvement in their performance, they lost again, with a 2–4 scoreline. The team consisted of:

> *Wade, Brown, Crosbie, James, Edgar, Logan,*
> *Bunner, Rodgers, Edwards, McMillan and Dalby.*

The dubious honour of the last goal in what became the final match played by the Star was scored by Dalby.

But a change in the Club's fortunes and renewed interest didn't materialise. The Club had to pay out for heavy travelling expenses – due to their very southern location, and gates at home matches were poor. Despite these burdens a credit balance was announced of £24. However for the recently completed season, the League had been regionalised, whereas the next campaign was to be a single division. The Club realised that they would not be able to keep their heads above water, and resigned from the League. A tentative suggestion of forming a more localised League (other than the Dumfries and District League which only catered for Clubs at a minor level) was made but never materialised. Another suggestion was to suspend activities for one year, and then review the situation to see if the Star could make a fresh start. But finally it was decided that they would attempt to enter the Carlisle and District League and if no support was forthcoming during the coming year then the Club would close down.

There appears to be no record of the Club either entering a League or playing any matches during the 1947/48, and therefore after so many years of struggle they eventually folded. It was not long before Annan Athletic, playing at Mafeking Park, became the new Senior Club in Annan.

Nithsdale glory years abruptly fade.

With non–League football not starting until the 1927/28 season for Nithsdale Wanderers, the Club entered the Alliance League in 1929, after one year of Friendly and Cup games only. For a Club so recently in the second division of the Scottish League, their fortunes had plummeted dramatically. The accounts at the end of the 1927/28 season showed that although £429 had been spent on players wages, the takings at the gate only produced £250, and a loss over the year of £134 was reported; the Club's plight would have been considerably worse if it had not been for £407 received for transferred players.

The return to league football was successful on the pitch but not financially as the Club struggled for survival before poor attendances at home games. During the close season, the Club made a forlorn application to re-enter the Scottish League, but Alloa and Brechin were both re-elected. The Sanquhar side rejoined the South of Scotland League, and after an excellent start on the 16th of August 1930, when St.Cuthbert's Wanderers were beaten 7–1, the team followed this up with a poor period.

With several players having left, it took some weeks for the Club to build up a good team, during which period they lost by five unopposed goals at Stranraer, and had a player sent off for the first time in six years. By the New Year an excellent recovery was made and the team topped the table. But no honours were won by the season's end in either League or major Cup competitions.

Even in the Scottish Cup the Club achieved little. The 1927/28 season saw a first round defeat at Partick Thistle with a 0-4 scoreline and one year later they lost by the same tally at St.Mirren. After exemptions in the qualifying rounds for the 1930/31 competition they were humiliated at the next stage when they were completely outclassed in a 0-14 defeat at Dundee United. Throughout the rest of the Club's life their fall from grace was so big that they never won another major Cup Competition, and up to the War in 1939, only three more appearances were made in the final rounds of the Scottish Cup - 0-2 at East Stirling in the 1933/34 season, 0-5 at Celtic (the second round) three years later, and a 2-5 home defeat to Buckie Thistle four years further on.

The relative isolation of the town, coupled with their exit from Senior football conspired to produce very little coverage of their exploits. It would seem that after leaving the South of Scotland League in 1933, two seasons were spent outside of any League competition. This was followed with two years in the Football Combination.

By 1937 most of the 'founding fathers' of the Club had died, although David Nivison was still prominent, and remained a Club Director until his death in 1949. From the 1937/38 season up to the War years they played in the South of Scotland League - but this whole period was passed without any major honours. Although still a Limited Company, this was in name only, and from 1929 they had operated as a purely amateur Club.

For a number of years the Clubs flitted between playing just Friendly and Cup matches and in a League, but even the post-second World War boom period for football failed to install any real interest in the Club. Ironically despite such a low ebb, it was during the 1947/48 season that the Club staged arguably the biggest match in their history.

The Scottish Cup holders - Aberdeen - appeared at Crawick Holm, for a second round match in that competition. On the 7th of February the Wanderers came close to causing a sensation.

The Dons, hardly impressive, were held to a scoreless first half, and if it hadn't have been for their poor marksmanship, the Amateurs may well have gone in for the break with one or more goals to their credit. Aberdeen opened the scoring early in the second period, a strike which appeared to demoralise the homesters, and after squandering further easy chances, they were finally overwhelmed with a 0–5 scoreline.

SOUVENIR PROGRAMME.

NITHSDALE WANDERERS V. ABERDEEN.

SCOTTISH CUP — 2nd Round.

(By courtesy of J. C. Gair, Dumfries).

At Crawick Holm, Sanquhar,

On SATURDAY 7th FEBRUARY, 1948,

Kick-off 2.45 p.m.

KIRKCONNEL PIPE BAND IN ATTENDANCE.

PROGRAMME — 3d.

TEAMS:

NITHSDALE WANDERERS.

W. GUNNYEON or ANDERSON

J. MAXWELL

A. PHILLIPS

J. LORRAINE   L. SADDINGTON

G. FLEMING   T. COUPLAND   S. CHISHOLM

F. M'COURTY   J. MILLIGAN   H. KEGGANS

REFEREE .... W. G. Livingstone, Glasgow.
LINESMEN .... D. Linley, Glasgow; R. Taylor, Glasgow.

KELLY

WILLIAMS   OWENS

HARRIS   BAIRD   TAYLOR
                          WADDELL
          COWIE   M'KENNA
                COOPER
                    JOHNSTONE

ABERDEEN.

Two young supporters present a 'lucky' horseshoe to the Nithsdale captain Arthur Phillips

They Carry South Cup Hopes v. Dons

Nithsdale Wanderers

After Stranraer's fine show against Rangers, South hopes are that Nithsdale Wanderers will go one better against Aberdeen, and provide the major shock of Round 2 of the Scottish Cup. Above are the men who will face the Dons at Sanquhar to-day. Left to right—back row—Phillips, Maxwell, Anderson, Flemington, Lorraine, Saddington; front row—McCourtney, Milligan, Keggans, Coupland, Chisholm.

'Keeper Dived To Save

One of the goalmouth thrills in the Nithsdale Wanderers v. Aberdeen Scottish Cup second round tie at Sanquhar on Saturday. Anderson, the Nithsdale 'keeper, dives to save, and just manages to reach the ball before Kelly, the Aberdeen centre-forward. After holding the Dons until half-time, the Wanderers lost five goals in the second half.

On the 6th of November 1949, the last of the 'old guard' disappeared, when David Nivison passed away. It was principally his experience and enthusiasm that had kept the Club going over the many years since its departure from the Scottish League. The acting–Secretary (William Nivison) made a last forlorn attempt in April 1950 to stir up interest in the Club, after a year in which there had been no financial transactions, with the team being run at a minor and purely amateur level. But it was all to no avail, and the Club hung on for another year, at which time the remaining three Club Directors resigned, and were replaced with William Nivison and just one other. Despite the promised enthusiasm and support it was not forthcoming but for a number of years the Wanderers played on.

On the 31st of May 1963 a public meeting was called to discuss *"The future of Nithsdale Wanderers"* and this was held three days later. The Committee had already decided back in April that in view of the apathy shown towards the Club, that it should fold at the end of the season. When this decision became common knowledge there was a show of dismay – despite the virtual non–attendance of spectators at home matches! Local schoolboys started a *" Keep the Dale alive campaign "*, and most of the players showed their support by agreeing to waive their match fees. The Committee considered whether one last effort should be made, but with only 25 people attending the public meeting, and twelve at the later A.G.M., it was obviously a forlorn hope. There was talk of Council help, but it appears that this never got past the talking stage! Over the previous season the total gate receipts amounted to £47, whereas ten years earlier they had been £447. It was obvious that fund–raising would be necessary to keep the Club alive, and urgent work was needed on the Ground, with necessary repairs to the enclosure fence and the pavilion.

On the 10th of June 1963, Nithsdale Wanderers entertained Glenafton Athletic in a Western League (Southern Section) match. The homesters took the lead through Hughes, but by half–time they were 1-2 behind. The second half was a rout, and ended in a 1-6 defeat. The Nithsdale team that day, the Club's last ever match, consisted of:

> West, Wilson, Hastings, Hetherington, Reid,
> McClue, McGowan, Hughes, Ferguson, Flannigan
> and 'New Man'.

On the 9th of July 1964 an offer of £350 for the Ground was accepted. On the 26th of August the Club was wound up and finally ceased on the 7th of December of that year.

The Grounds:

Mid–Annandale: The Club's forerunners, at the end of the 19th century, played at Mill Field and Broomhouse Park – probably one and the same venue – but in 1902 moved to Kintail Park. There is now no obvious evidence to pinpoint either Broomhouse Park or Mill Field, and in any event this venue (or venues) were almost certainly nothing more than open fields. *School Field* has also been referred to in past references to the Club, but no factual evidence has been found to substantiate this location as a former Ground; however the school is located near to the Kintail Park site (and also to King Edward Park – the Ground of the current Mid–Annandale Club), and therefore it is possible that these 'two' Grounds are one! In 1902 the Mids. forerunners moved to Kintail Park, and the same venue was used by the Mid–Annandale Club during their lifetime. Kintail Park was sandwiched between the railway line and Livingstone Place, and although houses were built on the site many years ago, the name lives on – the residential road named *Kintail Park* now dissects the former Ground. The venue never became anything more than a fairly basic Ground, with entrance probably off the current Beckton Road, and the main Glasgow Road. In the summer of 1923, a small Stand (at a cost of £13!) was erected on the South side of the pitch, and improvements to this structure – at a cost of £36 – were made during the close season two years later. Other facilities for spectators probably consisted of no more than a refreshment hut – close to the Stand – and a square building on the West boundary of the enclosure could well have been a pavilion containing changing rooms.

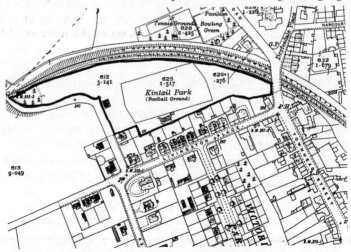

The O.S. Map of 1931 shows the sparse facilities at Kintail Park.

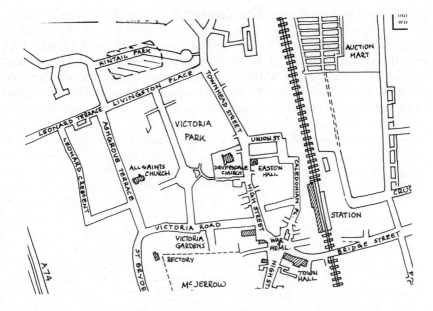

'Kintail Park' in Lockerbie is now just a residential street – with no traces of the former Ground.

Nithsdale Wanderers: The Club's first Ground, known as Castle Holm was situated to the South of the little town, behind the old Castle ruins. It is unlikely that this venue was anything more than a (probably fenced) basic enclosure. The move, in 1920, was to the opposite end of town, just South of Crawick Water, and to the West of the main road heading North. There was no terracing or embankments, but on the North–west side of the pitch, and close to the river, there was a fairly large Pavilion or small Grandstand, and a small uncovered enclosure in front.

The Grandstand was built of stone, complete with stone seating in ten rows, and with a capacity for about 250. Beneath the Grandstand were several rooms – dressing rooms for the teams and officials, a storage area and a small boiler room. Opposite the Grandstand there was a narrow covered enclosure that ran for about third pitch length. The only access to the Ground was via the main road, where turnstiles were installed. A feature of the playing area was a large hump in the middle of the pitch – it was said that if you lay in one goal mouth, then you could not see the other goal!

The Ground remained until well into the 1970's, before a small factory site was developed – right on the South–west boundary of the Ground. The football playing area was then once again used for football. By now there was nothing more than open field with a pitch laid out, located in virtually the same position as the former enclosed field, although in 1990 a degree of enclosure was reinstated when an open fence was erected adjacent to the road.

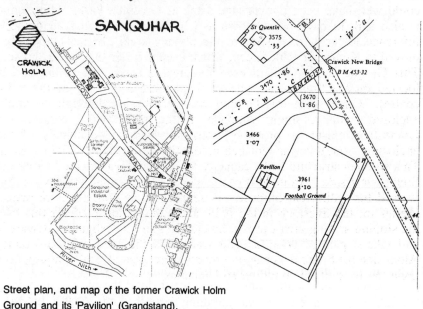

Street plan, and map of the former Crawick Holm Ground and its 'Pavilion' (Grandstand).

1990 – and the current football field that lies virtually over the old Ground site. (Photo Bill Gibbs)

Solway Star: At the Club's formation in 1911, Greenlea Park was used. This may have been the area of current open land adjacent to the road of the same name, or the site of the current Auction Mart (off Butts Street). In view of the status of the Club at this time the Ground was basic, possibly enclosed, and contained just a pavilion – for the players and officials – but probably no facilities for spectators. References to Mafeking Park have been made, but not obviously recorded, and this could well have been one and the same as Greenlea Park. This venue is also said to have been known as 'Old Mudhole', being an obvious reference to the normal state of the playing area! In 1921, the Club moved to Kimmeter Park Green, which became their final resting place. This Ground is now a field used for grazing sheep and cattle, and is located on the South-east side of Stapleton Road (East of the town centre). Once again this Ground was very basic, although no doubt enclosed, with a single entrance at the North-west corner. A Grandstand existed – probably from their earliest occupancy of the enclosure – but this was replaced before the start of the 1923/24 season. This wooden structure had a capacity for 300, and was located along the South-west side. Around 70 years later the Grandstand still exists, but is used for a different purpose. It now serves as nothing more than a shelter for the livestock in the field, and although adapted for this use, the sloping seating area can still be clearly seen; investigators beware – and take a pair of boots as you wade into the mud and cow dung! Alongside the Stand the changing rooms were located, and although now gone the base of this building still remains.

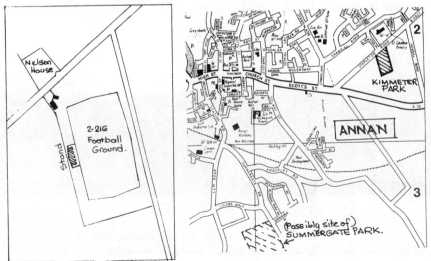

The compact Kimmeter Park Ground – with its tiny Stand in 1931 – now the site is just a field!

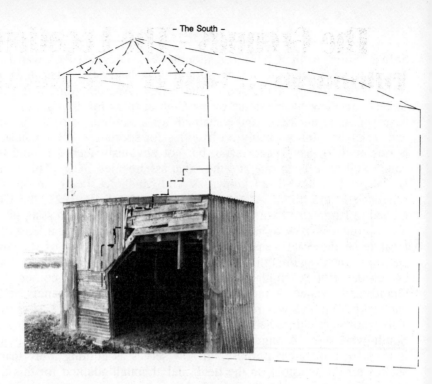

The 'Grandstand' is now a cow shed – watch the pancacks!
(Superimposed on the photo taken in 1990 is the outline of what the Stand **may** have looked like)

The 'Stand' is on the right of the picture (under the trees
(Top photo by Bill Gibbs. Lower by Dave Twydell)

The Grounds - The Locations
Edinburgh ... West of ... & The South

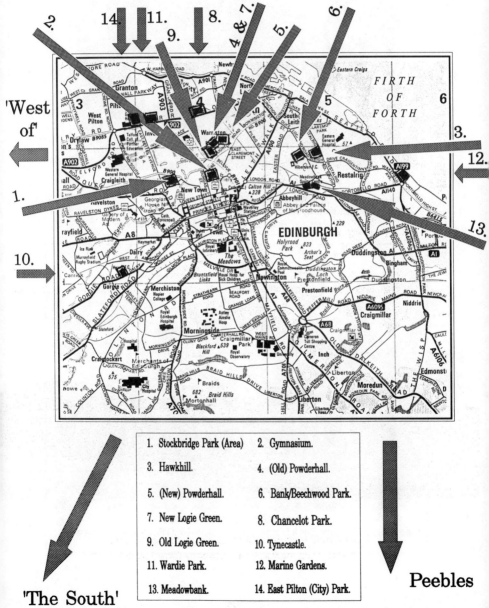

1. Stockbridge Park (Area)
2. Gymnasium.
3. Hawkhill.
4. (Old) Powderhall.
5. (New) Powderhall.
6. Bank/Beechwood Park.
7. New Logie Green.
8. Chancelot Park.
9. Old Logie Green.
10. Tynecastle.
11. Wardie Park.
12. Marine Gardens.
13. Meadowbank.
14. East Pilton (City) Park.

'West of'

'The South'

Peebles

WEST OF EDINBURGH.

ARMADALE FOOTBALL CLUB – 1920's.
(Back row) Harris, Black, Ballantyne, Leckie.
(Middle row) Ross (Trainer) Chambers, Rankine, Blair.
(Front) Hendry, Roberts, Jenkins, Menzies, Johnstone.

ARMADALE – 1910/11 Season.
(Back) Blair, J. Ballantine, Black, Mulheron, M'Nicholl, Welsh, O'Rourke, Brown (Trainer).
(Front) T. Ballantyne, Carson, Taylor, M'Call, Logan, Haddow.

West of Edinburgh.

BATHGATE FOOTBALL CLUB TEAM AND OFFICIALS.
THE SCOTTISH QUALIFYING CUP WINNERS.

1929/30 season: (Front) Frew, McAllister, Dick, Kerr, Walker, Somerville, Baird, Anderson (Dir.). (Middle) Cowan (Trainer), Findlay, Higgins, Currie, Greenhorn, Jamieson, Bryce, Nicholson (Asst.Tranier), Jack (Sec.). (Rear) Somerville (Vice Chair.) Henderson (Dir.), Walker, Nicol (Dir.), Welsh, Watson (Treas.) Hardy (Chairman).

BROXBURN 1910 – Qualifying Cup Winners.
(Rear) Heron, Cameron. (2nd row) Campbell, ?, ?, W.Bryce, S.Bryce, (3rd row) Paton, ?, Sharp, Bisset, Stevenson. (Front) Noble, Keast.

ARMADALE.

Founded 1879. Defunct 1894.
(Armadale Thistle 1893 –1894)
(Armadale Volunteers c.1888 – 1900)
Reformed 1910. Defunct 1935.

League career:

To 1891 –	Friendly and Cup Matches
1891/92 –	Eastern Alliance. †
1892/93 – 1894/95	Friendly and Cup matches.
1895/96 – 1898/99	Linlithglowshire League.
1910/11 –	Scottish Union.
1911/12 – 1914/15	Central League.
1915/16 – 1917/18	Eastern League.
1918/19 –	Inactive.
1919/20 – 1920/21	Central League.
1921/22 – 1932/33	**Scottish League Divsion 2.** *
1933/34 – 1935.	Inactive.

† *Competition abandoned before completion of fixtures.*
* *1932/33 season's fixtures not completed.*

....

Grounds:
To 1891 – Mayfield.
From 1891 – Volunteer Park.
Record Attendance: Approx. 10,000.
Scottish Cup, 4th round versus Kilmarnock (1–2). Season 1919/20.
Colours:
Blue. (To 1888: Navy Blue. 1888 – 1900: Blue and White stripes).
Members of Scottish F.A.
1910 – 1934 (Resigned).

Major honours and achievements:
Scottish Cup: Fourth round (last 8) 1919/20.
         Third Round (last 16) – 1920/21.
         Second Round – 1911/12.

East of Scotland Cup Winners: 1922/23. 1954/55.
East of Scotland Qualifying Cup Winners: 1912/13.
King Cup Winners: 1890/91.
Linlithglowshire Cup Winners: 1888/86. 1890/91. 1896/97.
Central League Champions: 1913/14. 1914/15.
Eastern League Champions: 1915/16.

Scottish League Division Two: Finshed third 1921/22 (First season).
         Finished bottom 1927/28 season.
         Expelled after 17 games, 1932/33 season.

BATHGATE.

Founded 1893. Defunct 1938

League career:

1893/94 – 1904/05	*Eastern League. †*
1905/06 –	*Football Combination.*
1906/07 – 1908/09	*Scottish Union.*
1909/10 – 1913/14	*Central League.*
1914/15 – 1916/17	*Eastern League.*
1917/18 –	*No Activity.*
1918/19 – 1920/21	*Central League.*
1921/22 – 1928/29	**Scottish League Division 2. ***
1929/30 – 1930/31	*East of Scotland League.*
1931/32 – 1937/38	*Inactive.*

† Seasons 1902/03 to 1904/05 also competed in Central Combination.
* Season 1928/29 resigned after 28 games.

....

Grounds:
Until 1902: Boghead Park.
From 1902 : Mill Park.

Record Attendance: *Approx. 10,000.*
Scottish Cup, 2nd Round versus Falkirk. 1921/22 season.

Colours: Until 1904: Red and White stripes.
          From 1904 : Maroon.

Members of Scottish F.A.
1894 – 1934 (Expelled, non-payment of Subs.).

Major homours and achievements:
Scottish Cup: Third Round   – 1921/22. 1925/26.
                Second Round – 1904/05. 1919/20. 1929/1930.
East of Scotland League Champions: 1929/30. 1930/31.
King Cup Winners: 1904/05. 1905/06. 1929/30.
Qualifying Cup Winners: 1919/20. 1929/30. 1930/31.
East of Scotland Qualifying Cup Winners: 1906/07.
Scottish Union Champions: 1907/08.

Scottish League Division Two: Finished third 1923/24.
                Finished bottom 1928/29 season (Resigned)

BROXBURN UNITED.

Founded 1912. Defunct 1932.

League career:

1912/13 – 1914/15	*Central League †*
1915/16 – 1916/17	*Eastern League.*
1917/18 – 1918/19	*No Activity.*
1919/20 – 1920/21	*Central League.*
1921/22 – 1925/26	***Scottish League Second Division.***
1926/27 –	*Scottish Alliance (Northern section).*
1927/28 –	*Mid–Lothian League.*
1928/29 –	*No Activity.*

† 1912/13 season took over fixtures of former 'Broxburn F.C.'

....

Grounds:
Sports Park.

Record Attendance: 9,000.
Scottish Cup, 3rd Round versus Falkirk (1924/25 season)

Colours:
To 1920: Black and White.
from 1920: Maroon.

Members of Scottish F.A.
1912 –1917 (Non–payment of subs.) 1919 – 1927 (Resigned)

Major honours and achievements:
Scottish Cup Fourth Round – 1924/25 (Quarter final)
Third Round – 1913/14. 1919/20.
Second Round – 1912/13. 1920/21. 1921/22. 1926/27.

Scottish League Division 2: 1921/22 finished sixth.
1925/26 finished bottom (Not re-elected)

SCOTTISH LEAGUE RECORDS:

ARMADALE:

Season	P.	W.	D.	L.	F.	A.	Pts.	Pos.
1921/22	38	20	5	13	64	49	45	3rd
1922/23	38	15	11	12	63	52	41	6th
1923/24	38	16	6	16	56	63	38	11th
1924/25	38	15	5	18	55	62	35	15th
1925/26	38	14	5	19	82	101	33	15th
1926/27	38	12	10	16	69	78	34	14th
1927/28	38	8	8	22	53	112	24	20th
1928/29	36	8	7	21	47	99	23	19th
1929/30	38	13	5	20	56	91	31	15th
1930/31	38	13	2	23	74	99	28	18th
1931/32	38	10	5	23	68	102	25	18th
1932/33	17	1	2	14	27	72	4	–

1932/33 season: Fixtures not completed – expelled from League.

BATHGATE:

Season	P.	W.	D.	L.	F.	A.	Pts.	Pos.
1921/22	38	16	11	11	56	41	43	5th
1922/23	38	16	9	13	57	55	41	5th
1923/24	38	16	12	10	58	49	44	3rd
1924/25	38	12	10	16	58	74	34	16th
1925/26	38	7	6	25	60	105	20	19th
1926/27	38	13	7	18	76	98	33	17th
1927/28	38	10	11	17	62	81	31	19th
1928/29	28	5	2	21	37	92	12	–

1928/29 season: Fixtures not completed – Retired from League.

BROXBURN UNITED:

Season	P.	W.	D.	L.	F.	A.	Pts.	Pos.
1921/22	38	14	11	13	43	43	39	6th
1922/23	38	14	12	12	42	45	40	8th
1923/24	38	7	8	18	48	58	32	19th
1924/25	38	12	10	16	58	74	34	16th
1925/26	38	7	6	25	60	105	20	20th

Football comes to West Lothian.

A few miles to the West of Edinburgh, there was an enclave of Scottish Football League teams, that contained a trio of Clubs, which all enjoyed for a few years – and and for a similar period of time – the experience of Senior status. The three – Armadale, Bathgate and Broxburn United – could be geographically compared to their Southern counterparts, i.e. the Mid–Annandale, Nithsdale Wanderers and Solway Star teams. The rapid growth of the game that originated from the affluent Society in England, rapidly spread, not only crossing the boundaries of Class, but also to the Urban areas North of the Border. After the formation of the Queens Park Club in the mid–1860's, other teams were soon formed in Glasgow and further afield, notably, and naturally, in Edinburgh.

For the small communities in the West Lothian district, the growth of the coal and ironstone industry, led to a rapid rise in population, and allied to the 'importation' of workers, football was not long coming to these towns. Probably the first published reference to football in the area came via the *'West Lothian Courier'* in 1878, although two years earlier Shotts first played in the Scottish Cup. The name of Bathgate first came upon the scene in 1879, although not the same team that were to eventually gain admittance to the Scottish League, but they doubtlessly were the forerunners of the later team. By September 1880, Armadale first received public acknowledgement – via the local newspaper – and within at least two years the name of Broxburn Shamrock also became known.

Armadale, the first of 'The Three'.

With regard to these three towns, football did not only first feature in Armadale, but the current 'Armadale F.C.' can be more readily identified with those original pioneers. The Armadale Club's formation year has been recorded as 1879, and although there appears to be no evidence to substantiate this claim, this date appears to be the most likely.

The first reported match of Armadale concerned the match between their second eleven and that of West Lothian (the later Bathgate Club), on the 4th of September 1880, when the latter triumphed with a 2-0 scoreline. One week later, the first teams of these two Clubs met, and Armadale again suffered a defeat, by the same score as their Reserves. The rapid spread of the game included the Lothian villages, and within a year or so, Armadale were playing regular matches with the likes of Plains Bluebell, Glengowan and Whifflet. The early Officials of the Armadale team, at least from 1881, included J. Sprott (Captain), H. Russell (Secretary) and J.Goldie the Club Treasurer.

At this time the 'Dale' were playing their home matches at the Mayfield Ground, which was situated near the Bathville Works, and in November 1881, a friendly fixture with East Stirlingshire provoked great interest in the town. The visitors ran out as 2-0 victors, thus reversing the previous scoreline when Armadale had visited Falkirk. The Edinburgh Association Cup (later named Shield), first saw the Dale's inclusion that season, but after a bye in the first round they were easily despatched by Kinleith in the next.

The following season saw the Club through to the semi-final of the competition. A bye in the first round was followed by a 3-1 defeat of Broxburn Shamrock and the Edinburgh Club, St. James, were beaten by three unopposed goals at Mayfield. The semi-final match brought about the most prestigious game in the Club's short history for they competed against Hearts, a match which they lost by only two (or three!) goals to nil. But by now the Club's stature had risen to the extent that they were a match for any of their local rivals; West Lothian were crushed with a 11-0 scoreline, and in February 1883, Bo'ness were beaten 4-2, in the first game between the two Clubs.

The Edinburgh Cup competition provided the main interest for the team and its supporters, in these pre-league days, but in the 1883/84 season the Club's interest died after a first round defeat to Greenburn Hibs. However, by now the Dale were known further afield, and one of their many friendly fixtures included an invitation to play the famous Hearts team in Edinburgh. For teams eliminated from the Edinburgh Cup in the early stages, a subsidiary competition – the Consolation Cup was devised.

This certainly brought some consolation for the team for they reached the semi-final stage, after victories over Broxburn Thistle and Cowdenbeath. Down to the last four, and the Dale easily overcame Broxburn Shamrock by 5-0, but the Club were then expelled from the competition for failing to provide the referee with details of the team members – apparently a somewhat harsh punishment!

The Club's Reserve team had fluctuating fortunes. For such teams the Edinburgh Association ran a second eleven competition, but despite reaching the semi-final stage in the 1883/84 season, they were then humiliated when beaten 16-0 by the Hearts Reserves. Such a heavy defeat during the season was not reserved only for the second eleven, for the first team were also completely overwhelmed when they lost by 1-12 to West Benhar! By now another worthy competition had been established, the Linlithgowshire Cup, a competition that was sponsored by the philanthropic Lord Rosebery. The Dale were losing finalists in the 1884/85 season, after victories over Grange Athletic (by 16-0!), Broxburn Shamrock and Bo'ness.

The latter match required a replay after two goals were shared on their opponents Ground – a game marred by drunken fans spilling out over the touchline – but before 400 spectators, the home replay was won by 3-0; in the final, the Dale lost by the odd goal in five to the redoubtable Mossend Swifts team.

Interest in the team had risen in the few years since their formation, and on reaching the final of the County Cup in 1886, at least 200 fans travelled to the Broxburn Thistle Ground, where they saw their favourites beat the town's Shamrock team, and hence recorded the first major honour for the Club. The townspeople were kept informed by way of carrier pigeons that were released at half-time, and carried the score, and by telegram at the conclusion of the match. On their arrival home, a Brass Band greeted them, and the team were carried shoulder high to the Strathbrock Hotel where they were presented with the Cup. The following season, the Dale declined to enter for the Edinburgh Shield – disputes (probably stemming from their expulsion in 1883) leading to this decision – and instead, the Scottish Cup was competed for.

The 1886/87 season produced a worthy run in the Premier Cup competition, when West Calder were first beaten 3-1, which was followed by a 5-1 victory over Newcastleton, and finally a 2-5 defeat to St. Bernards. The following few years saw little progress in this Cup, but some memorable matches, included a 12-0 victory over Champfleurie in 1888, and a narrow defeat (by the odd goal in five) at home to Hibernians, one year later. The Club's continuing support brought about the formation of other, but lesser, teams in the town, with the appearance of Armadale's Thistle and Athletic (around 1887), and Star in 1888. The latter team's formation was based upon the Star Inn, and their matches were played at the Volunteer Field, a venue which was shortly to become associated with the Dale.

The 1888/89 season saw the Club change their colours from navy blue shirts to blue and white stripes, and the honour of two players – Mathieson and Love – being picked to represent the East of Scotland team. The Club lost in the County Cup Final to Bo'ness, but the 2,000 attendance at Bathgate realised £36 in gate money, the second highest ever taken in the competition to that date.

By now it was agreed that a better home venue should be sought, and shortly after the start of the 1889/90 season, the Volunteer Field was secured, a Ground that has remained as the home of the Dale to this day. The site was part of the Barbauchlaw Estate which was owned by George Readman senior, and Colonel Hope of the 8th Volunteer Battalion Royal Scots secured a hall in South Street, for the Football Club's use.

The Ground was enclosed, and was first used by the Dale for their biggest match to that date, when the Hibernians ran out narrow winners in the Scottish Cup-tie. Efforts were soon made to make the playing surface more acceptable, and the Club's popularity – and support – continued to rise. In 1891, the Dale won the King Cup, and the final at Albion Park, Broxburn attracted an attendance of over 2,000, of which around half were Armadale fans.

With the formation of the Scottish League in 1890, and the legalisation of professionalism in England, Clubs such as Armadale were threatened on two fronts.

Now, the big City teams would be less inclined to compete in Friendly matches, and the retention of promising players was at risk. In the latter situation, Armadale were soon disappointed, for W.Booze 'defected' to England, and became a paid player with Burnley. But this did not prevent the Dale from appearing in three Cup Finals at the end of the 1890/91 season. Before a 2,000 crowd at Boghead Park, Bathgate, they overcame Bo'ness to win County Cup, but narrowly lost to Hearts (the Scottish Cup-holders) in the Shield and to Raith Rovers in the King Cup. The end of the season saw the formation of the Eastern Alliance (League), and together with other senior 'non-league' teams, Armadale were accepted as members.

At the start of the next season, the Club struggled to raise a full, and worthy, team, but in the their first ever League game, they nonetheless overcame Adventurers by 5-2, and followed this up with a resounding 5-1 victory over their main adversaries, Bo'ness. But this excellent start was not to continue, for six defeats followed, and two points were deducted for their use of an ineligible player! The Dale had a far from happy season, and to make matters worse, the Alliance was abandoned in confusion before the season's end; the team's last match being a 2-0 victory over Bathgate Rovers. The Club's fortunes slumped to their lowest level during the 1892/93 season, and apart from a surprise 4-1 win at Dunfermline Athletic in the Scottish Cup, heavy defeats in friendly games and early Cup exits were the outcomes of that year.

The Summer of 1893 saw the demise of the Club, but a new Club, under the name of 'Armadale Thistle' (and composed principally of players from the former Thistle Juniors Club) soon took their place. It was not long before the 'Thistle' suffix was dropped, and so the 'new' Armadale took to the football field. The Club were unfortunate to be going though this transition stage at this time, for doubtless this was the reason why they were not invited to join the newly formed East of Scotland League.

But the resurrection was shortlived and by 1894 the Club continued in little more than name only. Meanwhile the Junior Club, Armadale Volunteers, were going from strength to strength, and with no fixtures being played by the Armadale Club during the 1894/95 season, it was left to the Volunteers to represent the town.

The Dale were not alone in their adversity, for the mid 1890's saw a slump in the fortunes of many of the small town clubs. With the continued success of the Scottish League, and by now the full recognition of professionalism in Scotland, many fans were being lured away – and by way of easier railway travel – to watch the big town Clubs, rather than support their own local teams.

But early in the 1895/96 season a match report concerning Mossend Swifts and 'Armadale' (a 4–2 victory for the latter) appeared, and although this was probably in reality the Armadale Thistle team, this notable victory in effect heralded the return of a Senior team to the town. The season was not without its successes with semi–final Cup appearances, and the 'new' Club's entry – as founder–members – of the Linlithglowshire League. But any hope of the Club's re–emergence as force to be reckoned with was shortlived! The Scottish Cup was entered for in the 1896/97 season (without success), and although the County Cup was won, such a success was but a brief respite before the Club disappeared once again.

The Dale did reach the County Cup Final again in 1898 (when they lost by three unopposed goals to Bo'ness), but achieved little of note during the following season. Although entered for the Scottish Cup in the 1899/1900 season, they scratched to Mossend Swifts, and in the campaign that followed, no matches were played by the Club. The official end came at the meeting of the East of Scotland Association in September 1900, when Armadale Volunteers were expelled for non–payment of subscriptions.

Bathgate enter the fold.

In most respects the early history of football in the nearby town of Bathgate followed along similar lines to those of Armadale. Until the end of the Victorian era, the principal team in the town played in the same competitions and in Friendly matches against similar opponents. Even the origins of Bathgate F.C. started at a similar time, and the birth and subsequent rise in popularity of the game was brought about in the same way.

Football in Bathgate started under the guise of the 'West Lothian' Club in c.1880. although it was not long before the name was changed to plain 'Bathgate'. However, unlike Armadale F.C., competition for support in the town became more fierce as further Senior Clubs were created, and by the early 1890's, although by then the original Bathgate F.C. had ceased to exist, Bathgate Athletic (who played at the Cricket Ground) and Bathgate Rovers whose home venue was at Boghead Park had become the main protagonists with the Junior outfit, Bathgate Thistle, in the wings. Of the former two, the Rovers had been the most successful with a 4th round Scottish Cup appearance to their credit (at which stage they lost by eight goals to Abercorn) in 1891, and progress through to the second round one year later.

But despite winning the King Cup in 1892, by the end of the 1892/93 season they were at a very low ebb, to such an extent that a Scribe in the local newspaper was already referring to them as the *late* Club, in the summer of 1893! The Club's problems had been brought about by the competition they had to endure with the Athletic Club, and such rivalry brought about the inevitable wrangling with regard to the interchange of players between the two outfits. The size of the town could clearly not support two Senior teams, especially since football interest was at a fairly low ebb at this time, and by the end of the season serious considerations had to be given to an amalgamation between the two.

On the 20th of July 1893 a meeting was held at the Institute to consider the state of football in the town, for by now both senior teams were considered as having become defunct. It was agreed at the meeting that a completely new senior Club under the name of 'Bathgate F.C.' should be formed, with the proviso that the players would remain as amateurs and that they must be resident in the Parish. The new Club obtained membership of the Scottish F.A. for the 1893/94 season, and played their first match on the 5th of August. The Rovers old Ground at Boghead Park (complete with a Pavilion at one end) was available, and it was there that Broxburn were entertained before a large attendance that had gathered around the ropes. The locals' team consisted of mostly old Athletic and Rovers players, and it was Morris that gave the lead to the new Club.

By half-time the scoreline read 2-1, but the visitors came back strongly in the second period, and finished the match as 4-3 victors. The Club entered for the Scottish Cup, and although they obtained a goalless draw at Kirkcaldy, they were unsuccessful in the replay. Overall the Club made an undramatic start, but noticeably improved as the season wore on.

Halfway through the 1893/94 season, the local newspaper football reporter was urging for a complete revival of the game in the area, and it no doubt pleased him when Bathgate were accepted into the newly formed East of Scotland League (along with Broxburn, Broxburn Shamrock and Bo'ness). Since the League was not formed until January 1893, matches did not commence until the next month. The formation of the League, which evolved from a meeting of the East of Scotland F.A. in Edinburgh, agreed on a £1 entrance fee, with a £3 guarantee for visiting teams. Home teams would pay for all relevant match expenses, and for the initial (part!) season seven teams would participate.

Bathgate's first match produced a 3-3 draw at Broxburn Shamrock on the 3rd of February, and three weeks later they entertained Uphall (having lost by 0-4 to Kirkcaldy in the semi-finals of the King Cup during the interim). Bathgate protested with regard to the suitability of the Ground - their own! It was covered in snow, but their main reason for a hopeful postponement was more likely to them having only ten men available. Nonetheless by half-time they had taken a 3-1 lead, which must have depressed the visiting goalkeeper, as it was reported that:

"The Uphall Custodian had deserted his team in the interval".

And in the second period, during which time the teams were evenly matched with ten players each , Bathgate ran out eventual 6-1 victors!

Before the start of the 1894/95 season the Club were to lose their player, Battles, to the Hearts Club, a situation that was to be similarly repeated now that professionalism had come out into the open. Along with their near neighbours at Armadale, Bathgate were to find the next few years difficult, in having to keep their best players and vying with the City Clubs for support.

However, during the 1896/97 season, and one year later, they managed to reach the first round proper of the Scottish Cup, but on each occasion were easily beaten by fellow non-League opponents. This situation continued until the turn of the century, by which time the Clubs themselves appeared to have been doing little to attract extra support; in the East of Scotland Consolation Cup semi-final at Boghead Park in early 1901, the attendance for the match versus West Calder was stated as having been only 'fair'. However, this could have been improved upon, but spectators were fed up attending matches, only to find that the kick-off time had been considerably delayed - for matches were rarely started at the stated time! (the game was drawn 1-1, and Bathgate lost by six unopposed goals in the replay).

With a scarcity of suitable teams, the Club decided to enter the Central Combination for the 1902/03 season (together with their membership of the Eastern League), and the situation in general, and support, began to pick up. Friendly matches were still necessary to provide a full programme, one such game was played at home against the team with a most unimaginative name - Normal Athletic! In the Qualifying Cup, the Club had Bo'ness in opposition, a prospect that created great interest in the town. By now the Club were playing at Mill Park, and an attendance of 1,600 (which included 600 visiting supporters) saw an exciting game in which six goals were shared. Bathgate bowed out of the competition after a second replay was necessary.

The next season started with an impressive Friendly match when the reserves of Celtic visited Mill Park, and 2,500 supporters watched a 1-1 draw. The main event of this season, was the formation of the Club into a Limited Company, in April 1904. The A.G.M. attracted a large gathering of supporters, and it was announced that after a total expenditure of £367, the Club had made a modest profit of around £10. The increased interest in the Club was well merited, since the year had been highly successful on the playing front, for in the 38 matches played, only 9 were lost (and 8 drawn). But not everybody was satisfied, and a heated discussion developed with regard to who should make the decision in connection with the re-signing of players and team selections - the secretary or the Committee!

J. HASTIE.
(Outside Left, Bathgate F.C.)

JOE McGILL.
(Inside-Left, Bathgate F. C.)

ROBERT HOSSOCK
(Captain, Bathgate Football Club.)
(From a Photograph by Mr G. Townson.)

Is the latest "capture" of our local club, and a most fortunate and profitable one it has been, so far, to the club, while the supporters are jubilant at their club having found such a capable player to fill the position which he presntly occupies with much distinction.

But with the Club about to start, at an elevated status, it was hoped that a more harmonious situation could be restored. The company was floated with £500 capital, and there was some discussion with regard to ground improvements at this time.

Mill Park was located between Cochrane street and Russell Row, and for a number of years was little more than an enclosed field. The main entrance was on the North side (off Cochrane Street), with the pavilion tucked away in the far North–east corner of the Ground. But for spectators there was nothing more than raised banks down most of each side – at one end of the North side, the pitch was stopped abruptly by the rear wall of the malthouse. In 1904 there was talk of building a Grandstand, but such a development was probably not undertaken for a number of years.

The 1904/05 season was very successful, for the Club reached the second round of the Scottish Cup for the first time. After battling through the qualifying rounds, the Club entertained Arbroath in the first round, and despite being a goal down at half-time, they fought back strongly in the second period, to record a final score of 2-1. The next round created the greatest interest, for the Club had drawn Second Division Aberdeen, at Mill Park.

On the day of the match, the pitch lay under a carpet of snow, but following a pitch inspection at 2.30 p.m., the Referee decided that the game could proceed. By this time there was a crowd of around 3,000 in the enclosure, and aided by 300 travelling fans, this figure had swelled to 4,000 by kick-off time. Bathgate started well, but after 20 minutes the players had to leave the field due to a sudden blinding snow storm. After a three minute break, play resumed, and Aberdeen soon took the lead through Mc'Phee. By this time the visitors were playing with only ten men, but the injured Ruddiman returned, just before the homesters equalised in the 44th minute. Although Bathgate were playing against the strong wind in the second period they fought strongly, and the home supporters goaded the visitors with chants of:

"Where are the boys of the Gold Brigade",
(referring to Aberdeen's Blue and Gold team colours).

But after 20 minutes a further heavy snowfall led to the referee abandoning the match. The re-match was played at Pittodrie on the 18th of February, before a crowd of 6,000 which realised receipts of £169. Bathgate realised they stood little chance of winning, and Aberdeen played far better than in the earlier game. The visitors were overwhelmed in the first forty-five minutes and conceded six goals, but in the second period the homesters sat back on their lead, and Bathgate managed a consolation goal. It was reported that the Referee, Mr. Nisbet, was very popular with the Aberdeen fans, and when he entered the field at the start he was warmly cheered, to which he raised his cap in reply!

A more successful conclusion came in the final of the prestigious King Cup, when the Club won the trophy for the first time, a feat which was repeated one year later.

But even such matches were still often played in confusing circums-tances. In the County (Roseberry) Cup semi-final, Bathgate won at Bo'ness, although a week earlier the two Clubs had also met in a match which was designated as a friendly, but which was thought to have been the Cup–tie by both Players and supporters alike! The final was also played at Bo'ness, and special trains took the supporters of both Bathgate and Broxburn F.C., but after an injury to a Broxburn player near the end of the game – by which time Bathgate were leading 1–0 – a pitch invasion led to the match being abandoned. The re–match was held at Shamrock Park (home of Broxburn Shamrock), and before a 2,000 crowd Bathgate lost by the only goal of the game. However following a protest the match was replayed yet again, and ended 1–1 after extra time! Broxburn finally won the match. But success was also realised in the eight team Eastern League, although after leading the pack on several occasions, the club had to be satisfied with a final second place.

With six Directors, Bathgate became a limited Company on the 25th of June 1904, and took over the running of the former Club. Fifteen proprietory shares were purchased at £4 each plus sixty–nine ordinary £1 shares.

The achievements over the campaign resulted in the Club being admitted to the Scottish Union as founder–members for the 1906/07 season. Along with local Clubs Broxburn and Bo'ness, the Club competed with the reserve teams of Hearts and Rangers, and far from being overawed they finished the season as League leaders – on goal average above Rangers. But Rangers insisted that a a play–off should be undertaken to determine the true Champions, a demand that Bathgate refused; the Authorities, in their wisdom, decided to award the Championship to the Glasgow Club! However, undaunted Bathgate were undisputed Champions one year later.

Without doubt these early years of the twentieth century were the most successful in the Club's history, and in 1909, they were included amongst the eleven Clubs who reformed the Central League. This competition was probably the most senior outside of the Scottish League itself, and included such names as Alloa Athletic, Dunfermline Athletic, St. Johnstone and Stenhousemuir – Clubs that were to become long standing members of the premier competition.

But with the outbreak of the First World War, it became necessary for the Club to confine themselves to a more local competition, and so they joined the Eastern League on its reformation in 1915. But with wartime travel restrictions, and loss of Players to the forces, the Club along with many others decided to call a halt at the end of the 1916/17 season.

Broxburn become United.

The third Club of this trio came from Broxburn, a town nearer to Edinburgh, than Armadale and Bathgate, but one that was to also suffer badly from the economic depression of the 1920's. Whereas Armadale had only junior teams in contention for support, and in Bathgate there were two Clubs (before they combined), in Broxburn the competition was even more pronounced, since for many years, three different Clubs vied for support. Although probably the largest populated of the three towns, 14,000 around the turn of the century, this was clearly insufficient to support three Senior teams.

Broxburn Shamrock were probably the oldest of the trio in the town, being formed at least by 1882, and were therefore one of the pioneers of the game in the area. Influenced by the Irish connection, the Club not only adopted a name that reflected this viewpoint, but named their ground, simply, Shamrock Park. This was probably situated just West of the town, alongside the Canal, a site which currently embraces the Drill Hall. Goschen and Strathbrook Parks were also referred to as the Club's home Ground, which may have been earlier names of Shamrock Park, or former venues of the Club. The influx of thousands of Irish families to Scotland, following the great Famine of 1846, led to the formation of several prominent Clubs (notably Celtic and Hibernians) that were renowned for their insular outlook. Shamrock were prominent in local Cup competitions in the 1880's, and in the 1885/86 season first entered for the Scottish Cup; after a 2–2 draw with Bo'ness, they lost the replay by scoring only one goal to their opponents five.

They did not reach the second round until the 1887/88 season – and that only by default after Mossend Swifts had been disqualified – but lost in that tie to St. Bernards.

But by the early 1890's the Club had become a force to be reckoned with, and reached the second round again, in the 1891/92 season, at which stage they narrowly lost to Hearts, by the odd goal in nine. They then caused something of a sensation the very next campaign. After notable successes over Dunblane, Kings Park and St.Mirren (the latter of the Scottish League), they finally lost to Queens Park by 2–4 in the semi–final. By this time the Shamrock had become founder–members of the Eastern Alliance (in 1891), but then became less prominent, although they continued in existence until at least the First World War days, and therefore until after the creation of the rival United team.

Broxburn Thistle were also in existence by the early 1880's and they first followed their neighbours – Shamrock – into the Scottish Cup in the 1886/87 season. Their only achievement of note (in this competition), was the progress through to the third round in the 1890/91 season, at which point they were thrashed by Bathgate Rovers, with a six–nil scoreline. By now the Club had dropped the 'Thistle' from their title, and until their amalgamation with the Athletic they continued under the heading of plain 'Broxburn F.C.'. The Club's Ground was at Albyn Park – probably one and the same as the later named Albion Park, where the current Broxburn Athletic team play – which is situated off the, currently named, Greendykes Road.

The Ground was often used for representative matches, including local and County cup finals, but in 1904, the Club moved to the Sports Field (later named Sports Park).

By this time Broxburn F.C. were playing in the Central Combination. The team then moved on to the Scottish Union, as founder–members from 1906, and in the East of Scotland Qualifying Cup were highly successful, with a hat–trick of victories from 1909 to 1911.

OUR OLD FOOTBALLERS.

WILLIAM WARDROP,
BROXBURN.

It is three years past since William Wardrop came into our district an unknown nearly in the football world. Yet he was a keen lover of the game, and quickly his enthusiasm kindled in Broxburn, where he settled down, and soon he became a member of the club.

The third team of the Broxburn trio, were the Athletic. This team, at least in their early days were the more minor of the three Clubs, and first played their matches at a Ground in Station Road, possibly where the current playing fields are, at the junction with the main Edinburgh Road. The Club rarely hit the headlines, although they became more prominent around the turn of the century, at which time they progressed through to the final rounds of the Scottish Cup. In the 1902/03 season they reached the first round, when they lost at Leith Athletic, a stage that was repeated six years later, and then, in a final fling as an independent Club won through to the second round in 1911, when they were beaten by Third Lanark by 6–1. After a spell in the East of Scotland Junior League, they moved onto the modest Linthlithglowshire League, in 1904, before progressing on to finally the reformed Central League in 1909. By now the Athletic were playing at Albion Park.

As if the competition was not keen enough, the three Clubs had also to contend with the Uphall Club, who played off West Main Street, barely one mile West of Broxburn centre!

It was clear, by the enlightened pre–First World War years, that there was not sufficient support for even two, never mind three, senior teams in the town. Any question of the Shamrock combining with another Club was out of the question, for they still adhered to their religious and isolated background, but for both Broxburn F.C. and Broxburn Athletic, amalgamation was the only sensible answer. The idea had been mooted for several years, but the Athletic, as generally the lesser of such a proposed partnership would have exerted little influence, although their progress in the Scottish Cup which led to the match with Third Lanark, gave them greater credibility. It was after this match that the amalgamation was first seriously, but informally agreed. Negotiations between the two Clubs quietly took place between the committees, and on the 29th of March 1912, the proposal was made public.

It was agreed that the two Clubs would be formally dissolved on the 3rd of April, and members of both would form the initial Committee (twelve members from Broxburn and nine from the Athletic, with a Chairman being provided by the former). A newly elected Committee was to be chosen before the start of the 1912/13 season.

Under the name of 'Broxburn United', the new outfit took over the leases of both the grounds, viz. Albion Park and the Sports Field, and an annual membership fee for members of 25p was agreed upon. On the 23rd of March, Broxburn Athletic played their last match, when Armadale were beaten by the only goal of the game, in the semi-final of the Gardener Cup. Each Club was scheduled to play later, independent games, but rail strikes led to the cancellation of fixtures that would have brought down the curtain for the two teams.

The last game of the season was played on the 6th of April, in the final of the Gardeners Cup at Albion Park, when ironically Broxburn were due to play Broxburn Athletic, but by this time the two clubs were one! However, playing as different teams, a record attendance was attracted to the ground, and 'Broxburn F.C.' triumphed by a solitary goal, in a game which produced little excitement. The records of the two former Clubs revealed that in their last seasons, Broxburn F.C., from a total income of £328 had a surplus of 15p (home gates produced £278, and players wages, signing on fees and travelling costs amounted to £175). 30 matches had been played of which ten were won, and twelve lost. Over at the Athletic, the income of £268 had produced a healthy surplus of £5, and in the 26 games played (which produced eleven victories and thirteen defeats), Allan and Chambers had been ever presents.

BROXBURN F.C. – 1911

(Standing) Pagan, Black, Grieve, Nicol (Vice Pres.), Burns, M'Manus, Macnab, M'Phillips, Watson, Hunter, Marr (Sec.), M'Kenzie (Trainer) M'Queen (Pres.), (Seated) Clark, Fairley, Kennedy, Stevenson, M'Ewan.

Before the close of the 1911/12 season, the first match of the combined Club was played (in early April), and the friendly draw with Rangers (who included eight first–teamers in their line–up) attracted an attendance of 1,500. On the 24th of April, the full first team of Third Lanark came to Broxburn, for a match to raise funds for the new Club, and at Albion Park, 1,500 locals were encouraged with the 3–1 victory of their team; the Broxburn line–up contained four former Broxburn players, and seven from the previous Athletic team.

For the 1912/13 season, Broxburn Shamrock continued their independent existence, as new members of the Eastern League, while Broxburn United were elected to the Central league in place of the now defunct Broxburn F.C. There was great optimism within the new Club, and on the 17th of August, Bathgate were entertained in a pre–season friendly game.

One week later the same opponents were present for the first League game of the combined team, when 1,500 fans were present, and the newcomers won by 1–0. After six league matches this initial victory was the only one credited to the United, and they resided in bottom place in the League! The Club recovered from this disquieting start, and went on to play in the Central League until 1917, when the continuance of the War brought about a halt. Although no League honours were won, the United made their mark in the Scottish Cup, with a second round appearance in the 1912/13 season (when they were beaten by five unopposed goals at Raith Rovers), but went one better the next year. After a first round bye, Dumfries were beaten by 5–1, before the team succumbed at home to Motherwell, by two unopposed goals.

Armadale start afresh – again.

The start of the twentieth century saw no senior football representation in Armadale, although the town was well endowed with Junior teams. Armadale Daisy (County Juvenile finalists in 1901), as well as Armadales' United and Rising Star, vied for support, together with the lesser teams of Woodend Excelsior and Armadale Athletic.

By 1910, the main contenders were Armadales' Thistle, Rangers, Northern and Unity, but by now a body of football fans had decided that it was time to form a senior Club in the town once again. One hundred enthusiasts were present in Forsyth's Hall on the 15th of March 1910, when the creation of a new Club was agreed upon. Mr. H.Brown chaired the meeting, and the Armadale Thistle committee were prominent with their assistance given towards the formation of the new Club.

Towards the end of April 1910, a *'Grand Exhibition Football Match'* was played between a selected Armadale team and the first eleven of Bathgate. An entrance charge of 3d was made, but the crowd saw a far from grand match, which the newcomers won by the only goal, from Taylor. During the early summer, the new Armadale F.C. were held in limbo, as verification of their status was awaited from the Scottish F.A., and Armadale Thistle, who were to provide the nucleus of the new Club, proceeded in their Junior status. Eventually an application to join the Central League was able to be made, following the new 'Dale's' acceptance into the Scottish F.A., but this proved unsuccessful, and so an entry into the lesser Scottish Union had to suffice. A pre-season Friendly match versus Rangers was played in August, and the new team – composed almost entirely of 'foreigners' – lost to their opponents by 0-2. Dr. Anderson kicked off the match at Volunteer Park, and the team consisted of:

> *Black (former Broxburn Athletic), Easton (ex-Bathgate), J.Ballantyne(Motherwell), McCall (Hamilton), Mulhern (Shotts United), Blair (Clyde), T. Ballantyne (Partick Thistle), McGuire (Belfast Distillery), Haddow (Alloa).*

The only former Armadale players were (from the Thistle), Taylor and Cunningham.

In the first League game, the team came back with a point from West Calder Swifts, following a 1-1 draw. Broxburn Athletic were then beaten in the East of Scotland Cup, which was followed by a home game versus Broxburn Shamrock, in the Qualifying Cup; another 1-1 draw ensued and was then succeeded by four shared goals in the replay, and finally a comprehensive five goal victory by the newcomers.

A moderate start was made to the season, with more successes in the various Cup competitions, and the first League success did not come until January. However, by the end of the season, the Club had won a trophy for they beat Civil Service Strollers in the final of the East of Scotland Consolation Cup, which was played at Albion Park, Broxburn. Fortunately the Club improved in the second half of the season, in league matches, and finished the season in a comfortable mid-table position.

They were fortunate in being elected to the Central League in their second season, and looked forward to bigger attendances that would result from local derby games, and more prestigious opponents. During the close season levelling took place on the pitch, work on providing embankments for spectators was started and dressing room accommodation was built, developments which put the Club £50 in debt. In the Qualifying Cup, Duns sold Ground advantage for £10, to Armadale, and turned up for this second round match with only nine players; the homesters made up the Duns loss with two of their own men, and then proceeded to thrash their visitors by 10-0! After a victory at Bathgate, the Dale lost by 2-0 to East Stirlingshire in a decider at Ibrox, after two drawn games.

But the Club had already qualified for the final rounds of the Competition, and in their first Scottish Cup appearance for twenty years, they beat Peterhead, to produce a lucrative meeting with Aberdeen. More money was to be made by the Dale 'reversing' the tie (£40 and a half share of the gate money), but a lame showing resulted in a 0-3 defeat, and the sending off of Rankine.

This match at least secured their immediate financial future, and proved a godsend, for after finishing bottom of the Central League, they would otherwise have probably been voted out of this competition.

During the close season, Billy Harris (ex-Tottenham Hotspur and Bo'ness) plus the former Hearts player, Richardson, were the most notable signings, and further levelling - and drainage work - was undertaken at Volunteer Park. The 1912/13 season saw the Club find their feet in league competition, and the winning of two major trophies.

The East of Scotland Qualifying Cup was won when West Calder were beaten at Tynecastle (two goals in the last five minutes securing a 4–2 victory), and the County Cup was captured with a 2–1 victory over Broxburn United at Bathgate in the final.

After three years of moderate successes, the Club embarked on the next season full of optimism, which proved to be well founded. At the Ground, further work resulted in the building of a Grandstand, to seat 200, on the West side, and a pavilion – complete with a small Directors Grandstand – opposite. The Penman Cup was won, which had been carried over from the previous season, when Cowdenbeath were beaten on their own Ground before a record midweek attendance that produced gate receipts of £100. Although there was little else of merit in Cup competitions, of particular significance to the Club was their finishing the campaign as Central League Champions, a great achievement considering that only two years earlier they had been the wooden–spoonists!

The War in Europe caused a delay in the start of the 1913/14 League programme, and the hostilities resulted in difficulties of travel for some teams, and hence uncompleted fixtures. But in the League, there was no stopping the Dale, and after a defeat on the last day of October, the next reversal did not come until near the end of the campaign. Although one match remained unplayed, the Club became League Champions once again, this time five points ahead of second placed Arbroath. By now the Dale could seriously consider a bid for Scottish League status, but this unfortunately was out of the question, due to the wartime footing that the Country was now in. The Central League was suspended, and so the Club gained entry into the reformed Eastern League, which consisted of a majority of former Second Division Clubs. Aided by several auspicious – albeit – temporary signings (including Peter Currie from Bradford City and Jack Comrie of Reading), Armadale took the League by storm and won their first nine matches.

The Club became League Champions, and also won the Eastern Cup, and their record over the season, in all games, resulted in 26 victories, four draws and only four defeats. The next campaign was not so successful, but even so there were three Cup final appearances (at which the County and Gardeners Cup were won), and once again an overall successful season was the final verdict. By now Wartime restrictions were beginning to cause serious problems for all Clubs, and after doubts about starting, the Dale finally joined six other Clubs in the reduced Eastern League. But seriousness of intent was still apparent, and in March 1918, fighting broke out at the home game with Cowdenbeath, which led to the closure of Volunteer Park until May! This proved a severe drain on the Club's reduced resources, and with the abandonment of the league for the 1918/19 season, the Club had little choice but to cease operations until the end of the War, which fortunately was to come within a few months.

Central League Champions:
(Back) Ross (Trainer, T.Ballantyne, Burns, Christie (reserve), Thomson, Harris, Graham, Shaw. (Front) McKerley, J.Ballantyne, Tait (Capt.), Carlaw, Lawrence.

After the War was over.

So, the three Clubs all had a short period of inactivity, for Bathgate this time lasted for just one season, that of 1917/18. Armadale were also dormant for only one year, one season after Bathgate, and Broxburn United called a halt to the proceedings for both of those campaigns.

Hence it was Bathgate who were the first of the three teams back into the football fold.

The Club carried on where they had left off, and rejoined the Central League, a competition that had closed down in 1915. As before, most of the competing Clubs were former Scottish League Division 2 members, and their time in the Central League was expected to be just for the one post–war season, and afterwards they would rejoin the premier competition. For teams such as Bathgate, the way was also seen for them to join their fellow clubs in the higher competition. But the Clubs had not reckoned with the idiosyncratic views of the Scottish League governing body. During the summer of 1919, both Broxburn United and Armadale were ready for action, and they too were happy to re–join the Central League, with the thought that this route may immediately lead to the Scottish league itself, should, as expected, the Central be completely converted into the reformed and revised Division 2. When it became apparent that the Scottish League had no intention of confirming this expectation, the Central League decided to 'go it alone'.

They were in a very strong position, for the Scottish League Clubs (now one division of 22 Clubs, an increase of four, over the previous season's number) were restricted to certain rules, amongst which was a maximum wage, for players. For the Central League no such need for conformity was necessary, since they did not belong to the Inter–League Board. Therefore the Clubs within the League were able to recruit whomsoever they wanted, regardless of transfer fees, at a wage that was agreeable to both parties. For their part, the Scottish League members were bound to a post–war maximum wage that they could pay. With the post–war interest in the game at a high, and with well known – often of International status – players being lured to the Central League, then these 'non–league' Clubs found that their gates were up, and therefore the money was available.

The Scottish League appeared to be the losers in this situation. One anomaly concerned Falkirk and Hearts who, although members of the Scottish League, also had Reserve teams playing in the 'outlawed' Central League!

The main body of opinion within the Scottish League insisted that they should ride out the storm, reasoning that the Central League Clubs would not be able to afford the high wages for long.

Others considered that the Central League, en bloc, should be given Senior status, by 'promoting' the member Clubs into a new reformed Second Division. The latter situation was more or less the final outcome, but not for two years.

Bathgate enjoyed two moderately successful post–war seasons, and in the first one they won the Qualifying Cup, and reached the second round of the Premier Competition. The latter produced no real shocks, for they received a bye in the first round, and in the second lost by two unopposed goals at St. Bernards. The Club never looked serious challengers for Central league honours, and at the end of their first season, post–war stay, they only managed to finish below halfway up the final table.

The second campaign produced a far healthier finish. After their 3–0 home victory over Bo'ness on New Year Day, before a very encouraging crowd of 3,000 they reached to fourth in the table, and it wasn't until the fifteenth of January that the team sustained their first home defeat in the League when they lost by 1–2 to Lochgelly United, before a near 2,000 Mill Park crowd. At the finish they ended up in a creditable 5th place in the League, after sharing two draws in the last match at Stenhouse-muir. The Roseberry Cup final was reached (Bathgate lost to Bo'ness), and in the final game of the season, a prestigious Friendly match was played against Bradford City, from the English League, when over 2,000 fans saw their favourites win by 3–1.

In Armadale, a public meeting in March 1919, refloated the Football Club, and a Limited Company was later formed, which not only took over the name, but also the debts and liabilities, of the pre–war team. In Bathgate a similar step was taken.

The Dale signed on a number of former Scottish League players, including Ferguson, Gardner and McCaig from Partick Thistle, Devine from Ayr and Anderson, the former Airdrie and Albion Rovers man. The 1919/20 season started with a Friendly defeat at St. Bernards, and was followed with an easy victory over Civil service Strollers in the East of Scotland Qualifying Cup match at Volunteer Park, before a 700 crowd.

By the New Year, the team although only lying in a mid-table place (they were unable to repeat their pre-war Championship achievements) were about to cause something of a sensation in the Scottish Cup.

Having qualified for the premier competition, they entertained Clyde in January 1920. Although the visitors were only able to field ten men for much of the game, due to an early injury, the homesters were considered the better team, and overcame the opposition with a 78th minute goal, which pleased the majority of the 6,000 crowd. In the next round, Hibernians came to Volunteer Park, and a record attendance of 7,000 paid record receipts which totalled over £230. Additional (open) seating was provided each side of the Grandstand, and within the packed enclosure, the crowd were soon to be delighted, for Prentice put the Dale ahead after only one minute. Urged on by their partisan supporters, this lead was held, and so the club recorded their most notable victory.

But the Dale had not finished yet, for another home tie, brought Ayr United to Armadale. Once again all records were broken, with a gate of 8,000 (which included 1,000 visiting fans) and match receipts of £270. Ayr were a mid-table First Division team, but they too were shocked when the homesters took the lead, which was held until near the end of ninety minutes, when an equaliser (from the penalty spot), saved the blushes of the Scottish League team. Should Ayr win the replay, then the draw for the next round would produce a local derby match with Kilmarnock, but although written off by all but the most biased supporters, Armadale set out to cause yet another shock. Aided by around 2,000 fans in the 10,000 crowd, for the replay, the visiting eleven scored what transpired to be the only goal just before half-time, and by now all of Scottish football had heard of Armadale F.C.

So it was Armadale that were to play hosts to the strong Rugby Park team, and an all time record 10,000 crowd (approximately), was present to, hopefully, see their favourites progress on to the last four in the competition.

"A seething mass of humanity rolling and billowing, also bellowing around the primitive entrances to the arena"
Poetically described the scene at Volunteer Park that day.

A disputed goal put Kilmarnock into the lead in the first half, and this scoreline was soon doubled. Armadale had an uphill second half struggle, but gave their fans hope when they scored soon after the break. But the 1–2 score remained, although the match ended in unpleasant scenes which led to the Club being censured, and the Referee having to make his exit from the ground, inside a playing kit hamper! The rest of the season naturally became an anti–climax, although the Club were losing finalists to Bathgate, when a record attendance of 4,000 was present at the victors Ground, for the County Cup Final replay.

Such a successful Cup run could hardly go unnoticed, and Hearts bought Colin Dand for £650, but to show that their earlier run was no 'flash in the pan, the Dale came close to a repeat performance during the 1920/21 season. In the First round, they travelled, and beat, the struggling St. Mirren team with the odd goal in five, before a surprised crowd of 10,000, and then played a local derby with near neighbours Bo'ness. Bo'ness were enjoying an excellent run in league matches, and Armadale did well to force a scoreless draw at Newtown Park. The crowd of 5,000 produced record gate receipts of £250.

Once again Volunteer Park was packed, this time with 9,000 fans – a new record (receipts of £440) – for the replay. The homesters took the lead after 24 minutes, and sealed the game with a second goal fifteen minutes before the end. Through to the third round again, the last sixteen in the competition, Albion Rovers could hardly have relished the prospect of a visit to Armadale. After Spiers and Sneddon had given the Dale a two goal lead, no doubt the visitors worst fears were realised. But by half–time the Rovers had squared up the scoring, and this was to be the final result. An all time record attendance was present for the game, with estimates varying between ten and twelve thousand, and the higher figure was possible since the embankments around the pitch had been raised in height. In the replay, the Dale refused to be beaten, and a scoreless draw was watched by 21,000. A second replay was therefore necessary, and once again the non–League team were not overawed, for even after extra time the stalemate continued, once again scoreless, and before 12,000 at Hampden Park. Probably sheer exhaustion overcame Armadale eventually, for the third replay was staged the next day, and at the same venue, and finally they succumbed to a two goal defeat.

Volunteer Park in the early 1920s

Once again no honours were won in League competition, but by now the Directors had their sights set higher, towards the Scotttish League itself, as serious talks began with regard to a re-formation of the Second Division. On the 18th of June the Club was formed into a Limited Company, with nine directors who came from various walks of life. 1,000 shares at £1 each were issued, but by December only 267 had been taken up, with William Henderson holding 25.

Broxburn United were not to be denied their own moments of glory during this period, for they too had notable runs in the Scottish Cup, although on both occasions they produced no giant-killing deeds. In the 1919/20 season, after a bye in the first round, they then beat Queen of the South Wanderers – not the later Scottish League team (who in fact were founded that season) – before meeting their match in the third round. Their opponents were the mighty Rangers, but a three goal defeat at Ibrox was hardly a disgrace, and the share of a big gate was very welcome.

The following season, they received another bye in the first round, before losing at home to Hamilton, but by only the odd goal in three. The attendance for this match amounted to between five and six thousand, but an estimated 2,000 came from Hamilton by train and charabancs. Hamilton took the lead after 25 minutes, and this score remained until half-time.

Fifteen minutes into the second half, it looked as if it was all over for the United when the visitors doubled their lead, but Dunn pulled one goal back when a penalty was awarded and he scored from the rebound, after the goalkeeper had saved. Amid great excitement, the United applied pressure and deserved an equaliser, but it was not to be, and therefore the 1–2 scoreline remained.

Like their two neighbours at Armadale and Bathgate, they won no honours in the Central League. At the turn of the year of 1921, the team lay in a low mid–table position, and by the season's end this was not improved upon, for they finished twelfth, with 12 victories, 5 draws and 17 defeats. In their last match, at home to Bo'ness, the visitors required a win to ensure them of the Championship. Before a crowd of over 2,000 at Broxburn, the United were easily overcome when they were defeated by 3–0.

In March 1921, the Club followed the steps taken earlier by their two neighbours and were formed into a Limited Liability Company, with 10 Directors, which in effect took over the former Club. Despite the mounting problems in the shale Industry (which the town depended on), there was a satisfactory application for 50p shares, from the 1,000 that were issued. But the initial enthusiasm soon waned and by June only 241 had been taken up. At the first A.G.M. of the 'new' Club, on the 30th of August – that was held in the pavilion at the Sports Field – it was announced that extra equipment would be provided, plus a new pavilion, at a toal cost of £120.

After the Scottish League's denial of membership to the pre–war Clubs that had formed the Second Division, they finally succumbed to the wishes of the lesser Clubs. But it is dubious whether those Clubs really got a good deal. In exchange for the promise of membership of the Scottish League – the Second Division in reality a renamed Central League – and automatic promotion and relegation, the minnows would have to 'return' their stars that had been 'poached' from their big brothers. This in itself appeared fair, and did not provoke a great argument from the Central League Clubs as expected – no doubt the elevated status was a sufficient bribe to satisfy them – but with those big names gone, the glamour disappeared, as did the crowds!

In addition, for the first season (1921/22), relegation was to include the bottom three teams, whereas promotion from the Second was limited to just one fortunate Club, in order to return the First Division to it's somewhat elitist eighteen Club membership. Initially the Central League Clubs decided to 'go it alone', but had a change of heart in June. The prospect of this elevation of status was to be tempered by the disasters that befell many of these Clubs that were to, dubiously, enjoy membership for the first time. Eleven new Clubs were ready to do battle at the start of the 1921/22 season, but of these only five have survived in the Scottish League to this day, and of the remaining half a dozen, Armadale, Bathgate and Broxburn were to become three of the casualties.

The Dizzy Heights of the Scottish League.

On the 20th of August, the 1921/22 season kicked off, and for the first time since 1914, a Second Division of the Scottish League was included. Broxburn United were at home to Dunfermline, and a very encouraging crowd of between three and four thousand was present. After a scoreless first half, the visitors took the lead two minutes after the start of the second period, but following a great deal of pressure from the United they equalised through Williamson. The rest of the match passed off with ever increasing bad temper, such that at one point the Referee had to call the players of both teams together and give a stern warning. But the homesters maintained their pressure, and eventually ran out as 3–2 victors. The United team consisted of:

> *Kerr, Harris, McLeod, Coyle, Allan, Cairns, Hendry, Davies,*
> *Sutherland, Williamson and Dunn.*

One week later the United lost by 3–1 at Bo'ness, and on the 3rd of September entertained Stenhousemuir when a dour scoreless draw was fought out. The latter game attracted an excellent attendance of around 4,000, a quite remarkable figure considering the population of the town, and the fact that there were 2,000 unemployed in the District (caused by the ever increasing problems within the shale industry). Fortunately the candle making industry had been at a high, but this was was also on the wane, and just two weeks later the Club felt the effects when the crowd had dropped to 1,000 for St. Bernard's visit.

Despite these financial problems the Club maintained a good position in the League, and after eight games were placed sixth in the table. On the 5th of November, Mr. Kidd M.P., officially opened the new pavilion, but on the pitch it was a bad day, for the United lost by the only goal of the game, to Bathgate.

By the turn of the year the Club were in fifth place, but a spate of injuries then presented further difficulties for the Club. Meanwhile the Club progressed through to the second round of the Scottish Cup. A fine two goal victory was won at fellow Second Division, Dundee Hibernians, before a 5,000 gate, which earned the United a match with Hearts. Although drawn at home, the Club reversed the tie, in order to financially benefit from a big gate (over 20,000 were present), and went on to shock their Edinburgh opponents. Although one goal behind at half–time, they equalised and then took the lead through Davies in the second period. It was only an unlucky handball that presented the homesters with a penalty, and a goal, that prevented the United from winning. The replay was also at Tynecastle, and another 20,000 attendance produced match receipts of £971, which did wonders for the United's finances.

The Club were unlucky not to win the match against their First Division opponents, and so for the third time a large contingent of supporters made the short journey to Edinburgh. After six minutes, the United took a shock lead, but by half–time trailed by 1–2. Despite a spirited second half, the went a further goal behind, and so the score remained. The match attracted nearly 15,000 and further receipts of £686. Between these Cup ties, the Club played at St. Bernards in a League match, but the team for this game consisted almost totally of reserve players (and two men borrowed from Armadale!), and it came as no surprise when they were defeated , by four unopposed goals.

This defeat was the worst of the season, and at the end, the Club finished in a very satisfactory sixth in the League. However, it was only the near fortune that the Club received in shared gate money from the cup–ties that proved to be their salvation. Already the warning bells were sounding, and it was obvious that such highly lucrative matches could only be hoped for in the future!

Down the road at Bathgate, preparations to the Ground were made for the Club's introduction to Scottish League football, and improvements were made to the pitch and the enclosure in general. The dip in the centre of the pitch was filled in, and embankments were extended. By early August thirteen players had been signed on. A pre–season friendly match attracted 1,000 supporters to Mill Park, but they went away disappointed when their favourites lost by 0–2 to St. Bernards. But the team atoned for this with a 2–1 victory at East Fife, in their first League match on August the 20th. The team consisted of:

Wilkinson, A.Fleming, W.Fleming, McGibbon, Duncan, Johnstone, Mcneil, Henretta, Wilson, McCourt and Chalmers.

In the first period, Wilkinson did well to save a penalty, and Henretta became the first League goalscorer for Bathgate. After a 1–1 half–time scoreline, the winner came in the 80th minute. In the second League game, Armadale were entertained before a large crowd, of 4,000, and a scoreless draw transpired. After an unlucky 2–3 defeat at Alloa, Arbroath visited Bathgate, on the 10th of September, and were beaten by 2–0 after a scoreless first period. The crowd only numbered 2,000, due principally to heavy rain, although a similar number was present when Dundee Hibernians were beaten two weeks later.

After nine games, the Club lay 9th in the League, and on the 29th of October, only a last minute goal prevented a victory over St. Bernards, which was watched by an improved gate of nearly 3,000. After a home victory over Bo'ness the Club had risen to fourth in the table, and the improved attendance of nearly 4,000 contrasted strongly with the 500 that were present the next week, for the match at Clackmannon, which resulted in a 3–1 victory for Bathgate.

On the last day of 1921, Stenhousemuir were comprehensively beaten by four unopposed goals, at Mill Park, a victory which took the Club into 7th place, and was watched by 3,000. An intriguingly named late substitute for this match was *Junior*, who, two days later appeared for the Club under the name of *Newman*! The latter match brought high–flying Alloa (eventual Champions) to Bathgate, and nearly 5,000 saw a scoreless draw. The Club's outside chance for promotion became less likely, although hopes were raised on the 8th of April when Johnstone were thrashed by 4–0, a result which took the Club up to 4th place.

Despite the appalling weather, the crowd numbered around 2,000. A similar number of spectators were present for the visit of St. Johnstone, and a scoreless draw gave Bathgate an encouraging final fifth position in the League table.

Although the Gardener Cup was won (in the final, Bo'ness were beaten at Broxburn before an attendance of 3,000), it was the Scottish Cup that provided the main excitement, and financial rewards. In the first round, Helensburgh (their first season in senior football), were beaten at Mill Park by 3–2, aided in no small way by two penalties awarded to the homesters. The next round brought high–flyers from the First Division to Bathgate. The prospect was greeted with eager anticipation, and marked the first visit of Falkirk to the town, for thirty years, at which time a predecessor of Bathgate F.C. fought out an exciting 5–5 draw – despite being 2–5 down with 15 minutes of play remaining.

The most intriguing prospect was the opportunity for local fans to see Syd Puddefoot play for Falkirk, a player that had just been transferred from West Ham for the sensational fee of £5,000 – an unheard of sum for a Scottish Club to pay out. Bathgate fielded three new players, Fergus, Watson (from Celtic) and Black. The gates to the ground were opened at 1.00 p.m., and the enclosure quickly filled – aided by two trains from Falkirk – to a new record of 10,000. Additional seating was provided inside the enclosure fence and adjacent to the packed Grands–tand, and for one hour the spectators were entertained by the local public Band. Bathgate won the toss, and soon took control, despite being down to virtually ten men, following an injury to Robertson.

Although Puddefoot played well, it was the revitalised Robertson who was the star, when he beat two men and scored the first, and only, goal in the 78th minute; the exuberant fans carried him off the pitch at the final whistle. 850 supporters accompanied the team to Partick Thistle for the third round match, and Bathgate were again reduced to ten men for much of the game. Most of the 18,000 crowd would have agreed that the homesters 3–0 victory flattered them.

During the summer, Black was transferred to Hearts, and Wilkinson to Partick Thistle.

The Ground, which was the first in the County to have a Grandstand, and was owned by the Club (a rarity at this level), underwent further improvements. Turnstiles were installed and further entrances created, to cater for the hoped for increased crowds in the future.

Armadale were hardly overshadowed by their neighbours, and in view of their final position in the League, had arguably the best season of the three. Before the start of the 1921/22 season, the pitch was relaid, new drainage was installed, and a twenty year lease was arranged for the Ground. In August the plans for the Grandstand, which was to be built in brick at ground floor level (and to include gymnasium, baths, changing rooms, directors room, etc.) with a timber upper structure to seat 700, were submitted for approval. This initial cost amounted to £200, and was eventually finished around the turn of the year. In anticipation of larger crowds, turnstiles were also installed. After a number of new signings, the Club held a trial match, and 2,000 spectators were present.

The first League match was played on the 20th of August, when the Dale entertained St. Bernards. The crowd numbered 4,000, and the team consisted of:

McLeod, Hopewell, Dryburgh, Atkinson, McInally, Gibson, Stalker, Glen, Fleming, McNeilage, and Campbell.

Fleming opened up the scoring for the Dale, just before half–time, and further successful strikes by Glen and Campbell, gave the Club a comfortable 3–0 victory. The Club made a good start to the season, and by the end of the Year were still in with a chance of becoming Champions, and hence being promoted.

After a 4–0 home victory over St. Johnstone, the Dale travelled to East Fife and Kings Park over the New Year and added four more points to their tally. The only real point of concern was the attendances which at home only normally totalled 1,000 to 1,500.

But defeats in January and February put paid to any hopes of an elevated status for the next season, and when Vale of Leven were entertained on the 22nd of February, a 3–1 win), there was only a small crowd present at Volunteer Park, albeit the game was played on a midweek afternoon.

The somewhat indifferent form continued, enlivened by a 8–1 demolition, despite a 1–1 half–time scoreline, of the hapless Clackmannon team on April the 4th, a result which was to stand as the Club's record Scottish League win. A good near end of season run actually elevated the Club to second place at one time, but defeats at Johnstone and Dundee Hibernians finally settled any promotion hopes, and the Club had to be content with third place. A three goal defeat at Hibernian soon put paid to any Scottish Cup hopes, but one small consolation, was the Club's victory over Bo'ness in the County Cup Final.

Things had gone very well on the field, and the Club could look optimistically towards the following season, but financially the outlook was bleak. From a total income on the season of £3,129, a loss of £500 was made. In common with their neighbours at Bathgate and Broxburn, the Club had to suffer the consequences of the post–war depression and a miners' strike. Wage cuts were prevalent, and with only 492 shares taken up, of the 1,000 available, the outlook – at least in the short term – was far from rosy.

Armadale's promotion hopes die.

The 1922/23 season started well for Armadale, and it was not until the 13th of December that the first home League match was lost, to Kings Park, in what transpired to be the only defeat at Volunteer Park that campaign. Ten days later however, Johnstone were thrashed by 7–2, with Chalmers and McLaren each netting hat tricks. The Club's record on their travels however was poor, and victories were only obtained at Cowdenbeath and Arbroath.

There was little to enthuse over in Cup Competitions, and in the Scottish, the Club made an exit at the hands of Johnstone, despite the earlier League thrashing of these opponents. A final 6th place in the League was hardly a disgrace, but these high positions, following the Club's first two campaigns in the League, were never to be repeated.

The Armadale depression continued in several respects. In the town, many inhabitants were leaving for America to find employment, and at Volunteer Park, both the Secretary and the Club President resigned.

Wage cuts had to be imposed which led to difficulties in signing on new players to replace the better men who were transferred. Significant acquisitions were Peter Duncan, the former Hibernians and Brentford player, plus Joe Shortt the ex–Albion Rovers goalkeeper. By Christmas 1923, the League record was far from good, and it was only one Scottish Cup tie that helped to bail out the Club financially. A rail strike prevented many fans from travelling to Coldstream for the first round game, but before a crowd of 600 (a record attendance for this Club), new signing Meckle broke the deadlock ten minutes from the end. The second round required the Dale to make a lucrative journey to Hampden Park, where 15,000 saw Queens Park triumph by 3–1.

Although the away record in the League was improved upon, the Club conceded the two points on four occasions at home, and finished in a poor 11th in the League table of 20 teams. The 1924/25 season was to end with the Club in a worse position for they finished in 15th place. A few new players had been signed, including the former Tottenham and Queens Park goalkeeper A.C.Hunter, and it was to the team's defence that muted praise was given. By the time of the Club's entry for the Scottish Cup, all hopes of promotion had gone, in fact relegation (the Third Division was now in operation) looked the more likely bet!

The faithful continued to attend the matches at Volunteer Park, and 1,500 were present to see the Dale overcome the first hurdle, Civil Service Strollers. The godsend of a financially beneficial draw was the lot of the Club in the second round, when Aberdeen were the visitors. With the potential to attract a new record attendance in the region of 14,000, there was no talk of selling home Ground rights, but this figure was never reached.

Braziers were maintained on the pitch overnight, in order to beat the hard frost, but on the day no more than 8,000 fans were present. Aberdeen only brought forty diehards, and the supporters of neighbours Broxburn and Bathgate were content to follow their own teams' progress. The homesters were denied the lead early on, when a 'goal' was disallowed, but nonetheless took the lead through Chisholm. But this advantage was cancelled out before half–time, and the 1–1 score remained after 90 minutes.

The expected defeat came in the replay, by two unopposed goals, which was watched by 15,000. It was only thanks to the proceeds of these two Cup games that the Club's continued survival was assured, as unemployment meant low attendances for the League games. By now only 573 shares (of the 1,000 available had been bought), and with the final cost of the Grandstand amounting to £2,759, finance was inevitably to be related to the Club's success. Season tickets were priced at a moderate 15 shillings (75p), and although there was no money for Ground improvements, the centre of the pitch was attended to, in order to prevent flooding in this area. But all hopes of improved performances for the 1925/26 were soon dashed and it was not until the fifth match that the first victory came, when Kings Park were easily overcome by 4–1, on September the 12th.

The season was notable for it's high scoring matches. Both Bathgate and St.Bernards were beaten by 5–1 at Volunteer Park, whilst on the deficit side, the team losses included their visits to Alloa (0–4), Arthurlie (an incredible 4–7 reverse), Dunfermline (1–7) and St.Bernards (2–6); in no less than twelve League matches, at least six goals were scored!

These high scoring features were repeated in the Scottish Cup, when the Club made their exit at Arthurlie by 4–5 (20 goals scored in two games at Barrhead). But the balance went very much against the Dale and they finished 6th from bottom once again. The outgoings in wages and match expenses amounted to £1,905 over the year, and the gate receipts only realised £1,840. However by selling players – for a total of £1,905 – and buying in others at a cost of less than £100, the Club actually managed a profit over the year of £1,061 – but there was still a big debt that was owed on the Grandstand.

THE COMPANIES ACTS 1908 to 1917.

COMPANY LIMITED BY SHARES.

———

MEMORANDUM OF ASSOCIATION

OF

ARMADALE FOOTBALL CLUB LIMITED.

———

I. The name of the Company is "ARMADALE FOOTBALL "CLUB LIMITED."

II. The Registered Office of the Company will be situate in Scotland.

III. The objects for which the Company is established are :—

(1) To acquire and take over as a going concern, the undertaking and assets of the Armadale Football Club.

The 'Company' was registered in 1921.
(S.R.O. Ref. BT2/11767)

Broxburn's short stay.

Broxburn Utd. (unnamed) Team Group – Probably 1922/23 Season.

If Armadale thought they had problems, then Broxburn United's plight was even worse, for the end of this season, also saw the end of their Scottish League career.

Despite the financial restrictions that had to be imposed, Broxburn United announced their plans for a 400 capacity Grandstand at Sports Park, after their first encouraging season in the Scottish League. The Ground by now was almost totally enclosed, and season tickets went on sale during the summer of 1922, at 75p, and also at £1–05 which included a seat in the Stand. The 1922/23 season started very well, and after five League matches, the Club were well placed, second from top. But by the end of the Year, they had gradually slipped down the table. However reasonably good crowds continued to attend home matches, and for high flying Queens Park's visit on October the 6th, a crowd of 4,000 was present to see a goalless draw. The Glasgow Club's name invariably drew good crowds, and six weeks later, when bottom Club Forfar were the visitors, the attendance was a mere 1,500!

As the season wore on, the Club's fortunes continued to slide, both financially and on the field, and by early March – by which time the club were in the bottom half of the table – an attendance of only 900 bothered to attend the single goal victory over East Stirling.

One week earlier the United had visited Hampden Park, and were crushed 5–0 by Queens Park, where the crowd 'only' numbered around 9,000! (This figure would have been higher had it not been for counter attractions in the City).

Crowds picked up slightly as the season drew to an end, with 1,200 for Lochgelly's visit, although the local derby with Bathgate on the 21st of April (a 2–0 victory), could only muster 1,300 to the Sports Field, on a cold afternoon. After the early season results had promised so much, a final 8th place in the League had to suffice. The Scottish Cup efforts were best forgotten, for at the first hurdle, the Club were hammered by 5–0 at Kilmarnock. Finance was still a problem, and the Directors were not encouraged with the share purchases, which by now had only risen to around 550.

The 1923/24 season started deplorably for the United, and after losing their first two games by 3–0, they were bottom of the League. The next four matches led to a slight improvement, for they had risen by four places, but a further 6 games saw them slide back down to third from bottom. Generally the defeats were limited to only one or two goals, but it was turning out to be a bad campaign for the Club. In January, the United entertained second place Bathgate, and an above average crowd witnessed a scoreless draw, but two weeks later the Club's fortunes slumped. At home to high–flying Cowdenbeath, they lost by the only goal of the match, when two players were sent off – a rare disgrace in those days. A welcome 2–1 away victory over St. Bernards, before a 2,000 crowd, on the 12th of April, ensured the Club's survival in the Division.

Relegation was only just avoided, for they finished one place above wooden–spoonists Lochgelly (but 20 points clear), and only a single team was demoted. Despite the necessary financial restraints that the Club had to impose, it was announced at the Club's A.G.M. in August, that they had made a loss of £51 over the season. Gate receipts had brought in only £989, whereas wages, travelling expenses, etc. had taken nearly £1,400. Fortunately the debt on the Stand was reduced to £367, but after such a poor playing season – the only highlight being the winning of the Roseberry Cup – attendances had inevitably dropped.

In an effort to encourage more fans, season tickets were reduced to 12/6 (62p) for the coming, 1924/25 season. The Club could hardly have started the season with high expectations, but in a complete turnaround of fortune the campaign was fairly successful. The United got off to a flying start when they beat Johnstone by 3–0, before a good attendance that approached 2,000. After six matches, and following a 2–1 victory over Arbroath, the team were undefeated (with two draws), and found themselves in the unfamiliar second place in the League. But then they slumped, and after a six goal thrashing at newly relegated Clyde, on the 13th of December, they had dropped to sixth.

Worse was to follow as defeats became the norm, and after 23 League games they lay dangerously near the bottom of the table, in 15th place. A rare victory – by 3–0, at home to Bathgate, on the 10th of January (before an attendance of 2,000) – was followed by a special public meeting of the supporters. 500 fans were present, and the majority considered that the overall slump in the team's fortunes, after such an encouraging start, could not be tolerated. They were dissatisfied with the team selections, that were made by the Directors, and vowed to remedy the situation. An official Supporters Club was formed at the meeting, with the intention of raising money from which shares in the parent Club could be purchased, and then hopefully gain representation on the Board. Weekly contributions of 3d per member were agreed upon.

The lack of faith in the Club that was shown appeared to have given the shake up that was necessary, for the team proceeded to enjoy a highly successful run. One week after the Bathgate match, the United inflicted the first home defeat on Dumbarton, and then proceeded to embark on the most successful Scottish Cup run in the Club's history. Nithsdale Wanderers – Third Division Champions–elect – were first beaten in an exciting 3–2 match at the Sports Park before a crowd of 2,000. In the second round, another team from the lower division – Royal Albert – were defeated, on their own Ground, which led to a home tie with Falkirk.

The First Division team could hardly have relished the tie with Broxburn after their defeat just three years earlier at Bathgate, and any fears they may have had were fully justified!

9,000 fans (including a large visiting contingent) packed into the Ground, and an excellent victory by the homesters ensued. Graham gave the United the lead in the first half; *"amidst deafening roars and cheers"*, and when a late winner was scored, after Falkirk had equalised in the second period;

"The exuberance of the home supporters knew no bounds – men and women kissed each other for joy" (!)

This took the team through to the fourth round, and the last eight in the competition. A visit had to be made to the home of the strong Dundee Club, and in a very defensive match, the underdogs lost by the single goal that was scored in the 30th minute. The United fought strongly, particularly in the last 15 minutes, but all to no avail, and the only satisfaction was the Club's share of the £616 that was taken from the attendance of 15,541.

The Club's revitalised form continued in the League, and at the end of the season they finished in a most encouraging 7th place. But if it had not been for the lucrative Cup run, then the financial position would have been dire, for in only one home League match, was a profit made. With no end to the countrywide slump, it was all but impossible to improve attendances, but the Club were determined to build upon the improvements shown towards the end of the season; nobody would have forecast the fate that lay in store for the Club!

Over the season, £1,254 had been paid in wages. The Cup exploits had boosted the total share of gate takings to £1,404, but even so a loss of £140 on the season was reported. The balance of payments on the Grandstand stood at £367. The major summer signing was that of James Walker, from Coventry City, but a very poor start was made to the 1925/26 season, and after losing at home to top team Nithsdale Wanderers (before a gate in excess of 2,000), the team were placed fourth from bottom in the League. The East Sirling home game was a thriller, and after leading 4–3 at half–time, the United finished as 6–5 winners; but of particular concern was the attendance, which had dropped to less than 1,000.

By the time that Dumbarton came to the Sports Park and took away a point, in mid–November, the Club lay third from bottom, and only 800 diehards bothered to turn up for the game. Things went from bad to worse. With the club unable to win matches – just three victories and three draws in sixteen games to the end of the year – the fans could not be encouraged to come and support the team. With the situation in the shale industry still in a desperate way, it began to look likely that both enterprises would soon have to come to an end. After a crushing 4–7 home defeat by St.Bernards, on the 2nd of January, the Club had dropped to the bottom of the League, a position from which they were never to recover; another seven goals were conceded the next week (although they were only 1–2 in arrears at the break) when the team lost at Kings Park.

Despite such terrible displays, the United shook Hibernians when they forced a 1–1 draw in Glasgow, and at half-time were actually in the lead. The 14,000 gate that produced match receipts of £475 provided a financial godsend, as did the share from the replay, which was also played away from home. A kind gesture from their hosts allowed over 600 Broxburn fans free admission for the second game, and once again the underdogs produced a fine display, but lost by the only goal of the game. In the next match, in the League, there were 1,500 present to see the team lose to Dunfermline.

By early March, they were rooted to the bottom, and for Arthurlie's visit on the 20th of March (another inevitable defeat), the attendance was no more than 700, a figure – and result – that was repeated one week later when east Fife were in opposition. Just one victory was gained in the latter part of the season, when Alloa were beaten 4–3 on February the 13th, and by mid–April the Club were in an irretrievable position. A rare point was obtained, from Queen of the South on the 17th of that month, but was watched by only 600, and the last home – and last in the League – was played on the 24th. Armadale, who also had a poor season, attracted only 500 spectators, a pitiful number considering the local derby nature of the game, and after being 2–3 behind at the halfway stage, the homesters lost 3–4. The Broxburn team consisted of:

'Amateur', Struthers, Wilkinson, Fordyce, Anderson, Cowie,
Simpson, Muir, Davies, Dunsire and Taylor

(not one 'Mac' in the team!). Fordyce was the last Scottish League goalscorer for the Club.

The Club's (and the townspeople's) financial state, coupled with a terrible season, left little doubt that the Club would be voted out of the League. The team finished six points below the next Club (Bathgate), and recorded only four wins plus six draws in thirty–eight matches; the goal record stood at 56 'for' and a massive 127 'against'. Only three points were obtained on the team's travels, and the biggest defeats came at St. Bernards (0–8) and East Stirling (2–8).

Bathgate come close in 1924.

Things had started well at Bathgate. Encouraged by their first season in the Scottish League, the Club were pleased with the attendance for the first match of the 1922/23 season, a local derby with Broxburn United which attracted over 4,000 to Sports Park, and produced a 2–2 draw. A better result was obtained in the next home fixture, when, despite only having ten men for part of the match, Bathgate beat Forfar Athletic by 5–1, and were watched by a crowd of 3,000. Although the season started well, with this one victory and three draws (two away from home), things soon started going wrong, and by the time that nine matches had been played, the team were languishing near the bottom of the table.

The early season crowds – there was another 4,000 when Dunfermline were the visitors – inevitably started to decrease, and for the December visits of Lochgelly and of Stenhousemuir, they had dropped to around 2,000; these were in contrast to the 10,000 present for the clash in Glasgow with top–dogs Queens Park, when a special train took Bathgate fans to the match.

But the two December games at Sports Park produced excellent victories – 5–0 and 4–0 respectively, and by the end of the year the team had fought their way back to a mid–table position. The revival continued, and on New Years Day, an attendance of 5,000 were at Bathgate for the local derby with Armadale, when the homesters ran out as 4–2 winners. The Scottish Cup then took the attention, and for Bathgate their campaign started with a visit to, and a draw with, East Stirling. At the replay, more than 4,000 were present for the midweek game which was won 3–2.

This took the Club into the second round, and to a truly memorable tie with Queens Park. Three special trains took 2,500 supporters to Hampden Park, and the game was watched by an enormous gathering of 50,000. Royalty was also present – the first time at a Scottish match – and the Duke of York (left–footed) ceremoniously kicked–off for the teams. Highlights from the game were recorded for prosperity, by a Newsreel company of the day. McAllister gave the visitors a surprise early lead, and despite continuous attacks, in search of a second goal, it was Queens Park who scored.

The Second Division leaders finished the stronger of the two teams, but the 1–1 scoreline remained after ninety minutes. The midweek replay created enormous interest in Bathgate, and most factories stopped work in the afternoon! A record attendance was confidently expected, but heavy rain before the kick–off dampened the enthusiasm of many would–be spectators, and in the final event there were no more than 6,000 present. Bathgate's only consolation was a share in the combined receipts of £950, for after a scoreless first half, they were easily beaten at the finish, by 2–0.

The two exciting games appeared to have encouraged the team, for they continued to rise up the table, and after three League victories in March, they were place fifth from top. The team fell away to a degree in the last matches, and fifth position was their final placing.

A prosperous season was the end result, and encouraged by the reasonable degree of success, all available season tickets for the 1923/24 season were sold by early August. Hopeful of larger gates in the future, a useless piece of land within the boundaries of the Ground was 'exchanged' for another area, thereby giving room for more spectators in the North–east corner. The team got off to a reasonable start, and after beating Dumbarton on the 22nd of September, they had played six games, and were placed in mid–table. Although the team were playing well, the Club also suffered from the Industrial situation in the area, and attendances only averaged around 2,000.

A last minute goal against Arbroath on the 27th of October earned the Club two points, and took them to seventh, and a good run to early December saw the team rise another three places upward.

Alloa were beaten by 4–1, in a pre–Christmas encounter, and Forsyth scored all Bathgate's goals. After a 4–2 beating of Forfar on the 3nd of January 1924, the team had risen to second place, and hitherto unheard of talk regarding possible promotion was being freely discussed. The good form continued, mainly due to an excellent home record, and after the 2–0 victory over Alloa, attended by 4,000, the Club lay just one point behind the leaders, St.Johnstone.

Perhaps the team had their sights set on promotion, for after drawing with Bo'ness in the Scottish Cup – which had been watched by a season's best crowd of 7,000, the replay was lost. This must have quelled the enthusiasm, for when the table leaders – St. Johnstone – were the visitors to Bathgate, there was a crowd of only 3,000, and the 1–1 result was considered a fair reflection of the play. But this result was the signal for a series of disappointing results, which culminated in a 1–5 thrashing at fellow promotion chasers Stenhousemuir's Ground. A late recovery was staged, but the supporters knew that the team's chances had been allowed to slip away, and the 8th of March (lucky) single goal victory over Dunfermline, was seen by no more than 1,000 faithful supporters. The last League match was lost at Dumbarton by 2–6 , the worst result of the season, but even so the team finished in a praiseworthy third, although 12 points behind the Champions, St.Johnstone.

The Club's fourth season in the Scottish League was looked forward to with enthusiasm, after the two previous near–promotion attempts. But the campaign was to be the start of a slump from which the Club never recovered. The early matches started well enough, and for the opening game there was an attendance of 2,500 to see an exciting 4–4 draw with the newly promoted East Stirling club. After the 4–1 home victory over Dunfermline – when Muir netted a hat–trick – the Club lay fifth in the table, after five games. But a slump followed, and even after a 4–1 beating of East Fife, the Club were dismally placed, sixth from bottom in the League. Rain before the match didn't help the attendance, and there were barely 2,000 at the game.

But aided by a good home record the fortunes of the team picked up, and although they lost at Johnstone at the end of November, it was the first defeat for five weeks.

By the end of the year the Club had risen to seventh, and the fans started to dream of promotion once more, but the reality was a very different story!

The trio of Mid-lothian Clubs were lucky, or unlucky, with the draw in the Scottish Cup first round, for they were all scheduled to play at home. This inevitably affected the gates, and therefore the prestigious match at Bathgate, with high-flying Partick Thistle of the First Division, produced a disappointing attendance of 5,000. However, alternative competition was not the only factor that affected the paying public, for the Directors decided to cash in on the tie, and raised the prices for admission. The Grandstand was nearly deserted, as most refused, or were unable, to pay the four shilling (20p) price! The 'stay-aways' chose wisely, for a lack lustre display saw the Second Division team easily beaten by four unopposed goals.

Of more concern was the Club's inexplicable loss of form in the matches in the New Year. Although they managed to maintain a reasonably good home record, the team's travels were invariably rewarded with defeat. This of course led to loss of revenue through the turnstiles, and for Stenhousemuir's visit there were barely 1,200 present; of equal concern was the result, for despite holding a 2-1 half-time lead, the homesters collapsed during the second period, and ended up on the wrong end of a 2-5 scoreline. One week later the dreadful away form continued, and the team were thrashed by Forfar to the tune of five-nil. There was no recovery, and by the season's end, the team had finished fifth from bottom.

The situation at the end of the 1925/26 season was even worse! A reasonable start was made when four goals were shared at East Stirling, and one week later Armadale were overcome with a 3-1 scoreline at Bathgate. Interest in the Club, and affordability, by now was on the wane, and although great interest was aroused with newly relegated Third Lanark's first appearance at Mill Park, only 2,500 turned up. After sharing two goals at half-time, the homesters shocked their illustrious table topping guests, and triumphed by 2-1. Three weeks later, it was Nithsdale Wanderers who were in top position, but once again the attendance was only around 2,500, to see the 1-1 draw.

The Club at this time were in a low mid–table placing, and they were never able to improve upon this position for the rest of the campaign. By the end of the year, Bathgate had dropped to top fourth from bottom, but worse was to come. The New year home match with Stenhousemuir produced a crowd of 2,000, but a defeat by 1–4, and so the pattern continued. Following the Club's Cup run they were unable to stop the slide; after the 6th of March home defeat to St.bernards and the 3–7 crushing dished out by 3rd placed Clyde two weeks later (both games attracting 1,500 crowds), the team had slipped to one place off the bottom. But a surprise 5–0 victory over Dumbarton lifted everybody's spirits, although a 2–4 defeat at top team Dunfermline – before a 2,500 crowd – the following week brought back the gloom. Six points above wooden–spoonists Broxburn, and seven below next placed East Stirling was the Club's lot, and by a narrow margin their re–election bid was successful.

Once again it was the Scottish Cup that provided some much needed additional revenue. In the first round East Stirling were narrowly beaten (5–4) before 3,000 at Mill Park, and at the same venue – but with 500 more in the crowd – Bo'ness were entertained in the next round. The last kick of the game enabled Bathgate to equalise, through Pearson, and in the replay they won by 3–1. So despite their lowly League performances, the Club were through to the third round again, and were fortunate in being drawn at home. Airdrieonians were the attractive visitors, and the crowd numbered 7,000 (with receipts of £300). The first half was noted for the many missed chances by Bathgate, but eventually they took the lead, only for the visitors to equalise in the 37th minute, and then take the lead 60 seconds later. In the second half the homesters were no match for their opponents, and could only manage a second consolation goal just before the end, and lost the match by 2–5.

Bathgate started the 1926/27 season moderately, when they recorded two home wins (the first by 4–2 versus Ayr and before a crowd of 2,000), and two away defeats, in the opening games. Similar form continued to the end of the Year, by which time they were occupying a low mid–table position.

But a general lack of interest, coupled with lack of money in most cases, ensured that the traditional derby match with Armadale, on New Years

Day, would attract only 2,000 to Mill Park. One week later the Club secured an incredible home win, when Queen of the South were beaten 8–3, after a five goal lead at half–time. But such a result did not signal a change in fortune, for a single goal defeat at Raith Rovers seven days later was followed with a five goal trouncing by Third Lanark, at Mill Park.

The Scottish Cup could offer no consolation, for although drawn at home in the first round, the Club's opponents – Dunfermline (now in the First Division) – did not excite the locals, and the crowd only numbered 3,319. After two goals were shared up to half–time, the scoreline was doubled by the finish. There was a dispute with regard to Bathgate's player, Gardner, and Dunfermline threatened to protest should he be used in the replay. Intimidated in this way, the Club decided to leave him out of the team, and proceeded to lose the replay.

The situation continued to get worse in League games, and high scoring results – usually defeats – became more common; the 3–6 reversal at St. Bernards in March, was far from the attractive game that it would have appeared to have been! Even the visit of Champions–elect Bo'ness attracted no more than 2,000 to Bathgate, and although by now a well above average gate, doubtless the majority of the support was for the visitors! Whilst those neighbours made an upward move, Bathgate came close to moving in the other direction, for their final position of fourth from bottom was the result of their season's endeavour. It was only the single goal home win over Albion Rovers on the 23rd of April that ensured their survival in the Second Division.

The financial report on the Club made dire reading. For the third season running, a loss had been made on the year, this time a hefty £574. This figure would have been higher had it not been for a substantial donation of £349 from the Supporters Club. Home match receipts brought in only £1,095 (from a total income of £2,861) compared to the £1,733 received the previous season; this resulted in an average loss of around £50 per match at Mill Park. Only two matches were profitable, from the £125 taken in the Scottish Cup game, and the £1 surplus for the Bo'ness encounter! The Industrial troubles continued in the area, but even so the Club stated – somewhat optimistically – that better years lay ahead.

The 1927/28 season was to prove that rather than an upturn in fortunes, a continued slump was leading towards the Club's extinction. The season started in a predictable fashion with a home victory, and defeats on the team's travels. Although the pre-season trial match had attracted an encouraging crowd numbering over 1,000, the first League fixture enticed barely 1,500 for the visit of East Stirling. In contrast, the game at newly relegated Dundee United saw an attendance of 8,000. After four games the warning bells were sounding, for the team lay second from bottom, and two points from the next two games only lifted them by two places. Ayr's visit on the 17th of September produced barely 1,000 fans at Mill Park, and even the attraction of Third Lanark, two weeks later, could not lift the attendance above this lowly total. At least two good results were obtained from these matches, for a point was taken off the former, and two off the Glasgow club.

This lifted the team to a mid-table position, whereupon they proceeded to lose by five unopposed goals at Arbroath!

Although the team's showings were in general not too bad, the financial plight remained, and this was not helped by the profusion of home matches in November and December, months when attendances were normally at a low. Despite having fought their way into the top half of the table, there were barely 1,000 supporters sprinkled around the Ground at each of the games, versus Armadale and Queen of the South. After a ten game unbeaten run, the team had lifted themselves to 6th position, but the 1-2 home defeat to Dundee United was to signal the start of a very poor second half of the season.

Although Bathgate managed to maintain a good home record, their travels rarely produced a point, and defeats included hammerings at Ayr United and Third Lanark, by 7-1 and 6-1 respectively. At home the attendances had inevitably reached a low level, and for Leith's visit on the 3rd of January, the crowd of 1,000 was considered a reasonable one. At the end of March, the previous 5 games had produced just one point, and placed the Club 5th from the bottom. The final League table showed only seven points separating the 8th Club from the one second from bottom, Bathgate was in the latter position! But with no Third Division now available for relegated teams, the Club hung on to their Second Division status, when they applied for re-election.

In the Scottish Cup 300 keen fans travelled to Glasgow to see their team play the mighty Celtic. There was a crowd of only 3,000 (receipts of £150), due in the main to heavy rain, and after going in 1–2 down at half–time, the minnows finally lost by 3–1.

Tightened belts ensured that a deficit of only £18 was incurred over the season, but even further measures had to be taken to enable the Club to continue. With the recognition that large attendances were a thing of the past, the Club let out part of the large enclosure – to the North and East of the pitch – for allotments. But such moves were to prove to be pointless, for unknown to the Club, they were about to embark on fixtures that were never to be completed.

The season started badly with a 0–4 home defeat to Dundee United before a crowd of 1,000. But the next week a victory was secured at Queen of the South, and was followed by a 4–1 home win over east Fife, to put the team in 7th place. The latter game attracted an attendance of 1,500 – the biggest for three years – but the Club still made a £32 loss on the match (less than the usual)! Drummond returned to the team after his excursions to Burnley, Bristol City and Bourne–mouth, and helped the team to a 2–1 win at Alloa, which lifted them to 5th in the League. For the visit of table–topping Morton on the 8th of September, and unbelievable crowd of 3,000 was present, they but saw the locals lose by 1–3.

From then on the path was downwards, and the team soon found themselves in the bottom half. After a 2–8 thrashing at Forfar they had dropped to just two places above the lowest. By the time of Clydebank's visit in mid–December they had sunk to the lowest rung, with a four point gap to the next team. The fans had all but given up, and just a few hundred were present to see the two goal defeat.

The defeats continued into the New Year – 1–6 at Dundee United, followed by 2–6 at East Fife, although the 3–1 home win over Alloa brought some relief to the 1,000 or so that were present. Some respite came with the Scottish Cup, and after beating St.Andrews University away – before a crowd of 650 which produced receipts of £26, Bathgate drew Raith Rovers in the second round.

3,000 were attracted to the match and paid £110, to see the home team go in at the interval one goal down, but fight back in the second period and earn a draw with a Drummond equaliser. In the replay they were easily overcome with a 2–5 scoreline. A few days later a league visit to Dunfermline was made, and Bathgate were humiliated with a 0–8 defeat. This result prompted many changes for the next game – when the Club entertained Kings Park before *the smallest crowd for a long time.* After sharing two goals at the interval, the homesters eventually lost by 1–3. On the 23rd of February Bathgate travelled to Dunfermline to play, what became, their last Scottish League match. The team that day consisted of:

> *Dempster, Clark, Higgins, Gilmour, Westwood, Pearson,*
> *McPherson, Fairley, Ronald, Findlay and Hughes.*

The match ended as a 3–0 home win, with Kirk scoring all the goals.

Within days the Club formerly resigned from the League, the financial pressures were too much, and on the pitch the results had been awful; of the 28 League games played, just 5 victories had been obtained plus 2 draws. The Club finished nine points below next placed Armadale. So far as the League was concerened Bathgate's results were deleted from the record, officially the Club had not existed that season!

Armadale stay the course the longest.

Armadale had normally managed to hold their own in the Second Division, and of course had come tantalisingly close to promotion in their first season. But although just managing to keep ahead of their two near neighbours (only one after Broxburn's departure in 1926), these were hardly happy days at Volunteer Park. With most of the players from the previous year having re–signed, the Club set out on the 1926/27 season in the hope that a considerable improvement could be made over the previous one. After an opening victory over Bathgate, the Club maintained a good home record until Christmas Day, for during this period they suffered only one defeat at Volunteer Park, when the struggling Dumbarton team grabbed a narrow 4–3 victory on November the 6th.

On their travels, they had made a good start, with a point at Nithsdale and two each at both Albion Rovers and St. Bernards.

But these two early away victories were to be the only ones of the season, and the team slumped in the second half of the campaign. This slump was not so much a loss of form, as a loss of players! Goal scoring Morgan caught the eye after two quickly repeated hat-tricks against Nithsdale and Arbroath (the latter match a 3-4 reverse) early in 1927, and was sold to Hearts for £850. MacMillan had already moved on to Rangers, and in February, Downs 'deserted' to Newcastle. Such moves no doubt saved the Club financially, but led to a long string of generally poor results.

There was no solace to be found in the Scottish Cup, for although drawn at home to the, by now, non-League Broxburn United, they lost in front of a 2,500 Volunteer Park crowd. The team continued to do well at home in the League, the only 'blip' being a 2-6 defeat to fellow-strugglers Alloa on March the 26th; midway through the second half, with the scoreline blank, a draw looked on the cards, before the eight goal late blitz. But only two further points were picked up on the teams travels. The situation at the end of the season showed a similar record to a year earlier, for although two places higher, only one extra point was obtained.

Fortunately the Club were relieved of any money problems, at least in the short term, for transfer fees had ensured a credit balance (apart from the long term repayments required on the Grandstand), of over £1,000, and the funds were boosted from the proceeds of a Juvenile football tournament that was run by the Supporters Club during the summer of 1927. The total income for the season had amounted to £4,283, and was in sharp contrast to the loss of £1,041 that had been experienced one year earlier. Wardrope was signed from Queens Park and King became the club's new goalkeeper following his move from Port Glasgow Athletic. But the 1927/28 season was to unfold as the worst to date.

Ominous warnings were given following an opening day home defeat to Queen of the South (the attendance only numbered 1,500 despite many travelling supporters), and it was not until mid-September that the first victory was achieved, when St.Bernards were beaten 2-1 at Volunteer Park. On the 1st of October, Armadale conceded their worst ever Scottish League defeat, when Arthurlie won by ten goals to nil; the prolific scoring of McNally, who netted eight, has remained as a record in the Second Division. It is little wonder that no more than 1,500 diehards could be encouraged to Volunteer Park one week later, and a 1–3 defeat meant a continuation of the team's poor showings. After another home defeat, by 4–5 to Arbroath at the end of the month, the Club were rooted to the bottom of the League, a position from which they never recovered. The optimistic financial report of a few months earlier was now becoming a nonsense, and once again the Directors had to start dipping into their own pockets to ensure the Club's survival.

Highlights of the season were few and far between, but a hat trick by Wardrope in the pre–Christmas victory over Dundee United (repeating his similar feat against Alloa in a 3–3 draw), helped to redress the balance. On Christmas eve, the team were leading 4–2 at Queen of the South, and then in a remarkable turnaround ended up on the wrong end of a 8–5 scoreline!

As the season drew to a close, defeats continued, the worst being yet another ten goal thrashing when Third Lanark were the victors by 10–3. The season ended with two drawn matches, at home to East Stirling, and at Dundee United, but this did not prevent the Club becoming the wooden–spoonists. Only three points, from draws, were obtained away from home. Such a dismal record on the team's travels, ensured that they, along with neighbours Bathgate, would have to seek re–election. Although they were successful in this attempt, serious doubts were being expressed on whether the town could maintain a Scottish League club. In a bid to gain more support, an application was made to the Scottish F.A. to open an unemployed gate, at which only a 6d (2.5p) entrance charge would be made, a move that had become necessary due to the continual unemployment in the area.

Somehow the Club managed to survive, and continued to do so for a few more years, but it can only put down to the tenacity of the Directors and the supporters who held on to the Club's status, for in these final years, the Club achieved little of merit.

The 1928/29 season started with ten games without a victory, and the first two points came on October the 20th when Bathgate were played – for the last time in the League. It wasn't until the 1st of December that the next win was achieved, at home to Kings Park, and meanwhile continuous away defeats ensured that the team remained bottom of the table. There was nothing to remove the gloom, and by the season's end, only three points were picked up on the team's travels, although at home more matches were won than lost. But several of the defeats were far from close encounters – 1–9 at Albion Rovers, 1–6 at Arbroath, 0–5 at Dundee United and several others by four goals. With the mid–season resignation of Bathgate, there was no saving Armadale, and for the second season running they finished bottom, and perhaps somewhat surprisingly were once again re–elected.

A few new signings were made before the commencement of the following season, but by now costs were the all important factors, and these were all 'unnamed' youngsters. With such a gloomy outlook expected on the horizon, it came as a pleasant surprise to find that the Club's recent dismal record actually improved. After beating Stenhouse–muir in the opening fixture, the six goal defeat at East Stirling one week later gave the impression that the season was going to be as bad as the last two. But a good home record, including a 6–0 thrashing of Montrose in September, ensured a League position around mid–table by the Year end. But once again it was the team's dreadful performances on foreign soil that were to hamper them, although after only one away victory in three seasons, the three recorded in this one, was a definite improvement. But 0–8 at Raith, 0–6 at Dumbarton and 1–7 against Dunfermline resulted in 61 goals conceded (and only 15 scored), in 19 matches. However, the final record was undeniably an improvement, for the team finished 15th of 20 teams, 13 points above tail–enders Brechin.

Financial restrictions continued to bite, and for the 1930/31 season, the squad of players were composed almost totally of locals, and of the seventeen on the books, five were amateurs. But this style, although the only way possible for Armadale, left the Club hopelessly out of its class when compared to the majority of its contemporaries, and once again the year was full of struggles. As in the past few years, the supporters could rely on a majority of home matches being won, but the usual, sorry tale when it came to those played away. Fortunately there were no really bad defeats, but equally there was only one victory, a 2–1 success at nearby Bo'ness on January the 3rd; the elevation to the First Division of this team lasted for just one season, and in keeping with the other Clubs just to the west of Edinburgh, their time in the Scottish League was to be of a limited duration. Armadale benefited to the tune of £400 when local boy Jerry Kerr was snapped up by Rangers – after only one game in the Dale's first team – and by that time the team were already booked for yet another lowly placing in the final League table.

Even the administrators of the Club were seen to be lax, for a number of fines were imposed – money they could ill afford to part with – due to their inability to provide the League with match summaries, team line-ups, and the like. There really looked as if there was no hope for the Club, and with attendances at an all-time low – even the New Year match with Bo'ness could only attract 1,000 – it looked doubtful if they could continue on in the Scottish League after the end of the season. But fortunately luck played it's hand, and at least gave the Club a stay of execution.

On the 17th of January 1931, the Club received a home draw in the Scottish Cup, one that every lowly team dreamed of – Rangers! League Champions for the previous four years in succession – and Champions-elect for this season – the match was hailed as the biggest in the Club's history. Rather than accept their expected fate, the Directors took steps to upset their illustrious opponents. Four new players were signed on, two of whom were fullbacks Findlay and Hamilton from St.Mirren, men who were noted for their robust play.

New crush barriers and entrance gates were installed before the big day, and advanced Stand seats went on sale at the greatly increased price of five shillings (25p). Gale force winds on the eve of the match required urgent repairs to the Stand the next day, but all was finally ready for what was confidently expected to be a record attendance. No doubt discouraged by the high cost, and possibly the thought of discomfort from the crush, the crowd only amounted to 8,000, who paid match receipts of £350.

A rumour spread that Hamilton (also an ex-Rangers player) intended to ensure that the Rangers inside-forward, McPhail, would become ineffective – and not from legal play! Fifteen minutes into the game, McPhail was brought down by Hamilton, and the latter received his marching orders!

After 30 minutes the illustrious visitors took the lead, and from that point on, it was all but over. Brannan scored for the Dale after 68 minutes, but by this time the score was 5–1 to the visitors, and two further goals completed the rout. After losing at Dumbarton in the League the next week, both Findlay and Hamilton had their contracts cancelled, and so ended their short association with the Club. Two further matches without a win put the Club in serious danger of re-election once again, but a revival, which included five straight home victories, ensured that this process did not have to be repeated. The final position of 18th (third from bottom) was hardly anything to cheer about, but at least it ensured that the Clubs career in the Scottish League would continue. The economy measures, coupled with the Rangers gate, created an amazing profit of £426 over the year, but for how many more could the Club continue to be run on a shoe string?

The quality of players that the Club could now field was apparent when the 1931/32 campaign started with six straight defeats – and three of these were at home – in August. The first victory came when fellow-strugglers Brechin City were entertained at the end of September. Earlier that month, Hibernians made their first League visit to Volunteer Park, having been relegated from the First, and the Dale secured their first point from a 1–1 draw, which was watched by 2,000 spectators, by now a way above average gate. Armadale's poor record on their travels continued unabated – although three wins were recorded this season – and in one, ten goals were scored, at Edinburgh City in November, when the final result ended as 4–6. The City club had been formed as Edinburgh's answer to the all–amateur Queens Park, but they were not able to capture the imagination, or enjoy the successes of their Glasgow counterparts, and became the Second Division's regular 'whipping boys'.

By the time that the first round of the Scottish Cup was due, the team were in their, by now perennial, struggle at the foot of the table, and after beating fellow Second Division Club Montrose (before a crowd of only 1,000), they went out at Hamilton, thanks to two late goals. Of usual concern, at this time of the season, was the worry of possible rejection from the League, and the Club's performances hardly gave cause for optimism, but two home victories in April, against Montrose and Albion Rovers ensured their survival for another year.

But third from bottom again, and only goal average from having to seek re-election was hardly anything to celebrate, nor was the trouble that the Directors faced when they had to answer to the League for non-payment of guarantees to visiting Clubs! These debts were eventually settled during the summer of 1932, but the Club were then called to task with regard to the Whippet Racing that was being held at Volunteer Park. Such use of the Ground had given the club some much needed extra revenue, but the new sport was frowned upon by the League authorities, in the same way that Greyhound Racing was deplored in England.

The last away match of the season ended in a 1-3 defeat.

Reluctantly Armadale had to serve notice on the organisers of the dogs. This was not the only problem at the Ground, for it had come under severe criticism from opposing teams, as one scribe of the day wrote:

"The Armadale pitch has no challenger in the League for the title of the worst, and to attempt to play football there is prectically useless.... it is covered with miniature bunkers" (!)

The prospects for the 1932/33 season were very grim, and such thoughts were well founded for the team were not able to complete barely more than half of their fixtures. On August the 13th Arbroath were entertained, and happily returned home with two points from their 4–1 victory, a match watched by barely 1,000 spectators.

A brief respite from the Club's troubles came at Kings Park the following week, when a last minute equaliser secured a point for the Dale. But with constant team and positional changes being tried in order to try to find a winning combination, the following six matches were lost.

On September the 24th, the first win of the season was secured from a 5–3 victory over Dundee United, when Scoular netted a hat–trick. Another point was obtained, at home to Leith Athletic a few weeks later. Scoular scored both the goals, and one week later put the team ahead after only 30 seconds, at East Fife, but Armadale lost in the final event by 1–8! Dark clouds were on the horizon, as the Club were at loggerheads with the League once again, over the payment of guarantees, as were Bo'ness, and a call to a meeting with the League on October the 21st was ignored by both Clubs.

By now the (professional) players were being paid a pitiful 50p per week, and with average gates of £18 – not enough to even cover the minimum guarantee to visiting Clubs – the situation had reached a really desperate state. After fourteen matches played, Bo'ness were expelled from the League for their non–payments, a Club that a few years earlier had reached the First Division, and had only 200 watching their last home match. This probably served as a timely warning to Armadale, because money owing to Stenhousemuir was promptly paid, but with the visit of Alloa on November the 5th attracting only 300 spectators, it really looked as if there was no way out for Armadale.

The match at Hibernian one week later produced a good attendance for this team were riding high, but Armadale received little for their appearance – and subsequent 2–8 defeat – as their share, all but £6, was seized and used to pay other creditors.

On the 19th of November 1933, Armadale F.C. entertained Raith Rovers, for their last ever Scottish League game. The team included two apparently unregistered players (shown in parenthesis):

> *Meek, Boyle, Kerr, Donnelly, "Brown", Hamilton, Fleming, "Thompson", Newman, Michie and McDonald.*

Cowan gave the visitors a three goal half–time lead, and the match finished up as 5–1, with Michie scoring the only, and last, goal for Armadale in the 78th minute. The match was watched by 300 spectators.

In view of past experiences, the Club were informed that Raith Rovers must be paid their guarantee that day, or else they too would be ejected from the League. The sum was not paid, the Club were informed that their membership of the League was terminated, and Forfar were informed of the cancellation of their match with Armadale for the following Saturday.

At this stage the team were rooted firmly to the bottom of the League, with only four points from their seventeen games, six points behind next placed Edinburgh City. However, the Club decided to fulfil their Scottish Cup commitments, and even signed on four new players for the occasion; no doubt hoping for some sort of miracle, that could ensure their future survival.

The only team that Armadale had defeated that season, Dundee United, appeared before a Volunteer Park crowd of 1,000 on the 21st of January, for the last Senior match played by the Dale. After having a goal disallowed, the Dale never looked like winning, and two second half goals gave the visiting side a 2–0 victory. The much changed team from the final League match consisted of:

> *Wilkinson, Boyle, Scott, Hamilton, Forrester, Fleming, Connelly, McInally, Michie, Miller and Imrie.*

There was no question of the Club continuing in any form, unlike their neighbours, Bathgate and Broxburn United, who continued in non–League football. Once again Armadale F.C. were dead! The name of the Club was not erased from the records until the Company were dissolved in 1935, but after that last Scottish Cup match in 1933, they never played again. Armadale did not have to endure a slow lingering death, but within a year of their demise, a Juvenile team under the name of Armadale Juniors was formed. Two years later the Club 'grew up' and became a fully fledged Junior Club, with the new title of 'Armadale Thistle'. This Club are still the 'town' team, and like their predecessors play at Volunteer Park.

ARMADALE THISTLE – Midlothian Lge. Champs. & Roseberry Cup Wins. 1939/40
(Back) Marjorianks, Hunter, Prentice, McKay, Louden, McMillan.
(Middle) Beveridge, Hailstones, ?, Inglis, Johnstone, Welsh, Peden, Robertson.
(Front) Russell, McConnell, Swan, Henderson, Banks.

After The League – Oblivion.

With no Third Division into which Broxburn United could be relegated, they were elected to the next best thing, the Scottish Alliance. This League increased it's membership, and formed two geographical divisions for the 1926/27 season, due to the former Third Division Clubs who joined en-masse. Member clubs were able to compete alongside the likes of the reserve teams of Rangers, Aberdeen and Hearts. Competing in the Northern section, the Club were now relieved of the severe financial requirements that were experienced in the Scottish League, but it was still a severe strain to make ends meet.

With only £15 as a guarantee at their away fixtures, it was realised that home gates would have to show a profit to balance the inevictable deficit. A successful season seemed unlikely when the first match was lost at home to Dundee reserves, and was followed with a 0-2 defeat to the Falkirk second eleven.

The attendances started well, but by the end of the year rarely rose above a few hundred, in the match against Lochgelly there were only 200 present on a bitterly cold day in January 1927. The Club did little more than hold their own in this competition, although they reached the second round of the Scottish Cup, after a surprise victory over Armadale. The second round brought old Scottish League adversaries, Montrose, to Broxburn, and before an attendance of 2,000 the homesters held their opponents to a creditable 2-2 draw. In the replay, true to form, the new non-Leaguers lost. The last match in the Alliance was played at home to the powerful Aberdeen 'A' (reserves) team, and after the visitors took the lead in the first minute, they went on to an easy 5-0 victory.

The Club were facing an impossible situation, for the local shale industry had come to a standstill. The shale works were closing down, one by one, and for many families the outlook was desperate; some menfolk had been unable to pay the rent on their houses for eighteen months and were now on the point of being evicted. Against this background, there were more important issues than the local Senior football club, and with no hope of any influx of funds, the Club had little choice but to revert to Junior status, or fold altogether. They chose the former course and joined the local Mid-Lothian League.

The likes of Queens Park and Clydebank as League opponents were now a memory of the past; the first Mid-Lothian match was played at home to Wallyford Bluebell! For a while support, in the circumstances, was reasonable, but the Club now had to compete on the same level, as other Junior teams in the town, such as Broxburn Rangers - who opened their new Ground at Albyn Park during the latter months of 1927. For the United the situation became ever worse, and by now the fans had all but deserted them. On a wet afternoon in the autumn they entertained Edinburgh Emmet, and there were barely 150 spectators dotted around the enclosure.

The Club ceased their activities at the end of the 1927/28 season, although it was not until April 1932, that the Broxburn United Football Club Limited was finally, and officially dissolved.

Amongst a number of Clubs that have appeared and disappeared to date, the town has not been host to a long standing Senior status Club since 1927 (Broxburn St. John made a brief appearance at this level in 1933). Currently Broxburn Athletic – who were first formed in 1928 and first played at Uphall – are the town's representatives. Reformed after the Second World War, they have played – since 1968 – in the Junior 'East' League, the successor to the old established Edinburgh and District League, and home matches are played at Albyn Park.

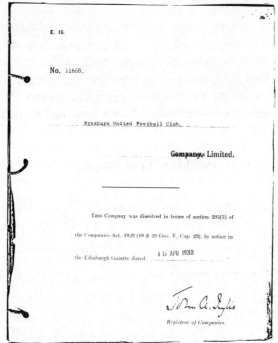

E. 16.

No. 11668.

Broxburn United Football Club,

Company Limited.

This Company was dissolved in terms of section 295(5) of the Companies Act, 1929 (19 & 20 Geo. V, Cap. 23), by notice in the Edinburgh Gazette dated   1 5 APR 1932

John A. Lylis
Registrar of Companies.

The Official End of the United (S.R.O. ref. BT2 11668)

– 1928/29 season –

BATHGATE FOOTBALL CLUB: THE SIGNED PLAYERS.

We give a photograph of Bathgate F.C. players with their trainer.
Top row:—Robert McIntosh (custodian) Bo'ness, who came this season from Castle-park Thistle, Philpstoun, Jas. Gribben (inside right or inside left), Baillieston, who came from Clyde, and prior to that was with Bo'ness. John Clarke (right back) Kelty, from Lochgelly Celtic. Wm. Waugh (custodian), Bathgate, from Durhamtown Rangers. Hugh Bolton (left back), Glasgow, came from Bridgeton Waverley and is on his third season for Bathgate. William Westwood (centre half) Shotts, from Shotts United and is on his second season with Bathgate. Andrew Pearson (left half) Kingseat. He came from Kingseat Juniors to Bathgate seven seasons ago. Alexander Ronald (right half) Bathgate, from Woodend United.
Bottom row:—John Higgins (right or left back) Bathgate. From Queen of the South and Third Lanark. Second season with Bathgate. James Macpherson (outside right) Livingston Station. Came from Livingston Amateurs last season. John Warrender (inside right), Methil. From Arbroath. Robert Drummond (centre forward) Bathgate. He joined Bathgate from Kingseat Juniors. After a season's play with Bathgate he in turn played for Burnley, Bristol City and Bournemouth. He returned to Bathgate this season. David Findlay (inside right or inside left) Bathgate. From Bridgend Violet. William Hughes (outside left) Winchburgh. He came to Bathgate three seasons ago from Bellstane Birds. Mr George Cowan, Bathgate's veteran trainer.
Photo by Mr Benzie, Bathgate.

Although Bathgate resigned from the Scottish League (on the 26th of February 1929), they suffered from the same problems which were caused by the same circumstances, as their earlier departed neighbours, Broxburn United. The oil bearing shale industry was actually founded in Bathgate by Dr. James Young in 1850, and although it became a flourishing industry, when the raw materials began to run out in the 1920's, so did the principal employers in the region. Like Broxburn, Bathgate retained their senior status, and in their case joined the East of Scotland League. At this level the Club were very successful, and during their two seasons membership were Champions on each occasion. Additionally they played in the first round of the Scottish cup in both seasons (losing in each case to Scottish League opponents), and were also the Qualifying Cup winners in both years – a remarkable success story for a Club that had to resign from the Scottish League!

The Club also won the King Cup during the 1929/30 season, but this was not retained, for one year later Bathgate lost to Pencuik; the match turned into an ugly brawl after Bathgate's goalkeeper went off injured, a player was sent off for the offence, and the Mill Park team were defeated 0–7.

On the field the two seasons could hardly have been bettered – only four League matches were lost during this period – but the perpetual financial struggle remained. Even the Club's share from the final of the Qualifying Cup in 1931 showed a profit of only £50.

The 1930/31 season was perpetuated with bad weather which inevitably affected the already poor gates. The total gate receipts for the year amounted to a meagre £173 – season ticket sales had produced little more than £5 – and the Club were £370 in the 'red'. It was only thanks to the fund–raising activities that kept the Club going, a bazaar producing £190 and additional donations which amounted to £45. When it was announced in July 1931 that all of the Shale Mines were to shut for good, the Club had little choice but to drop into Junior football.

– 1929/30 Season –

The above is a photograph of the Bathgate F.C. team and officials present at Ayr, when Bathgate, for the second year in succession and for the third time since the war, won the Scottish Qualifying Cup. Top row reads.—players—J. Gordon, J. Greenhorn, A. Jamieson, G. Kerr, W. Currie, R. Smith. Officials, J. Hardy, president; A. Jack, Secy., Jno. Love, director. Second row reads—players, J. Frew, D. M'Allister, T. Dick, J. Walker, and P. Somerville. The officials are—J. Anderson, director; G. Cowan, trainer; and J. Bain, Treasurer. It is interesting to note that in the team which won the Cup this year, there were only three changes from the team which won it in 1929. The new men are J. Gordon, right back; R. Smith, left half, and J. Walker, inside left. In 1929, after winning the Qualifying Cup, the team won the King Cup and finished by securing the League trophy. This season they have done well in their League fixtures. The first round of the King Cup will be played next month. If the team keeps up the same enthusiasm as has marked the season so far, they should be able to win the King Cup and League trophy again. In the first round of the Scottish Cup, which is to be played on 17th January, Bathgate are visitors to Motherwell. While it is not expected that they will put the heather on fire, it is pretty certain that Bathgate will worthily uphold their East of Scotland reputation.

The economic situation affected many Clubs in the area, which led to closures, and for the 1931/32 season, the Club although entered into the well established Edinburgh and District League, found that they had only eight other clubs in opposition! The financial accounts of the Club made pathetic reading, for both gate receipts and season ticket sales were half those of the previous year, and although the rent on the Ground was a modest £24, with the players expenses which totalled £68, the overall loss on the season was £122.

Although the Club enjoyed another successful season, there appears to be no record of them playing in the 1932/33 campaign, and like Broxburn United, the official end did not come for some years after their effective demise, in Bathgate's case, in May 1938, when an announce-ment that the Club was to wind-up was issued; the final end came on the 25th of Ocotber 1938.

The parallels continue in respect to Broxburn, for the town of Bathgate does not have a Senior team, and currently Bathgate Thistle (who were founded in 1937) are the leading Club, and also play in the Junior 'East' League.

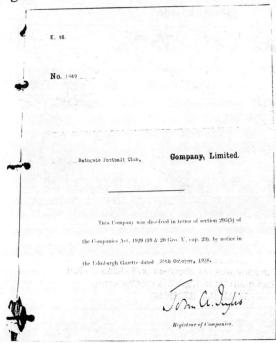

Bathgate's final end comes in 1938. (S.R.O. Ref. BT2/5649)

Although the Company was not dissolved until October 1938,
the Club had given up all hope five months earlier.
(S.R.O. Ref. BT2/5649)

The Grounds.

Descriptions of the Grounds of the Clubs, and their predecessors have already been detailed. The current situation with regard to these enclosures is as follows:

Armadale: Volunteer Park has always been the only properly enclosed Ground in the town, and remains today, the home of Armadale Thistle. For a Junior Club it is a substantial and well enclosed Ground, and is a fitting memorial to the days when it was host to a Scottish League team. The original enclosure walls are crumbling in places, and until 1990, the substantial concrete and gravel terrace behind the South goal remained in it's entirety, but is now much reduced in area. The East side with its embankment and lower terraced strip still remains intact – but the pavilion has long since gone. Opposite, on the West side of the pitch, the original Grandstand has been replaced with a covered standing enclosure, but with limited seating. The Community Centre overlooks the Northern end, where there was once a slaughter house.

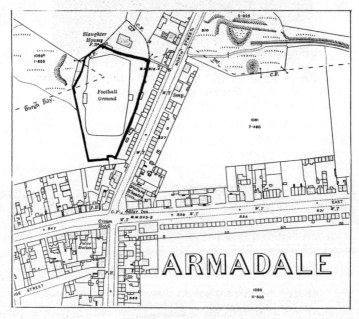

O.S. Map of 1916 (The current Stand is in the same location as the original one)

Old terracing remains along the East side.
A view of the (West side) Stand from the large embankment.
(Photos by Dave Twydell)

Bathgate: The large and irregularly shaped Mill Park Ground was located between Cochrane Street and Russell Row, and was named after Mill Road which still runs – North to South, and just to the West of the site of the former Ground. During the 1930's the Ground was built over, and although Cochrane Street and Russell Row – the latter now renamed Waverley Street – are much the same, nothing remains of Mill Park; Marmion Road now connects these two residential roads, and runs a few metres to the East of what would have been the halfway line of the pitch!

The O.S. Map of 1917 showing the sparse Mill Park Ground.
Now covered with housing.

Broxburn: Albyn Park, the home of one of the United's predecessors, is home to the current Broxburn Athletic, and although with limited facilities has no doubt undergone development since those turn of the century days. The Sports Park site is now the Sports Centre, although the present car park substantially overlies the former Ground. Church Street, which has now been extended, runs alongside what would have been the narrow East side of the pitch. There are suggestions of former embankments at the North and South ends of the car park; the remains of former embankments to the Football Ground, or just a romantic interpretation?

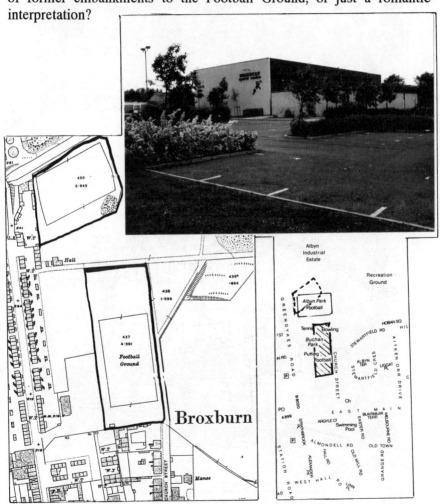

O.S. Map of 1917. The upper Ground is Albyn Park the site of the current Club. Sports Park is now the site of the Sports Centre (Photo by Dave Twydell)

PEEBLES ROVERS.

Peebles Rovers F.C.

Unnamed Team Group – 1932/33 season.

Peebles Rovers who meet St Mirren in the Scottish Cup—Back Row—Dodds (trainer), Cochrane, Kilner, Haywood, Napier, Pride and Sked. Front Row—Gill, Waterston, Turnbull, Sterricks and M'Dermott.

Peebles Rovers Team Group – January 1935

Peebles Rovers.

Founded 1893.

To 1902/03	Friendly and Cup Matches
1902/03 – 1908/09:	Border League.
1909/10 – 1911/12:	Scottish Union.
1912/13 – 1914/15:	Eastern League. *
1915/16 – 1918/19:	Inactive.
1919/20 – 1920/21:	Border League & Scottish Amateur (East) League.
1921/22 – :	Eastern League.
1922/23 – :	Western League.
1923/24 – 1925/26:	**Scottish League Division 3.**
1926/27 – :	Alliance League.
1927/28 – :	Midlothian Junior League.
1928/29 – 1938/39:	East of Scotland League.
1939/40 – 1944/45:	Inactive.
1945/46 – 1965/66:	East of Scotland League.
1966/67 – 1973/74:	East of Scotland – Mid-East Junior League. **
1974/75 – 1975/76:	(Probably) Inactive.
1976/77 – 1977/78:	Border League 'B' Division.
1978/79 – 1979/80:	(Probably) Inactive.
1980/81 – 1986/87:	East of Scotland League.
1987/88 – 1988/89:	East of Scotland League (1st Division).
1989/90 – to date:	East of Scotland League (Premier Division).

* 1914/15 season, fixtures not completed.
** Probably also known as 'Edinburgh and District Junior League (East Div.)'.

....

Grounds:
Early years: Villa Park and Victoria Park.
c. 1900 to 1906:   Victoria Park.
1906 to date: Whitestone Park.
Colours:
To 1924 – Maroon.
1924 to 1928 – White.
1928 to c. 1980 – Maroon.
c. 1980 to date – Red and White.
Members of Scottish F.A.
1907 – 1915 (Resigned). 1919 – 1927 (Resigned). 1928 to date.

Major honours and achievements:
Scottish Cup: Third Round (last 16) – 1912/13. 1913/14.
                Second Round – 1922/23. 1924/25. 1925/26. 1953/54. 1958/59. 1959/60. 1960/61.

                Qualifying Cup (South) Winners: 1953/54.
East of Scotland Qualifying Cup Winners: 1911/12. 1913/14. 1914/15. 1921/22. 1922/23.
1937/38. 1948/49. 1949/50. 1951/52. 1953/54. 1961/62.
East of Scotland Cup Winners: 1922/23. 1954/55.
King Cup Winners: 1908/09. 1950/51. 1951/52. 1961/62. 1962/63.

East of Scotland League Champions: 1928/29. 1932/33 – 1935/36 (incl.). 1945/46.
(First Div. Champs. 1988/89).
Scottish Union Champions: 1910/11.
Border League Champions: 1903/04.

....

Scottish Cup 1960/61 lost to Hibernian : 1–15.
East of Scotland League 1982/83 season, obtained only 2 points throughout season.

Scottish League (Division 3) – Complete Record.

1923/24 season:

August	18	(Home)	1–2.	Mid–Annandale.
	25	(Away)	1–2.	Solway Star.
September	8	(Home)	3–1.	Montrose.
	22	(Away)	1–4.	Dykehead.
	29	(Home)	2–6.	East Stirling.
October	6	(Away)	0–0.	Clackmannon.
	13	(Home)	1–3.	Arthurlie.
	20	(Away)	3–5.	Galston.
November	3	(Away)	2–3.	Nithsdale Wanderers.
	10	(Home)	4–0.	Clackmannon.
	17	(Home)	1–1.	Queen of the South.
	24	(Away)	0–4.	Royal Albert.
December	1	(Away)	1–1.	Brechin City.
	15	(Away)	1–2.	East Stirling.
	22	(Home)	2–1.	Dykehead.
	29	(Home)	0–0.	Dumbarton Hibs.
January	1	(Home)	2–2.	Solway Star.
	2	(Away)	2–3.	Mid–Annandale.
	5	(Home)	0–0.	Nithsdale Wanderers.
	19	(Home)	5–2.	Helensburgh.
	26	(Away)	1–1.	Arthurlie.
February	2	(Away)	0–0.	Dumbarton Hibs.
	9	(Home)	3–0.	Royal Albert.
	16	(Home)	2–0.	Brechin City.
	23	(Away)	4–2.	Helensburgh.
March	1	(Home)	0–0.	Beith.
	15	(Away)	0–1.	Montrose.
	22	(Away)	0–4.	Queen of the South.
April	5	(Away)	0–2.	Beith.

		Home:				Away:						
Played	W.	D.	L.	F.	A.	W.	D.	L.	F.	A.	Pts	Pos.
30	6	5	4	27	21	1	3	11	16	35	22	14th

1924/25 Season:

August	16	(Away)	1–1.	Dykehead.
	18	(Home)	7–1.	Beith
	30	(Home)	4–0.	Mid–Annadale.
September	6	(Home)	4–3.	Clackmannon.
	13	(Away)	1–1.	Beith.
October	11	(Away)	2–2.	Royal Albert.
	25	(Home)	1–1.	Lochgelly.
November	8	(Home)	0–1.	Queen of the South.
	15	(Away)	1–2.	Vale of Leven.
	22	(Away)	1–2.	Montrose.
	29	(Home)	2–0.	Dykehead.
December	6	(Home)	3–1.	Brechin City.
	13	(Away)	3–2.	Leith Athletic.
	20	(Home)	4–3.	Montrose.
	27	(Away)	1–2.	Solway Star.
January	1	(Home)	1–1.	Royal Albert.
	3	(Away)	2–3.	Mid–Annandale.
	10	(Away)	1–7.	Nithsdale Wanderers.
	17	(Home)	5–0.	Helensburgh.
	31	(Away)	0–6.	Queen of the South.
February	14	(Away)	2–3.	Clackmannon.
	21	(Away)	1–4.	Brechin City.
	28	(Away)	1–2.	Lochgelly.
March	7	(Away)	1–3.	Helensburgh.
	14	(Home)	1–1.	Solway Star.
	21	(Home)	3–2.	Nithsdale Wanderers.
	28	(Home)	1–0.	Vale of Leven.
April	11	(Away)	2–5.	Galston.
	20	(Home)	1–1.	Leith Athletic.
	29	(Home)	4–0.	Galston.

	Home:					Away:						
Played	W.	D.	L.	F.	A.	W.	D.	L.	F.	A.	Pts	Pos.
30	10	4	1	41	15	2	3	10	23	42	31	8th

N.B. Dumbarton Hibs did not complete their fixtures.

1925/26 season:

August	15	(Away)	2–1	Beith.
	22	(Away)	0–1	Helensburgh.
	29	(Home)	2–4	Vale of Leven.
September	12	(Away)	4–2	Clackmannon.
	26	(Away)	3–5	Montrose.
October	10	(Away)	3–5	Lochgelly.
	17	(Home	5–0	Solway Star.
	24	(Home)	3–0	Brechin City.
	31	(Home	5–0	Lochgelly.
November	7	(Away)	1–4	Dykehead.
	21	(Away)	2–4	Mid–Annandale.
	28	(Away)	2–1	Galston.
December	12	(Away)	2–4	Vale of Leven.
	26	(Away)	1–3	Mid–Annandale.
January	1	(Home)	0–6	Leith Athletic.
	2	(Home)	0–4	Beith.
	9	(Away)	0–2	Leith Athletic.
	30	(Away)	2–5	Forfar.
February	13	(Home)	2–1	Johnstone.
March	6	(Away)	1–7	Solway Star.
	13	(Away)	1–3	Johnstone.
	20	(Away)	3–5	Royal Albert.
	27	(Home)	3–1	Dykehead.
April	3	(Home)	2–3	Helensburgh.
	10	(Home)	2–1	Forfar.
	17	(Home)	1–4	Royal Albert.

		Home:				Away:						
Played	W.	D.	L.	F.	A.	W.	D.	L.	F.	A.	Pts	Pos.
26	6	0	6	27	28	3	0	11	25	48	18	15th

N.B. Home games versus; Clackmannon, Galston and Montrose plus the away match at Brechin City not played.

Rovers the Minors.

Unlike the others in this geographically sectioned set of ex-League Clubs, Peebles Rovers stand out alone, rather than being within a group. They are also unique in this 'Edinburgh and the South' section by virtue of the Club being essentially the same as that which graced the Scottish Football League.

The exact formation date of the Club is difficult to establish, although 1893 has been the accredited year in past references to the Club. Until the early 1890's, sport was dominated in the town by Rugby, but by 1893 soccer had rapidly taken over the mantle as the most popular pastime, and this was evidenced by the proliferation of teams in the immediate vicinity. Among the many teams, the most dominant appeared to be Peebles, Peebles Strollers, and Bonnington Thistle Peebles – all three using Villa Park as their home ground. Peebles Wanderers, Peebles Athletic and Peebles Hibernians also received frequent newspaper references as did several Clubs from neighbouring districts. Without doubt the two most senior teams were Peebles and Bonnington Thistle, the former organising a 5-a-side football competition in the summer of 1893, and support at the matches of the latter Club was such that big matches were accompanied by Brass Band entertainment at Villa Park.

The start of the 1893/94 season was greeted with great anticipation by the locals (or so the local newspaper reported), and the interest was directed towards the top two Clubs, viz. Peebles and Bonnington Thistle. Up to this time it is noticeable that there was no reference to Peebles Rovers Football Club. The first regular references to the 'Rovers' Club appear to be in the 1894/1895 season when matches were played in Victoria Park. Noticeably there were no references to the Bonnington Thistle Club, either then or later, and it is therefore quite possible that the 'Thistle' were in fact the forerunners of the 'Rovers'!

There is no doubt that the plain 'Peebles' were a completely separate Club (the two named teams often played separate games on the same day), and although the Rovers at this time were the lesser of the two, they nonetheless had their moment of glory in the 1893/94 season when it was later revealed (in the local newspaper) that they won through to the final of the Border Cup. The more progressive Peebles F.C. were able to secure the use of Bonnycraig Park for their home matches for the start of the 1894/95 season.

Meanwhile the Rovers continued to use both Villa and Victoria Parks for their fixtures. The Rovers' fixtures were few and far between, and by the end of April 1895, only eight matches had been played that season, although their success rate was high for these few encounters produced a goal difference of 45-15!

By the turn of the century the Rovers were using Victoria Park on a regular basis, but they were still playing 'second fiddle' to Peebles F.C., and it wasn't until the 1902/03 season that the Rovers took positive steps towards establishing themselves as the senior team in the town. Until this time, they had contented themselves with playing Friendly and localised Cup games, but on the 29th of November 1902, the team played their first truly competitive match, following the Club's acceptance into the Border League.

Appropriately enough they joined the Border Association in 1902. This League was a very sparsely supported competition, as it contained only seven teams, amongst them the elevens from Vale of Leithen, Gala Renton and Selkirk; the latter – who became the League leaders after five matches – were the Rovers first opponents, and the Victoria Park homesters ran out as winners with the only goal of the game.

Peebles Top Team.

The first season of league football produced no major honours, but one year later the Club established themselves as the undisputed top town team. Although still only containing a handful of teams, the Rovers enjoyed a long and successful run from October to the near end of season, when they remained undefeated in all games. The last League match was played at the Caddon Park ground of Vale of Leithen, and one point was required to ensure that the Championship came to Peebles. The Rovers team duly obliged with a 1-1 draw. In League matches the Club were undefeated with eight victories and six drawn games.

The Club also reached the final of the Border Cup, which was played at Innerleithen. Their opponents were the strong Selkirk team, and before a record attendance for the competition – which produced a gate of nearly £16 – an exciting match ended with two goals shared. In the replay the Rovers went down by two goals to nil. In all thirty games were played that season, and the six defeats were all sustained in friendly and Cup games towards the beginning and near the end of the campaign.

The Club continued in the seven Club Border League for several seasons, where they had mixed fortunes. The 1905/06 season was particularly bad – they had dropped to second from bottom in the table by the end of the year – and support naturally waned. For a Border Cup–tie second replay match at Kelso, a special train was chartered for supporters, but with only fifty fans travelling the venture was a financial loss – and the team went down by three goals to Duns! But the Club was still ambitious, and arrangements were made during the summer of 1906 for the team to play at the more suitable Whitestone Park.

The Club's debut at this new venue was delayed until October, but the season started in fine fashion (with the early matches being played at Villa Park), when they thrashed Renton with a 7–1 scoreline, before a good attendance which realised £2–70. After five league games the Rovers headed the table, and by the end of the year – despite playing fewer matches – they lay in second place. The 1907/08 season was particularly notable for three achievements. By reaching the first round of the Scottish F.A.Cup, the Rovers appeared in probably their biggest match ever, when they were called upon to play at Celtic Park.

Although the attendance of 4,000 was not large by Glasgow Celtic standards, the non–Leaguers share of the gate was most welcome, even if the 0–4 scoreline wasn't! Later that season, on the 22nd of April, the Rovers entertained Celtic in a friendly match, and the attendance – a record to that date – was over 1,000, and produced gate receipts of £25; the visitors won by 3–1. The Border Cup was won (after an emphatic four goal victory over Duns), as was the King Cup. The latter competition was won after a replay at Tynecastle Park, and the Club's share from the 1,300 attendance amounted to £34.

The Club's achievements did not go unnoticed amongst the football fraternity, for the end of the season saw the 'defection' of Tommy Taylor, South to Lincoln City, where he joined up with other former Rovers' players, Ormiston and Wilson.

The A.G.M. at the end of the season was attended by a very large crowd, and the Club's followers were heartened to hear that after the total expenses of the season that amounted to £277, a profit of £3 was realised. Over the previous year, the Club had played a total of 30 games, of which eight were drawn and only six lost. Despite the Club's decision to resign from the Border Association (this followed their acceptance as members of the Scottish F.A. one year earlier), they embarked on their seventh – and last – season in the Border League. The close season saw much activity, for with all their debts paid off, they were able to effect a number of Ground improvements that were conditional upon their acceptance into the Football Association. The surface of the pitch was improved (and the length extended by seven yards) and the facilities were improved upon. Two pavilions were built, one for the Club's exclusive use and the other for the Referee. These were in addition to the pavilion which the Club shared with the Cricket Club. For spectators, there was a covered and seated Stand.

The success of the 1908/09 season saw the Club progress through to the final of the East of Scotland Qualifying Cup Competition. Berwick Rangers were first beaten (by 2–1 at their own enclosure), and the next round required three matches before a victor was found. After two drawn games with Vale of Leithen, the Rovers finally won the second replay at Whitestone Park with a 2–1 scoreline before a large attendance which produced gate receipts of £15.

The final was played at the Gymnasium Ground in Edinburgh, where the Rovers were beaten by Broxburn Athletic. Two notable Friendly encounters occurred at Whitestone Park, the first when Queen's Park Strollers (the Reserve team of the illustrious Queen's Park Club) were beaten by 4–1 in what was regarded as the best game ever seen at the enclosure. A few weeks later a Celtic eleven were entertained, and the homesters ran out 2–1 winners.

An elevation in status.

The Club was elected into the Scottish Union (League) for the 1909/10 season, and the years whilst playing in this competition were generally successful. With such opposition as Galston, Dumbarton Harp, Johnstone, Dykehead, Renton and Port Glasgow Athletic, there was no doubt that the Rovers were matched with more senior competitors. Notable in the pre–First World War period, were the Club's successes in the several Cup Competitions. In the immediate pre–war years, they reached the third round of the Scottish Cup – the last sixteen – in 1913, and also one year later, but defeats at Celtic (0–3) and at Stevenston United respectively halted any further progress. Three successes also came with their capture of the East of Scotland Qualifying Cup during this successful period. The final of the prestigious Edinburgh City Cup was reached in 1912, at which stage they lost to St. Bernards. The Club's solitary Championship of the Scottish Union came in 1911, and after just one more season in this competition, they joined the Eastern League, which had first started in 1903, ceased in 1905, but had been revived for the 1912/13 season. This League initially contained only ten Clubs, but worthy competitors included Lochgelly, Vale of Leithen and Broxburn Shamrock. Although no League honours were won they maintained a challenge for the Championship, and such was the Rovers' confidence that they made a bid for membership of the Scottish League Division 2 at the end of that campaign.

The newspaper of the day referred to the Rovers having been in existence for nine years (i.e. since 1904), and it can only be assumed that at this time the Club were reformed. The Club's (unsuccessful) bid for Scottish League status was based on their recent successes, not least their performances in Cup competitions, and they argued that with a catchment area within a six mile radius of the town of 10,000, then support would be forthcoming!

The Scottish F.A. Cup run that season saw the team through to the Competition proper for the second time (they had earlier appeared in the first round in 1907, when they had also lost to Celtic). Their Cup exploits were not without drama, for in a qualifying round when they met Leith, at Peebles, before a crowd of 3,000, the match was abandoned with ten minutes remaining on the clock.

The Rovers were winning by 2–1 – the same half–time scoreline – when the pitch was invaded by hordes of visiting supporters; in the circumstances it came as no real surprise when it was ruled that the tie should be awarded in Peebles favour. One year later the same opponents were encountered in the 4th qualifying round again, but on this occasion there were no crowd problems, and Leith progressed by virtue of their two goal win; another crowd of 3,000 was present, although an estimated 2,000 were visitors! Crowds of around 1,000 – of home fans – were not uncommon at this period for Cup, and attractive, League matches.

With the onset of the First World War, football for the Rovers became impossible. By the start of the 1914/15 season the Club had lost many players to the War effort, and in the Borders area only three teams remained that could raise full teams for their League matches, and by January 1915, the Rovers remained the sole representatives in the district. The situation became impossible, for few competitive games were possible, and long distance travelling to matches ruled out any chances of financial stability. Therefore it came as no surprise when the Club opted to close down until the cessation of hostilities. During the War, interest in football in the town was maintained as various military teams used the Ground, with entrance charges to matches of 4d. (2p) and half–price for men in uniform.

Post–war Football.

For the start of the 1919/20 season, the composition of the Peebles Rovers team was unrecognisable from pre–war days, with few players returning to the Club. But interest was high, and with several members of the fairer sex joining the Club, it was decided to make a small charge for Ladies attending matches, a facility that had previously been free. The Club entered, for this their first post–war season, both the Border and Scottish Amateur (East) Leagues. Such competitions were doubtless of a lesser standing than those of earlier years, but until full normality returned the measure at least ensured that football was played in the town at a reasonable level. Many teams had not returned to playing by this time, and in the meagrely composed Border League, matches did not start for the season until after the New Year!

The first match for the Rovers was an East of Scotland Qualifying Cup game against Gala Fairydean on August the 30th. A 'huge crowd' was present, but they could not lift the local team, who succumbed to a defeat with the odd goal in five.

The season was quite successful, for after a poor start, the Rovers eventually improved. The same two Leagues were entered the next season, and the Rovers showed themselves to be superior to their opponents, although many fixtures remained unplayed. In the Eastern League only nine matches were played, of which six were won and none were lost (of twelve games originally scheduled), but even so the Club finished top of the table! The situation was similar in the Amateur League.

The Club re-entered the Eastern League for the 1921/22 season, but alongside only five other Clubs. Even so support was good, with excellent crowds being recorded at Whitestone Park matches, despite the rising unemployment in the area. Before the start of the season there was doubts on whether the Club would be allowed to continue the use of the Ground. With few other pitches available the Club may well have folded.

The Eastern League only made a brief appearance in the post-war years – for two seasons – and in 1922, the Rovers, along with Queen of the South, Solway Star, Helensburgh and Nithsdale Wanderers, joined the Western League, arguably the most senior competition outside of the Scottish League itself. But even so, some episodes were not condusive with a competition of such high standing. For the long journey to Dumfries for the match with Queen of the South, the Rovers arrived very late and with only seven players to call upon. Rather than cancel the fixture and having to repeat the long journey at a later date, the Club agreed to use four junior Queen's players in their line-up! By the start of the game, dusk was already approaching, and it was agreed to play for just 35 minutes in each half, but even in this reduced time the depleted Rovers succumbed to a 0-7 defeat!

But such a defeat was not an uncommon occurrence in a generally unsuccessful campaign, although by the season's end, after a poor start, the Club finished in a mid–table place.

The highlight of the season was undoubtedly a match in the Scottish Cup. The Club played through to the second round, their victories including a four goal victory over Moorpark Amateurs in the first round, and the next game required the Club to travel to the mighty Hibernians. There was little doubt with regard to the outcome of this encounter, and a prominent Edinburgh newspaper stated that:
"The Hibs. task is as easy as taking pennies from the youngsters bank".

Despite the awesome prospect 600 Peebles supportrers were amongst the crowd of 14,000, which produced match receipts of £416. The Rovers team consisted of Hodge, Veitch, Allison, Maxwell, Duncan, Dickson, Hannigan, Aird, Houston, Gordon and Pearce. Ironically Maxwell, Hannigan and Gordon were all ex–Hibs. players. Directly from the kick–off the homesters nearly scored, and the first half was dominated by the Scottish League team. But despite the visitors playing with only ten men for the latter part of the first period – Hannigan going off with an injury – the non–Leaguers held their opponents to a no scoring first half. Hannigan returned for the second half of the match, but was virtually a passenger, but even so against all the odds the final result remained scoreless. The Rovers agreed to stage the replay at Easter Road, and a generous gesture by Hibs. ensured that all travelling supporters (200 for the second encounter) were admitted free. The attendance was 8,000 (£230 receipts), but the fitter and fully professional team comfortably won this replay by three unopposed goals. The only other point of merit during the 1922/23 season was the Club's appearance in the final of the East of Scotland Cup. At Logie Green, Edinburgh, they lost by 1–2 to Leith Athletic before an attendance of 3,000.

On the 23rd of May 1923, the Scottish Football League, at their meeting in Glasgow, took the surprising decision to create a Third Division. Surprising since it had already been shown that with it's sparse and scattered population, the League could barely sustain just two divisions! But for Peebles Rovers and fifteen other Clubs an opening was provided for glory in the Scottish League.

Although on paper the formation of another division opened the way for progression, in reality it was little more than a renamed non–League competition. All Clubs had to guarantee a modest £15 to visiting Clubs, the Scottish Cup had still to be entered from the qualifying stages, and the little teams rise in status was only rewarded with Associate Membership of the League, with no voting rights! However, credibility was given with the chance of automatic promotion, but since only three of these original entrants have progressed onto a sustained membership of the League, then it is obvious that the move was far from a successful one, either from the Clubs' standpoint or the League's.

Quartette of Peebles Football Personalities.

W. Wilson and J. Rutherford, who have taken part in all Peebles Rovers' games during the season.

Peeblesshire Photo.
G. Turner, top scorer for Peebles Rovers.

T. Litster.
Schoolboy R. Carrick, capped for Scotland against England.

The brief flirtation with the Scottish League.

Peebles Rovers opened their Scottish League career on the 18th of August 1923, when accompanied by many travelling supporters, Mid–Annandale (from Locherbie) were the visitors. Heavy rain during the day did not subdue the enthusiasm, and a 'good' crowd was present. It was not an auspicious debut for the Rovers, for they went in at half-time, by a goal in arrears, and during the second half fell further behind. The homesters came into the game late in the second half, and Turner became the Club's first goalscorer in the Scottish League with his shot in the closing minutes. The players who represented the Club in this 1–2 defeat consisted of:

> Hope, Veitch, McVicar, Miller, 'Junior' (presumably
> an unnamed amateur player), Mackie, Watson, Turner,
> E.R. MacLauchin, Pearce and Ritchie.

The Club's second League match produced another defeat (with the same scoreline), although the Rovers were considered unlucky to lose this game at Solway Star. Vale of Leithen were beaten in the Scottish Cup, but the Rovers progressed no further in this competition. The next round required them to visit the new Ground of Leith Athletic at Wardie Park, a venue that was described as a neat enclosure surrounding a poor pitch.

The Club's first League victory came on September the 8th when Montrose were beaten 3–1 at Whitestone Park, but overall it was a disappointing start, and after seven games the club lay second from bottom in the table. The worst defeat of the season occurred on September the 29th, when the Rovers were beaten at home to East Stirling with a 2–6 scoreline. The Club's goalkeeper, Hope, had been injured, and his replacement – Doolan – could hardy have expected a more testing debut! Two new players were signed at the end of October, but it was not until November the 10th that a second league victory was recorded, when Clackmannon were convincingly beaten by 4–0 at Peebles. But this encouraging victory did not trigger off a run of good results, and by the turn of the year, after 16 League matches, the Club still lay in a lowly second from bottom in the table. Despite introducing more new players in the New Year, the dismal results continued, and even after a notable 5–2 victory over fellow strugglers Helensburgh on January the 19th, the Club were still placed just one off the bottom.

Poor performances inevitably affected attendances, and when the team visited League leaders Arthurlie (a creditable 1-1 draw) one week later, the attendance was 1,200 - their lowest of the season - but a figure that the Rovers would have gladly settled for at their home matches.

At the tail end of the season a slight improvement raised the Club to fifth from bottom, but final defeats at Beith and Queen of the South, resulted in a final, and disappointing two places lower in the table. On their travels the Club picked up just four points (from two draws and one win), and at home four defeats were sustained. The Club didn't even have any success in the final of the Western Cup (the Western League Cup carried over from the previous year) when they lost, over two legs to Arthurlie. But even after such a dismal start the Club looked ahead with confidence, and for the spectators, serious discussions were held with regard to covered and seated improvements at Whitestone Park.

The 1924/25 season started with a creditable 1-1 draw at Dykehead, and the Club's better performances continued, such that after four games they remained undefeated with two victories to their credit. Cup matches resulted in them having played less League matches than the other teams, and they were placed only seventh in the table. The first defeat came on the 8th of November, when high flying Queen of the South scored the only goal, at Whitestone Park. After their good start, it was a disappointment when two further defeats, on their travels in November, resulted in a slide down the table, but a pre-Christmas improvement resulted in a sixth League table placing by the turn of the year. The composition of the team had changed quite drastically from a year earlier, and the inclusion of these new faces appeared to be paying off, also the change in colours - from red shirts to maroon - may have brought about a change of luck!

The attention in the town was for a time focused towards the Scottish Cup, when a good run led the team through to the second round. Arbroath were first comfortably beaten by three unopposed goals, on their own Ground, and this result was followed with a 1-1 draw at Clackmannon before a poor crowd of only 300. The replay, on the following Wednesday attracted 500 spectators to Whitestone Park, a good turnout for a mid-week match (a fair crowd for Peebles on any day), and two goals were again shared between the two teams. In the second replay the opposition were beaten by the odd goal in five, and this victory took the Rovers through to the 1st round proper. After a scoreless draw at St. Cuthberts Wanderers, the visitors were thrashed by 5–0, in the replay at Peebles which attracted 800 spectators to the match. One hundred travelling fans boosted the attendance to 1,100, at Dykehead, for the 2nd round match. After going one goal up early in the match, the homesters increased their lead by half–time, and at the end, the Rovers had lost by 1–3.

This Cup defeat was followed by several League losses on their travels, but this run came to an end when Nithsdale Wanderers were entertained on March the 21st. The League leaders visited Whitestone Park in a confident mood, but were brought down to earth by a 2–3 defeat. In a bad tempered match, the situation came to a head near the end when one player from each side was dismissed. This led to a pitch invasion by supporters of both teams, and required the intervention of the police to bring order to the proceedings! Troubled Galston were easily beaten by 5–2, on their own Ground, on April the 11th – one of only two Peebles victories on their travels – and the curtain was brought down on the season in fine style eighteen days later, when the same team were thrashed by four unopposed goals. The final outcome for the Rovers was at least encouraging, for they commanded a final 8th league placing in the League of sixteen teams. But once again the Club were let down by poor performances on their travels. Just two draws were added to their pair of victories, whereas at home there had been just the one defeat. Notable victories included those against Beith (7–1), and Helensburgh by 5–0. A total of 44 games were played during the season, and of note were three players; Wilson and Rutherford who ever–presents, and Turner, the leading goalscorer with a total of 24.

The fortunes of Peebles Rovers could be considered satisfactory, but of a more wider concern, was the League itself, where large cracks were already showing! The number of competing clubs had dropped by four, to sixteen, and of those that were left many were experiencing financial distress. The Meadows Park Club of Dumbarton Hibs had folded in February, and therefore did not complete their fixtures, and Galston only just struggled through. It was only the encouragement of the Scottish League that ensured that the latter team completed all their games.

For Peebles Rovers the next season, their third – and final one – in the Scottish League started well with a 2–1 success at Beith. The Rovers team was very much the same one as a few months earlier, the only notable absentee being goalkeeper Wilson, who had been transferred to Newcastle United. The opening victory was not to be a sign of good things to come, for a run of several games, including a 3–5 home defeat to Montrose, followed without another win until the 5–3 success at the Recreation Park of Lochgelly. A marvellous trio of home victories followed, when no goals were conceded but five were scored against Solway Star, three versus Brechin and another five over the hapless Lochgelly. The Brechin victory was soured with the sending off of a player from each side.

These successes ensured that the Rovers attained respectability with a mid–table place in the League, after nine games, but they were now without Gavin McVicar who had been transferred to Third Lanark. By November the situation looked decidedly poor for most Third Division Clubs. Johnstone announced that they could not continue, but somehow pulled through and completed their fixtures. For Galston the end finally came, for in mid–February, and after only fifteen matches, they were unable to continue. For Peebles Rovers the situation was also dire, for by the end of the year they were in debt by around £200, and although the ever willing Supporters Club helped financially, the parent Club announced that unless more funds were forthcoming, then they too would have to resign.

By the turn of the year, the Rovers lay in a mid–table position with six victories and eight defeats, but then, despite the introduction of several new players, their fortunes dipped alarmingly. New Years day brought no cheer when the team succumbed to their biggest home defeat when they lost 0–6 to the high–flying Leith outfit. The next day four (unopposed) goals were conceded to the mediocre Beith team, at Whitestone Park. Despite introducing more new faces together with positional changes, the team suffered a two goal defeat at Leith on the 9th of January, by which time they had slipped to third from bottom in the League.

The poor form continued on the team's travels, and convincing defeats were sustained, including a 1–7 thrashing at Solway Star in early March which dropped the Rovers into the bottom of the League position. The previous month, a rare victory – over Johnstone – produced pathetic match receipts of only £17 at Whitestone Park, barely sufficient to pay the visitors their guaranteed fee!

Despite their poor results the team managed to progress through to the second round of the Scottish Cup, but these games hardly alleviated the Club's financial problems. Keith were easily beaten in the 1st round, at Whitestone Park, with a scoreline of 7–3, but the poor weather produced match receipts of only £25.

In the next cup encounter a surprisingly good result ensued at the home of Second Division Albion Rovers when their opponents were held to a 1–1 draw (after a shock half–time lead held by the Rovers), before a crowd numbering 3,500. The replay, admittedly in midweek and in poor weather, attracted no more than a normal saturday League match crowd for this prestigious game, and the team disappointed their followers when they succumbed to a four goal defeat.

One of only three away victories was deleted from the records due to Galston's resignation, and on the field the team struggled through to the end of the season. On the 10th of April they still languished at the bottom of the table, but a surprise 2–1 home victory over table–topping Forfar lifted their morale, although the match was a bad tempered affair, and three players were sent off. One week after the Forfar victory, the Club played their last home League match, and what transpired to be their last in the Scottish League. Royal Albert were the visitors, and another defeat was sustained, when the homesters scored only one of the five goals. The Peebles team consisted of:

> *Wilkinson, Bryce, Haggerty, Kane, Mason, Peden,*
> *Craig, Turner, Carruthers, Findlay and Bennet,*

Turner (one and the same as the Club's first League marksmen ?), had the distinction of scoring the last League goal for the Club, near the end of the ninety minutes.

Disaster and exclusion.

The season had been a disaster! The team finished bottom of the League – on goal average from next placed Clackmannon – although this position was, perhaps slightly misleading. With several Clubs floundering towards the end, including the disappearance of Galston, the Rovers were unable to complete four of their fixtures (having played less games than most of the other teams in the League), and all of them home encounters. There were few worries about being re–elected, since by May 1926, it was freely admitted that this ill–conceived League was doomed! Most of the Clubs came from small towns, several from little more than villages, and it had become apparent that they were just not big enough to sustain Scottish League teams, together with the additional expenses that had to be incurred. In view of the Rovers earlier statement with regard to their precarious financial situation, it was most surprising that they managed to pull through to the end, for their 1926 record which had produced nine defeats and only three victories had been hardly the form to attract extra support! During the Club's short Scottish League career they managed to create two records. The season had seen them play 26 League matches without one drawn encounter – a situation only matched in earlier years by other teams having played far fewer matches, and to their discredit, by conceding 76 goals (in 26 games), this had not been surpassed during the three years existence of the Third Division.

Back as a non–League team for the 1926/27 season, the Rovers were nonetheless still in familiar company. The folding of the Scottish League Division 3 resulted in many Clubs having to find a new competition to play in, and the Peebles Club, together with several of their former opponents, and together with reserve teams of five League Clubs (including Aberdeen and Hearts) opted for the (new) Alliance League. Away to Montrose in their first League match, and watched by a very healthy 2,000 crowd, the Rovers were easily cast aside with a 1–5 defeat, after being 1–3 down at half–time. The next match was even worse when they lost by five unopposed goals to Dundee Reserves. The first victory did not come until the return with the Dundee team, by which time Peebles had played seven matches and lost five, giving them an uncomfortable second from bottom position in the League.

Fortunately some solace was obtained from a reasonable run of Cup victories, which saw them winners at home to Coldstream (6-2), Vale of Leithen by 3-1, and a crushing of Arbroath Athletic with a 9-3 scoreline. There were 150 travelling supporters at Broxburn United for the East of Scotland Cup match, but the Club bowed out of the competition when they lost by 2-4 after sharing the two goals scored in the first half.

As well as playing troubles on the field, the Rovers also had other problems on the pitch, since before the Dykehead home game, the local fire brigade had to be called out to drain the pitch after a very wet spell. Overall it was to prove a dismal re-introduction into non-League football, for further heavy defeats, including 0-5 and 0-10 to the Reserves of Falkirk and Aberdeen respectively, ensured a lowly placing in the League throughout the season. Overall it was a disastrous season, and for the next campaign they had to lower their sights and their status quite considerably, when they entered the Midlothian Junior League.

A brand new start.

But one season out of senior football was probably the best prescription for the ailing Club, as from the 1928/29 season, and right through to the Second World War they competed in the East of Scotland League. During these years, the Club more than held their own in this reasonably high level competition, and this period could reasonably be considered their halcyon days. They claimed the League Championship in the first season, and this feat was repeated in 1933. By the early 1930's the Club were without doubt the most successful in the East of Scotland League as they ruled supreme with four consecutive Championships from 1933 through to 1936. During the 1932/33 season, the Club had commanded a high placing throughout the campaign, and after topping the table from the New Year, they remained in this position to the end. Ironically the season had started badly with two League defeats, but then from the 8th of September through to mid-February 1935, they maintained an unbeaten run. In this twelve team League they became Champions – despite one match remaining unplayed – and amazingly used only eighteen different players throughout – and four of those only played one game each!

By the season's end 33 matches had been played in all, with only two drawn matches and twelve defeats, with Haywood topping the goal-scoring list with 51 successes.

The 1936/37 season saw 14 teams entered in the League, as opposed to the previous twelve, and although the season started with a 3-1 away win at Berwick Rangers, the Rovers made no more than a moderate start. But by the end of the year they had risen to 2nd in the table, with seven victories and one drawn match in the nine games played until then.

However, the League Championship eluded the Club, although they fought their way through to the semi-finals of the qualifying competition of the Scottish Cup, but a 2-7 defeat at Bo'ness put an end to any glory in that direction. Support had risen for the Club, and that season a Supporters Club was formed once again, an organisation that first appeared for the Rovers in pre-First World War days. Although the 1937/38 campaign saw the Club win the East of Scotland qualifying competition, they were back on a downward slide once again.

At the A.G.M. despite the runners-up spot in the 1938/39 season, a proposal was put forward for the Club to turn to the Junior ranks once again, since wages and expenses had again outstripped the Club's meagre income. The Club's Officials recognised the value of the cash donations raised by the Supporters Club, but after the motion to revert to Junior status was defeated, they informed those fans that their money-raising schemes would have to be increased!

There had been a £50 loss on the season, and home gates had only produced £146 during the year, with an extra £70 from the Supporters Club. The players wages were a moderate total of £36, but despite the Club's relative success, such gate receipts as the £3-2-6d. taken for Berwick's visit - of which £3 had to paid as a guarantee to the visitors - clearly things were far from happy.

An amazing number of 43 different players were used throughout the season, a figure in sharp contrast to those few used four years earlier. The 1939/40 season started with a 2-7 thrashing at Chirnside United, although the second match, at home was won.

On the 26th of August 1939, the Rovers shared four goals with Raith Rovers, at Whitestone Park, in a Friendly match, and were prepared to play their next fixture at Dunbar Town, one week later. The match, but not any others for several years, was played, as the intervention of the second World War resulted in a cessation of activities until 1945. Football was occasionally seen during the War, in the town, by virtue of Servicemen based in the area and local Junior players. But the name of *'Peebles Rovers'* did not appear, but instead the 'name' of *'Number 330'*, the Wartime League consisting totally of numbers rather than names! Home matches were generally played at Whitestone Park, but also Peebles High School was used. Over these years of hostilities, Whitestone Park suffered, for it was requisitioned for the War effort during part of the period.

With the War virtually over, a degree of football normality returned to Peebles in 1945, and on the 1st of September the trial match of Peebles Rovers was well attended; the locals had a 'thirst' for football, one that was not apparent in pre–war days! Still playing in their familiar maroon coloured shirts, the reformed (and now amatuer) Rovers, played their first match on the 8th of September, when Edinburgh City were the visitors for a friendly encounter. The game turned into a goalscoring bonanza, for after sharing equally six goals by half–time, the homesters ran riot in the second period, and ended up winners by 11–4. With a mixture of old (pre–war) and new players, the team made a hesitant start to their East of Scotland League matches, but this was soon overcome, and at the end of the season, they were once again crowned as League Champions.

The 1940's and 1950's were moderately successful, for despite no League Championships, various successes came in the different cup competitions. The East of Scotland Qualifying Cup once again produced it's successes for the Rovers, for they were winners in the 1948/49 season, one year later, 1951/52 and in 1953/54. The East of Scotland Cup itself was won in 1955, as was the King Cup in 1951 and 1952. During the 1953/54 season the club reached the second round proper of the Scottish Cup, a feat repeated in 1959 and 1960. On the first of these occasions, after a notable single goal victory at Montrose in the first round, the Rovers then lost to Buckie Thistle by an embarrassing scoreline of 2–7 – after a 1–1 draw.

The second appearance saw their progress halted in no uncertain manner when they were thrashed by ten unopposed goals at St. Mirren, and one year later lost at home to Ayr United by 1–6.

The earlier defeat at St.Mirren was almost respectable compared with the debacle suffered at Hibernian in 1961, when after easily overcoming Gala Fairydean in the first round, they lost the next with a 1–15 scoreline. Although a few Cups were won in the early 1960's, the Club gradually descended in status, plagued as ever by poor support. For the 1966/67 season the Rovers adopted Junior status, and played in the East of Scotland, Mid–East (Junior) League – where typical opposition were the likes of the Hearts third team – and for several years continued in a similar minor capacity. Although the records show the Club playing in the Border League 'B' division from 1976 to 1978, much of this period appears to have been spent in virtual hibernation!

Another new start!

It wasn't until the 1980/81 season that the Club re–emerged at a reasonably high level, when they were once again accepted into the East of Scotland League. But the 1980's proved to be years of struggle, not least the 1982/83 season when they finished as wooden–spoonists and obtained just two points throughout the campaign! When the League was reformed for the 1987/88 season, the Club were in reality demoted, and became founder–members of the First (Second) Division. One year earlier, the Club were delivered a body blow when they discovered that their proposed re–entry into the Scottish cup, there first since 1965 was barred. Whitestone Park had in those earlier, more lenient days, been considered a suitable venue, but due to the Club's break in contention for the premier Cup they now came under the scrutiny of the more stringent legislation of the 1980's. To comply with the Association's requirem–ents, it was decreed that an eight foot high chainlink fence would have to be erected around the full perimeter of the football area. This not surprisingly produced protests from both local residents and other Park users, and at a Planning meeting the Club's proposal was turned down.

This action effectively bars the Club from entry into the lucrative competition for the conceivable future.

Red card for football club's cup hopes

By WILLIAM CHISHOLM

A BORDERS football club's dreams of Scottish Cup glory were shattered yesterday when plans to make their ground comply with Scottish Football Association safety regulations were shown the red card.

Peebles Rovers last took part in the competition 22 years ago and joined the game's lesser ranks as the club struggled for survival. But Rovers have since recovered and hold a mid-table position in the East of Scotland League. They hoped to enter the Scottish Qualifying Cup, a stepping stone towards a tilt at Premier League opposition and the financial rewards that can bring.

Unfortunately the Peebles ground at Whitestone Park where the club has played its home fixtures since 1893 no longer meets SFA standards.

Before Rovers could stage cup ties, an 8ft high chainlink fence would have had to be erected to enclose the pitch and terracing.

Such a proposal has not gone down well with owners of houses facing the ground, with 21 of them lodging objections. The Whitestone ground is part of an attractive public park where several sports clubs have their pitches.

Mr Douglas Hope, deputy director of planning with Borders Regional Council, told a planning committee meeting yesterday that while the fence might be acceptable on three sides of Whitestone Park, he was not in favour of it going all the way round.

The meeting heard that local discussions surrounding the Rovers' proposal had become heated, but even if permission for the fence were granted there was no guarantee the SFA would restore the club's status.

After Councillor Tom Hunter (Ind), the council convener, claimed the fence would ruin the park and Councillor George Turnbull (Con) said the development would have a dramatic impact on the beauty of the area, the committee voted 6-4 to refuse the application.

So for the moment Peebles Rovers will not be figuring in the draw for the cup they once contested regularly. Some of their once-contested performances were memorable, but there was one the club would sooner forget.

On February 11, 1961 Rovers took on the then mighty Hibernian in the second round of the cup and provided the Easter Road side with a record victory, a 15-1 triumph, with Joe Baker scoring nine times.

But on the playing front, things at least were improving, and at the end of the 1988/89 season the Club became Champions of their Division and with this honour came promotion upto the Premier Division. After years of struggle and near extinction, perhaps they have reached a turning point when they can once again become a force in non–League Scottish football.

It has to be admitted that Peebles Rovers have never been, or are likely to become a household word in football. Their brief existence in the Scottish League was no more than a passing phase, and this elevation was due more to them being 'in the right place at the right time', as it was for the majority of Clubs that constituted that ill–fated League. Their close proximity to Edinburgh – and the variety of Scottish League teams – coupled with a small population that have never been renowned for their following of football is always likely to inhibit the Club.

A neat Stand and adjacent terrace steps – but enclosure is all but impossible.
(Photos: Dave Twydell)

Whitestone Park – a long walk from the pavilion to the pitch!

Grounds of the Rovers.

In the Club's early years both Victoria and Villa Parks were used as home venues, as they were for several other Clubs. There is no doubt that these were nothing more than large open areas, and maps of the period confirm this. In October 1906, the Rovers moved to Whitestone Park, or Kerfield as it was also known to that time. Since the smaller Kerfield Park now adjoins Whitestone Park, it is probable that around the turn of the century the two were as one. Over the years the facilities for the team and the fans have been improved, such that at present they are worthy of a team of this status, particularly in view of the Club's such recent years of struggle. The Park, which lies just to the East of the town centre, contains a large pavilion and changing rooms on the West side. But, together with an adjacent large grassed embankment, it is somewhat remote from the football pitch. Close to, and down one side of the football playing area, there is currently a quarter pitch length seated Stand, and four steps of concrete terracing are located each side of the Stand.

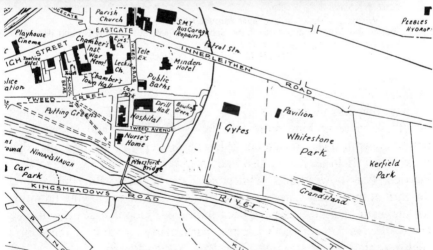

Viewed from the side opposite to the Stand there is the appearance of
a neat Ground, however from the impressive entrance gates off the
Innerleithen Road, the Club's enclosure problems can be appreciated.
The area of neat and well kept grass extends to provide perhaps three
full sized football pitches, and it is obvious that any desire to enclose as
a Football Ground, can only be a forlorn hope.

EDINBURGH CITY.

EDINBURGH CITY PLAYERS AND OFFICIALS

Edinburgh City F.C.—Standing (left to right)—Councillor J. R. Coltart, Bailie Wilson M'Laren, E. Gardner, T. Robertson, J. Jones, J. R. Johnston, J. Macdor, D. Bannatyne, D. Arbuthnot, and G. H. Mitchell. Seated (left to right)—R. Perry, J. Monaghan, J. Henderson, H. Strachan, and F. MacNabola.

15th August 1931.
Line–up before the Club's debut match in the Scottish League, at their new Ground (Powderhall).
Note the Stand and adjacent building, not much changed in 1990 (see page 181).

Unnamed Line–up August 1932.

Edinburgh City.

Founded 1928 – Defunct 1954.
(New Club created/changed name from 'Postal United' – 1986)

League Career:

1928/29 – 1929/30:	East of Scotland League.
1930/31 –	Edinburgh & District League.
1931/32 – 1939/40:	**Scottish League Division 2. ***
1939/40 – 1944/45:	Minor local competitions.
1945/46 –	Eastern League.
1946/47 – 1948/49:	**Scottish League 'C' Division..**
1949/50 – 1954/55:	Edinburgh & District Junior League.

* 1939/40 season, Scottish League fixtures ceased after four matches.

1986/87 –	East of Scotland League.
1987/88 – 1988/89:	East of Scotland League – Premier Division.
1989/90 –	East of Scotland League – First Division.
1990/91 –	East of Scotland League – Premier Division.

....

Grounds:
1928 – 1931: Marine Gardens.
1931 – 1934: (New) Powderhall.
1934 – 1935: Marine Gardens.
1935 – 1954: East Pilton (City) Park.

1986 –   Paties Road, Colinton.

Colours:
White Shirts, Black Shorts.

Members of the Scottish F.A.
1928 – 1931 (Associate)
1931 – 1949 (Full – resigned)

Major Honours and Achievements:
Scottish Cup – 2nd Round: 1930/31 1931/32 1937/38 1938/39.
East of Scotland (City) Cup Winners: 1947/48.

Amateur International Players:
(Scotland): F.Russell (30/31) J.Cumming (31/32, 32/33) R.Wann (31/32) P.Gardiner (32/33)
E.Hamilton (32/33) J.McKell (33/34)
D.White (34/35) W.Hamilton (35/36) J.McShane (35/36) G.Hall (38/39) J.Mooney (38/39)
S.Duncan (38/39).

Record Victory: (Scottish League) 1937/38, (Home) 6–1 and 7–2 (Away) v. Brechin C.

Record Defeat: (Scottish League) 1937/38, (Away) v. East Fife 2–13.
                        (Scottish Cup) 1928/29, (Away) 1–11 v. Raith Rovers.

Record Attendance:
30th January 1932. 6,000 versus St.Bernards (Scottish Cup) – at Powderhall.
25th January 1936. 5,740 versus Cowdenbeath (Scottish Cup) – at East Pilton Park.

Scottish League record:

	P.	W.	D.	L.	F.	A.	Pts.	Pos.
2nd Division:								
1931/32	38	5	7	26	78	146	17	20th (Bottom)
1932/33	34	4	4	26	39	133	12	18th (Bottom)
1933/34	34	4	6	24	37	111	14	18th (Bottom)
1934/35	34	3	2	29	45	134	8	18th (Bottom)
1935/36	34	8	9	17	57	83	25	15th
1936/37	34	2	3	29	42	120	7	18th (Bottom)
1937/38	34	7	3	24	77	135	17	17th
1938/39	34	6	4	24	58	119	16	18th (Bottom)
1939/40	4	1	1	2	9	8	3	12th
(Matches ceased after 4 games)								

'C' Division:								
1946/47	18	3	3	12	40	44	9	10th (Bottom)
1947/48	22	6	3	13	54	60	15	11th
1948/49	22	2	4	16	26	85	8	12th (Bottom)

The new home of the Leith Athletic and Edinburgh City football clubs at the Marine Gardens, Portobello.

The new home of the Leith athletic and Edinburgh City football clubs at the Marine Gardens, Portobello.
– August 1928 –

Formed with high ideals.

There can surely not have been a Senior football club that met with such a complete lack of success, than that experienced by Edinburgh City F.C. A Club that can measure its real success by virtue of one season (in a total of twelve) in the League when they finished fourth from bottom says it all!

The Club were founded, in 1928, with noble intentions, wishing to provide a top class and purely amateur club in Edinburgh, with the ambition of emulating the equivalent team that represented Glasgow – Queens Park. But there were two main factors that would doom this bold venture. Queens Park had – and still have – tradition in their favour, and tradition cannot be contrived or manufactured. Secondly the 'age' of the Amateurs by this time had all but died. Although Queens Park were of course still thriving – as were their English counterparts, the Corinthians, the day of the amateur club at a high and respected level had already gone, for since the introduction of professionalism, the romanticism of such teams had gradually disappeared and was now little but a fond memory.

The founders of Edinburgh City were Councillor J.R. Coltart, Baillie W. McLaren and Mr. G.H. Mitchell. Their aims were simple, if in the final event, impossible to achieve. It was intended that the Club would provide an outlet for the undoubted talent that must have abounded within the famous Edinburgh schools, colleges and the University itself. A team that could compete, on a purely amateur basis, at the highest level, and perhaps reverse the trend which had seen such organisations turn their winter sporting pursuits towards the oval balled game of rugby. Reasonable ideals, but ones which were never realised.

The Club's beginnings were relatively humble, and at this level quite successful. Having being refused admittance to the Scottish Alliance, the City were accepted into the East of Scotland League for the 1928/29 season, the second campaign of this new competition. The Club also had a reserve team who were to play in the Lothian Amateur League. As a home Ground, the use of Marine Gardens was secured, and they groundshared with Leith Athletic who also moved there that season, from New Powderhall.

The newcomers had honoured the renowned amateur team by choosing the same club colours. The first match was played against Queens Park – in the circumstances, the ideal choice – on August the 8th, and the result was a 2–5 victory to the visitors.

The first League match for the City resulted in a 4–4 draw at Selkirk. It soon became apparent that their opponents were going to make it tough for the new club, for more games were lost than won. 0–5 at Duns and 3–5 at home Gala Fairydean were typical of the early season results. However there was some later success in the league campaign, and they were able to qualify for the final rounds of the Scottish Cup. Their first match in this competition being a 3–1 victory at Selkirk. The City could not have wished for (or dreaded?) a more stern test in the 1st round proper, than a trip to Ibrox, to face the mighty Rangers. The gulf that lay between the amateurs, and the top League Club in the country was demonstrated with the final result of 1–11, after the City went in 0–8 down at half–time, before 10,500 curious spectators. Even at their own (amateur) level the going was tough, and in the Amateur Cup they made an exit after losing by 1–2 to Civil Service Strollers, the Club that had beaten them in an earlier Scottish Cup qualifying round match. Even the King Cup was beyond the team, for they lost (in a replay) by 1–5 to Murrayfield Amateurs. The Club however, had made a reasonable start in league competition, and this was followed by another good season, but no glory in the various Cup competitions.

The 1930/31 season saw them move to the rival Edinburgh and District League, which despite its localised name catered for quite senior Clubs, and was in effect on a par with the East of Scotland League. Other Clubs in this competition consisted of Civil Service Strollers, Murrayfield Amateurs – previous members of the East of Scotland League – together with Edinburgh University, Leith Amateurs, Lochgelly Amateurs, and Argyle and Sutherland Highlanders; a total of only seven teams in this League's inaugural season. Alongside these few, but still relatively modest competitors, the City were able to hold their own, despite not being amongst the honours at the season's end. In the Scottish Cup the team had a good 3–1 away victory at Brechin, but did not progress on and qualify for the Scottish Cup proper, for they fell at the next hurdle, at Arbroath.

A fortunate League entry

In May 1931, despite having no real form to back up their ambitions, they applied for membership of the Scottish League. Their eventual entry into the League was a somewhat bizarre choice and was based on luck, rather than their ability. Their application, in May, was unsuccessful, for the two re-election candidates – Bo'ness and Clydebank were given votes of confidence. This on its own was a somewhat strange decision, for not only were the two Clubs all but bankrupt and only just able to complete the fixtures of the previous season, but the chance to cut down on the number of clubs in the League was lost, at a time when an influential committee had only just reported that this course was the one that the League should be aiming for. To illustrate this bad judgement, Clydebank tendered their resignation on the 1st of July, just a few weeks before the start of the 1931/32 season. A second chance to cut down the numbers was missed, when new applications to replace Clydebank were received from Edinburgh City and Nithsdale Wanderers. The Sanquhar based Club had little reason to feel optimistic about their application, but they had only recently been members of the League, and had shown themselves capable when they were promoted from the Third Division to the Second. On the face of it Edinburgh City's attempt was almost laughable, for they had only been in existence for three years, and had achieved nothing of note in the football world. Yet by 25 votes to 7 it was the amateurs who won the day!

That the Club was almost certainly doomed to failure was even more likely when it was considered that Edinburgh – with a population of under half that of Glasgow – would now be expected to support five League teams as against the Western City's six. By coincidence a similar situation arose in England around this time when the comparatively new (and not particularly successful) London based Club, Thames F.C., were voted into the Football League – although in their case they only survived two dismal seasons! There was no suggestion that there was anything untoward regarding this amazing decision to welcome the City into the League, for it was clearly a romantic notion that did not take into account pure commonsense. In their defence the Edinburgh City officials proceeded with enthusiasm and honest endeavour, with the assurance that adequate financial backing was

Powderhall in 1990 – in several respects little changed from the 1930's. (Photo Dave Twydell)

available, and confident that large crowds would be attracted to the Capital's top amateur team.

Unable to secure a long term lease at Marine Gardens, the Club switched to the West and moved into the (New) Powderhall Stadium, a Ground that at one time had been used by both Leith Athletic and St.Bernards. The first League match for the City was played at Brechin, before a 2,000 crowd, and Robertson scored the Edinburgh team's opener after 21 minutes, in reply to a Brechin goal just one minute earlier. By half–time the scores were level at 2–2. In the second half the visitors had to face the strong breeze, and conceded a further goal. The team, on this not very auspicious occasion consisted of:

*Johnston, Jones, Bannantyre, McDonald, Gard-
iner, Robertson, Lowe, Henderson, Monaghan,
Kerr and Strachan.*

On August the 15th, Bo'ness were entertained at Powderhall, in the first home League match. The amateurs must have been severely disap–pointed when the crowd only numbered a few hundred for this historic match, although there were other local attractions to keep away the crowds. The homesters went in at the interval one goal down, and the final result was a 2–3 defeat, although it was reported that they had the basis of a good team, and were unlucky to lose.

But defeats immediately became the norm, and the first five matches were lost before a point was won, when a visit was made to Dumbarton. By Christmas the newcomers lay 2nd from bottom in the League (the first win coming on October the 10th versus near neighbours Hibernian), a position above which they were seldom to rise, in all their League career. Along the way some heavy defeats had been suffered – 4–8 at home to Queen of the South on August the 29th and just two weeks later 0–7 versus East Fife. High scoring defeats on their travels were also not unusual, and included 2–8 at Alloa, 2–6 at Arbroath and 2–7 at Raith.

The New Year was not a happy one, for the defeats just continued, and often with embarrassing scorelines, such as the 0–6 reversal in the return with East Fife on the 2nd of January. By the season's end the record was dismal, for only 5 wins and seven draws, from 38 matches had been achieved, and the team finished clear at the bottom by eight points. However this was their first season in the League, and they were given another chance when they were re–elected. The Club received represen-tative honours when Cumming and Wann were both given 'caps' and played in the Amateur International match versus Wales – one year earlier Russell had been similarly honoured in the International game versus Ireland.

In the national Cup competition they faced Murrayfield Amateurs, a Club that one year earlier they were on a (league) par with, and showed their superiority in the game that was played at Tynecastle before a

4,000 crowd. The City comfortably won by 3–0, after a single goal half–time lead. In the second round they were drawn at home to St. Bernards. An excellent crowd of 6,000 was present for the local derby match, and the City bowed out 2–3 in a tight game.

Undismayed with the poor start to their League career, the City set off on the 1932/33 campaign with confidence. But it soon became obvious that yet again the Club were to become the Division's 'whipping boys'. The season started badly on August the 13th at Stenhousemuir, with a 1–4 defeat, followed by a 2–4 home reverse to Montrose seven days later. Two more away defeats followed, as a foretaste of what was to come – 0–4 at Dunfermline and 2–6 at Dumbarton. At the City's lowly level, the late Autumn became a relatively successful period, for Leith (1–0), Armadale (4–3), and Forfar (4–3) were each beaten at home – three of a total of only four victories throughout the entire season! Sandwiched between these games came the inevitable defeats on their travels (including an 8–1 thrashing at St.Bernards). On October the 15th there was a crowd of 5,000 at Powderhall – although doubtless most spectators were supporting the visiting Hibernian team – and the City started well, but soon fell away, and ended up on the wrong end of a 0–4 defeat. In contrast the home match on the 26th of November, versus Arbroath, was watched by only 200 diehards, when the City were swamped with a 0–7 defeat. The team were said to be outclassed in every department, and it was only goalkeeper Gardiner who stopped the opposition running up a 'cricket score'.

By the start of 1933, the Club were anchored to the bottom of the League, and the New Year commenced with the inevitable defeats. Hibernian – the Champions–elect – attracted a crowd of only 1,500 (no doubt the fans were deterred by the winter weather and the unattractive opposition) for their match with the City on February the 18th, and an inevitable defeat for the amateurs, by 1–7. The losses continued to the end of yet another highly disappointing season, which finished with the City inevitably in the 'wooden spoon' position, with only 12 points – nine less than the next club, Montrose.

In April, Bo'ness and Armadale gave up and their results were removed, which was a shame for of the 2 matches played against these two unfortunate teams, one had been a City victory!

The Scottish Cup came to an abrupt end when the City lost by 1–3 at home to Ayr United, but before a far greater than average attendance of 3,540. On the International front, the Club undoubtably had quality at this amateur level, for no fewer than five players received caps during the season, including three for the match versus Wales.

The successful re–election bids continue

In the normal circumstances the Club's future in the Scottish League would have been in grave danger in view of their two disastrous seasons, however with the resignation of Armadale and Bo'ness, the number of Clubs in the competition had automatically been reduced by two, and the desirable reduction in the number of Clubs was thus achieved. Without any strong enough Clubs available to replace Edinburgh City, they were highly fortunate when their re–election became more or less a formality. The Club were realistic enough to appreciate that their very existence hung in the balance, and that drastic steps had to be taken. Only one player – A.R.Ross – was retained for the 1933/34 season, and when the first match, against Dumbarton at Powderhall on the 12th of August, was won with a 2–1 scoreline, it looked as things were on the up for the City. The only black mark was the sending off of goalkeeper McIlraith. All such thoughts were soon dispelled when the team lost by ˙four unopposed goals at Morton one week later! The all to familiar weekly defeats started, and it wasn't until just before Christmas that the next two points were won, when Kings Park were beaten 1–0. Between times the team's horrendous record on their travels continued, and included heavy defeats at Albion Rovers (1–8) and at Dundee United (3–9). After 11 games the City were 'only' second from bottom, but by the Year's end they were back in their familiar tail–end position.

In the second half of the campaign they managed to double their number of home victories – to four – but at the end, their lamentable away record produced just two points from early season drawn matches at Brechin and East Stirling. The total of fourteen points obtained were two more than a year earlier, but they finished in the bottom slot again, and ten points behind the next placed Dundee United. Their Cup aspirations came to an early end with a 2–5 defeat at Queen of the South, and only one player was capped at Amateur level – J. McKell – in three matches.

It was obvious that after three consecutive finishes at the bottom of the League, and well below the next team on each occasion, the Club realised that their re–election application bid was very likely to be turned down. But the Club always showed the sportsmanship that was the epitome of the true amateur, and they were always popular visitors – no doubt influended by the two points that their opponents were almost guaranteed to win! Perhaps it was therefore not such a surprise they they were given another chance to prove themselves.

Although the previous three seasons could be considered awful, then Edinburgh City's performances during the 1934/35 campaign were even worse! The Powderhall Ground was far from ideal, the main objection being the size of the pitch which was barely 50 yards wide, and so a move was made back to the Leith Athletic home venue at Marine Gardens. The first match defeat at demoted Alloa by 0–5 gave an accurate foretaste of what was to come. This was followed by two more defeats on foreign soil before the first home match on September the 1st. This encounter was won (3–1 over fellow strugglers Montrose), and after another victory the next week – 3–2 over Dumbarton (another poor team), their two consecutive victories represented their best run of success in over three seasons of League football! But the latter victory on the 8th of September was to become the last in the League until the 4–2 win at East Stirling on April the 6th, and this deplorable run between times represented one of the longest periods without success at this level of football. From 5th from bottom after 5 games (their best ever position to that date), they soon slipped to the familiar bottom rung. By Christmas there was an eight point gap between them and the next placed Club.

The Club were normally watched at home by crowds in the low hundreds, and it was only their amateur status that ensured their continual financial survival. But there were still expenses to be paid (Ground rent, travelling costs, etc.), and it was only thanks to the social side of the Club, with smoking concerts and dances, etc. for both players and supporters, that kept its head above water. By the end of the season the Club's League record was their worst ever, even by their incredibly low standards, for just eight points had been won (12 less than next placed Montrose), and the goal difference produced 44 in credit and 94 against.

On two occasions they had conceded nine goals on their travels. They lost by 2–8 at home to the much improved Dundee United team, and twice seven goals had been scored against them, plus three occasions when matches ended up with a six deficit – one of which was a 1–6 home drubbing by the mediocre Cowdenbeath team. Surely this was the end of the City's Scottish League career! yet amazingly for the fourth time they were voted back into the fold, and by this time there seems to have been no logical reason why they were given yet another chance.

EDINBURGH CITY FOOTBALL TEAM
Back Row (left to right)—J. M'Kell, W. Hamilton, W. Ferguson, J. Crichton, R. Hope and J. M'Shane.
Front—A. C. Anderson, P. Carruthers, W. Hope, A. R. Waterson and H. Gallagher.

Team Group taken in November 1935

The first true home

A move was made at the start of the 1935/36 season to City Park (later named East Pilton Park), the first true home of the Club. The Ground was officially opened on August the 12th for the visit of relegated Falkirk. By now the crowds at the club's home matches were almost non–existent, but there were encouragingly several hundred at the start, that had increased to over 1,000 by half–time. After a scoreless first 45 minutes, the visitors took the lead early in the second period. But Hamilton levelled for the City, before two late goals ensured yet another dismal defeat for the amateurs.

Another defeat and two draws followed, leaving the Club holding up all the others, and the first victory didn't arrive until September the 7th, when St. Mirren were beaten 3–2 before 500 City Park faithfuls. However, with two drawn matches in between, the Club moved up to the dizzy heights of 6th from bottom!

Another victory one week later – by 2–1 at Brechin lifted the team a further three places, and when the third victory in succession was achieved at home over previously unbeaten Alloa (but watched by only a few 100), the team were placed 6th in the table; a promotion challeng-ing position! But a defeat at Raith and then a home hammering by St. Bernards (but in front of 2,000), showed that the earlier success rate was no more than a flash in the pan. Although a near sensational 5–0 City Park victory against Kings Park, after the team had undergone a changed defensive pattern, showed that there may be hope. But by Christmas the City had dropped to 6th from bottom, and once again the second half of the season was one of disappointment.

On February the 1st, the poorly supported Leith team attracted a crowd of 1,000 to City Park, but a 2–3 defeat showed that the amateur team was going to find it a struggle to maintain even their lowly position. However by the season's end things could have been worse, and without any of the high scoring thrashings of the past, they actually managed to end up in fourth from bottom place in the League table. For the first time re–election did not have to be sought, which was very fortunate, for it is difficult to imagine that they would have been given yet another chance to prove themselves.

In the Scottish Cup 1st round, an all time record City Park attendance of 5,740 was present for the visit of Cowdenbeath. If the fixture had been a League match then it probably would not have attracted more than the customary few hundred. But defeat came yet again at this stage (by 2–3), as it had one year earlier when Kings Park put paid to the City hopes. Over the season two Amateur International caps were each won by Hamilton and McShane.

In a more optimistic mood the Club set out on the next season, but in the final event it became their worst ever! Just two victories were obtained – both at home – over Kings Park in September and with a 3–2 scoreline versus Aidrie in January. From the outset the City languished at the bottom, and with a final record of only seven points – an all–time record low for the Scottish League – they trailed 18 short of next placed Kings Park. Apart from two horrendous home defeats (both by 2–8 against East Fife and Alloa), their goals against record could have been worst, although seven goals were conceded at Morton and six in the return game with Raith. For the East Fife home game in April, the crowd had dwindled even more, and there were no more than *a few* spectators present. There was surely no hope of retaining their League status, but amazingly they did, although this was no doubt reinforced with their relatively successful position one year earlier. The season had seen another early exit from the Scottish Cup, following a first round defeat at home (attendance 1,066) to non–Leaguers Duns, by 2–5.

The 1937/38 season was the second successful one, for the team finished second from bottom in the League! It really must have been depressing to have been one of the few City supporters, as game after game was lost, season after season. In this campaign, it started with a 1–3 defeat at Stenhousemuir on August the 14th, and was followed by a 0–4 thrashing, at home to Aidrie. On August the 28th the first League point was obtained, when Forfar were held to a 4–4 draw (following a 2–2 half–time scoreline). Amongst the crowd of some 500 was the Earl of Strathmore, the Queen's father, and in the match N.Bruce, a former Watsonian *rugby* player made his debut for the amateurs. The first victory of the season was a welcome 6–1 win over the equally struggling Brechin City team, and this lifted the team to 5th from bottom. But this elevation was shortlived and after three further matches the City were back into their more familiar surroundings – 2nd from bottom.

EDINBURGH CITY F.C.
Back Row—J. M'Kell, A. S. Greig, D. Stewart, J. Hamilton, J. Mooney, and J. Mulvey.
Front—P. Carruthers, R. Hope, N. R. Bruce, A. Lumsden, and E. Y. H. White.

Team Group of the 1937/38 season

Although the team as usual suffered some bad defeats – the worst by 2–8 at home to Forfar – in fairness they also achieved a few notable victories. The only win on foreign soil was a somewhat amazing demolition of Brechin on the 27th of November, an unlikely 7–2 scoreline (this produced an aggregate score of 13–3 in the two matches with the League's eventual wooden–spoonists). Also the 5–2 win over Stenhousemuir and 4–0 versus Dumbarton proved that they could at least score goals, even if they couldn't stop them going in at the other end!

But whatever merits that could be attributed to the amateurs, the fact remained that their finish just one place off the bottom, meant another year of failure. Yet they were once again voted in to the League. This confidence in a team that was clearly never going to make the grade had by now become quite unbelievable!

It was in the Scottish Cup that the only worthwhile victory in the Club's entire history was achieved. Drawn away to First Division neighbours Hibernian, a crowd of 8,920 was present at Easter Road for the expected slaughter of the amateurs. But the fans were silenced in the first half when the City took a 2–1 half time lead.

Their surprise must have turned to amazement when two more goals were scored in the second period – one for each team – which therefore earned Edinburgh City a surprise 3–2 victory. But the second round match at Raith Rovers, an in–form team although only fellow occupants of the Second Division, became a farce as the City were hopelessly outclassed and lost by 2–9.

Although the 1938/39 season was no better than previous campaigns, the team got off to their best start ever, with a 4–2 home win over Montrose, followed by four goals equally shared at Kings Park. But the third match at Alloa put things back in perspective with a 1–5 defeat. By Christmas only one point had been picked up on the team's travels, and at home one draw also; the inevitable bottom place in the League – already seven points adrift of the next club – was the outcome. The second half of the season picked up slightly – notably a 4–1 victory over Morton, a middle of the table team who in view of their position had a very poor away record.

But the improvement was very marginal, for at the end only 16 points had been obtained – but nonetheless the third best League total for the City – and the inevitable bottom position in the table, six points behind East Stirling. The last League game was played in front of only a handful of spectators at City Park, but at least it produced a victory. Forfar, who themselves only obtained four points on their travels during the season, were narrowly beaten 3–2, although the homesters had taken a commanding 3–0 half–time lead. The winning goal came from Evans in the 74th minute. The City team consisted of:

McDonald, Hall, Greig, Mooney, Hope, McLeod,
McLennan, Evans, 'A.N.Other', Forbes and Stout.

In the Scottish Cup, the team once again won a game! At home in the first round to non–League Stranraer, and before a crowd numbering 600, the City could only manage to share six goals, and at half–time were losing by a single goal. The replay four days later required a long trip down South, and before 1,360 fans the City had a surprise 2–1 victory. On the first day of February the amateurs entertained the struggling First Division St. Mirren team. An excellent crowd numbering 4,383 saw the locals hold their competitors to a 1–1 half–time scoreline, but were outplayed in the next forty–five minutes and finally lost the tie by 1–3.

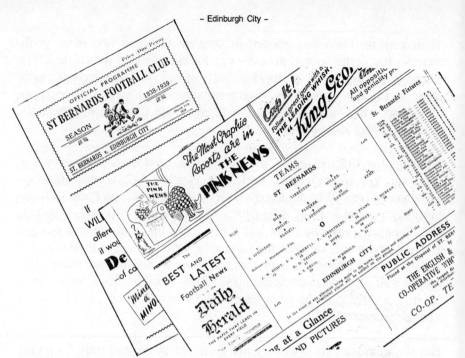

Perhaps with the inevitable War looming up, the Scottish League had more important things on their mind, for Edinburgh City's re-election bid was yet again successful! Although only four matches were played in the severely curtailed season, the City could at least claim a 'final' position of 12th, seven places off the bottom! After losing 2–3 at home to Dundee United on the 12th of August, they drew at Montrose one week later, then beat Morton 3–0, before their final pre-War League match, a 3–2 defeat at Dumbarton. The first match had produced a four figure crowd – good by the City's standards. In the final match due to train delays the kick-off was delayed for nearly an hour. The City team was an almost completely new line-up from a few months earlier:

MacDonald, Hope, McDermid, Leitch, Haldane, Veitch, McLennan, Forbes, Brown, Turnbull and Stout.

Although a number of Scottish League clubs closed down for the duration of the hostilities, particularly the less successful teams, the City – due to their amateur status – were at least able to carry on in some form. But it was only in minor local competitions, which were rarely reported upon in the newspapers.

A struggle to the end

In direct contrast to Leith Athletic's reasonable claims to continue their Scottish League career in the post–War years, Edinburgh City's case was hopeless. There was the assurance that the reformation of the Scottish League for the first season was only a temporary measure, and in 1945 – along with eight other Clubs (all first teams, 'cast–offs', except for the two Dundee clubs reserve elevens) – they joined the new Eastern League in its one season post–War existence. Needless to say no honours were won by the Club! By now there were even fewer people who cared whether the Club lived or died, and in the home match versus East Stirling the gate receipts totalled £1–50, which represented an attendance of under 100!

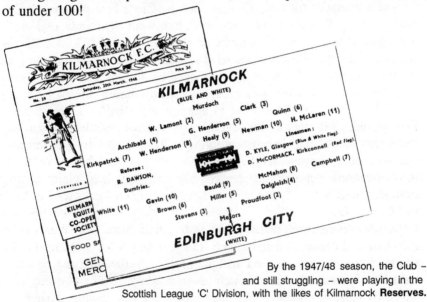

By the 1947/48 season, the Club – and still struggling – were playing in the Scottish League 'C' Division, with the likes of Kilmarnock **Reserves.**

Yet even now the Club felt that could make a go of it, and along with the 'minnows' of the old Scottish League, they helped to form the new Scottish 'C' Division. The Club managed to struggle through another three seasons at this level, but on the field, despite the lower standard – several reserve teams were included – they still found that they were unable to compete with the others. The 1946/47 season saw them finish in their usual bottom place, although only on goal average below the Dundee United second eleven.

One year later they managed six victories and three draws in their twenty-two games - finishing one place above bottom team Raith reserves. Finally they were back to the lowest spot in the 1948/49 season. In the Scottish Cup they had some success and actually won something - the Qualifying Cup - in the 1946/47 campaign, on defeating Stranraer 1-0. But they made a quick exit at Morton in the first round proper, with a 4-0 reverse, and after that, they never made it to the first round proper again.

Abandoning the very principle by which they were formed, they turned professional for the 1947/48 season, but this radical move did little to improve their performances on the field. This campaign also saw them appoint a manager for the first time, but the City's best player - Willie Bauld - moved on to Hearts, and with him went their only real asset. During these three seasons the gate receipts fell from £723, to £436 and finally £422. Run on professional lines, the Club's income became an important factor, and at long last they gave up all hope of further Senior level football. A move was made down into Junior football for the 1949/50 season, and the modest Edinburgh and District Junior League was entered. Yet even at this level they were hardly a success, for they could only finish in 11th position in the 14 team League. Five further years saw little improvement, and in 1955 they abandoned hope and ceased all football activities.

Very little was reported on the Edinburgh and District League, but it is likely that the match versus Ormiston on the 20th of April 1955, was the last match ever played by Edinburgh City. Yet the Club itself just would not die, and as a social club only, the name lived on. In 1986, an approach was made to the City directors by Postal United who offered to change their name to *Edinburgh City,* and combine with the social club. This offer was taken up, and so the name continues - albeit at a fairly minor level, in the East of Scotland League.

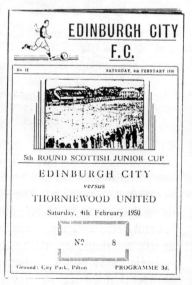

EDINBURGH CITY F.C.

No. 12   SATURDAY, 4th FEBRUARY 1950

5th ROUND SCOTTISH JUNIOR CUP

EDINBURGH CITY
versus
THORNIEWOOD UNITED

Saturday, 4th February 1950

N?   8

Ground: City Park, Pilton   PROGRAMME 3d.

The Grounds:

1928 – 1931: Marine Gardens
The City groundshared with Leith Athletic for three seasons (See Leith Athletic section).

1931 – 1934: (New) Powderhall
The Ground had a few years earlier been used by Leith Athletic – until they moved to Marine Gardens. By now New Powderhall had been well developed and offered good facilities for spectators, but the size of the pitch and its often waterlogged condition made it far from ideal for football (See also Leith Athletic and St. Bernards sections).

1934 – 1935: Marine Gardens
This move for just one season was no more than a temporary measure, whilst the building of City Park was undertaken.

1935 – 1945: City or East Pilton Park

The Stand at City Park (Photo Bill Gibbs)

This Ground was, and still is, located to the North of the City, at the junction of Ferry Road and Pilton Drive. It had previously been just open land but was developed into a very reasonable enclosed Ground by the Club. Fairly wide embankments were formed all round, and on the East side a moderate sized seated and covered Stand was erected. The Stand cost £1,000 and although cramped contains dressing rooms and offices under. Two entrances were incorporated, one off Pilton Drive, and the other via a narrow passage at the end of the row of houses in Ferry Road. On todays standards it can be regarded as only a modest enclosure, but even now – substantially as it was in pre-war days – it has charm, with good viewing (but from only grassed embankments).

Despite the Club's return to football, albeit substantially as the renamed *Postal United*, it is sad that they are unable to return to the former Club's Ground, the one that could truly called their own. The Ground is to this day very well enclosed (when not in use access is impossible, and with a few vantage points that give only a glimpse of the 'treasure' beyond), with the only entrance now being off Ferry Road. The Ground came close to becoming a Scottish League club's home venue in 1974, when Ferranti Thistle (who had used City Park since the late 1950's) were elected into the competition, but it was not considered suitable. Although the use of the wooden Stand is now forbidden, the Ground is still used – by Spartans and Craigroyston (both are members of the East of Scotland League). City Park has the unique distinction of being the only Ground – and still substantially the same – that remains, of the many enclosures that were used regularly by one or more of the three ex-League Edinburgh clubs.

Although still a neat and compact Stand, the use of it is now banned.
(Photos Bill Gibbs)

The Ground remains similar to the pre-War days (for the location see also page 71).

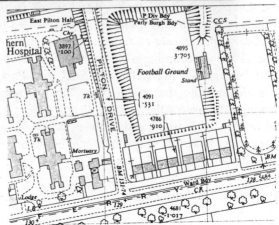

LEITH ATHLETIC.

Team group – August 1931
(Back) McNeil, Henderson, Boyce, Lockie, Forrest and Crawford.
(Front) Pullar, Forbes, Laidlaw, M'Coll and Johnston.

LEITH ATHLETIC F.C.
Back Row:—Macfarlane, M'Gachie, Mair, MacGillivray, Harrison, and Meikleham.
Front Row:—Wilson, Paterson, M'Cormack, M'Intee, and O'Rawe.
September 1934

Leith Athletic.

Founded 1887 – Defunct 1957.
(Folded and reformed: 1902)
(Reformed 1906 – changed name to 'Leith'.)
(Folded 1916. Reformed 1919 as 'Leith Athletic.)
(Reformed 1927)

League Career:

1887 – 1891	Friendly and Cup matches.
1891/92 – 1892/93	**Scottish League.**
1893/94 – 1894/95	**Scottish League Division 1.**
1895/96 – 1914/15	**Scottish League Division 2.**
1915/16 –	Eastern League.
1916/17 – 1920/21	Inactive.
1921/22 –	Western League.
1922/23 – 1923/24	Scottish Alliance.
1924/25 – 1925/26	**Scottish League Division 3.**
1926/27 –	Scottish Alliance.
1927/28 – 1929/30	**Scottish League Division 2.**
1930/31 – 1931/32	**Scottish League Division 1.**
1933/34 – 1939/40	**Scottish League Division 2. ***
1940/41 –	Inactive.
1941/42 –	Scottish League – North-East Div.
1942/43 – 1944/45	Inactive.
1945/46 –	Eastern League. †
1946/47 –	**Scottish League 'C' Division..**
1947/48 –	**Scottish League Division 2.**
1948/49 –	**Scottish League 'C' Division.**
1949/50 –	**Scottish League 'C' Div. S.E. Region.**
1950/51 – 1952/53	**Scottish League 'C' Div. N.E. Region.**
1953/54 –	Cup and Friendlies only.
1954/55 – 1956/57	Inactive.

* 1939/40 season, Scottish League fixtures ceased after four matches.
† Resigned in October 1945 (no matches played).

....

Grounds:
1887 – 1890: Hawkhill.
1890 – 1894: Bank Park.
1895 – 1899: Beechwood Park.
1899 – 1900: Hawkhill and New Logie Green.
1900 – 1904: Chancelot Park.
1904 – 1916: Old Logie Green.

1919 – 1924: Chancelot and Wardie Parks.
1924 – 1926: Old Logie Green.
1926 – 1928: (New) Powderhall.
1928 – 1936: Marine Gardens.
1936 – 1942: Meadowbank.

1946 – 1947: Old Meadowbank.
1947 – 1954: New Meadowbank.

Colours:
1887 – 1889: Chocolate and White Quarters.
1889 –   Black and White Stripes

Members of the Scottish F.A.
c.1890 to 1902. August 1903 – August 1917 (expelled for non–payment of fees)
May 1919 – 1954.

Major Honours and Achievements:

Scottish League Division 1 – 4th: 1891/92.
Scottish League Division 2 – Champions: 1905/06. 1909/10. 1929/30.
                          Runners up: 1895/96. 1896/97. 1914/15.

Scottish Cup:
6th round (quarter–finals):   1890/91.
3rd round (quarter–finals):   1903/04.
2nd round (last 16) :   1891/92. 1892/93. 1893/94.
                               1896/97. 1897/98. 1911/12.
3rd round (last 16) :   1929/30.

Qualifying Cup Winners: 1905/06. 1909/10. 1925/26.
              (South): 1948/49. 1949/50.

East of Scotland Challenge Shield Winners: 1896/97.
King Cup Winners: 1922/23.
East of Scotland (City) Cup Winners:
1921/22. 1923/24. 1926/27. 1928/29. 1935/36. 1936/37.

International Players (whilst with Club):
(Scotland): M. McQueen (1890 and 1891). R.Clements (1891)

Record Victory: (Scottish Cup) 1890/91: 12–0 v. Adventurers.
                         (Also 1893/94 11–2 v. Orion)
                         (League) 1891/92 (Home): 10–0 v. Vale of Leven.

Biggest defeat: (League) 1932/33 (Away): 1–9 v. Falkirk.

Record Attendances:
22nd January 1927: 14,000 v. Rangers (Scottish Cup) at Powderhall.
8th August 1931:   21,000 v. Celtic (League Division 1) at Marine Gardens.
22nd January 1949: 11,625 v. Raith Rovers (Scottish Cup) at Meadowbank.

Scottish League record:

	P.	W.	D.	L.	F.	A.	Pts.	Pos.
1st Division:								
1891/92	22	12	1	9	51	40	25	4th
1892/93	18	8	1	9	43	31	17	6th
1893/94	18	4	2	12	36	46	10	9th
Successfully re-elected								
1894/95	18	3	1	14	32	64	7	9th
Not re-elected relegated to Second Division.								
1895/96	18	11	1	6	55	31	23	2nd
1896/97	18	13	1	4	55	27	27	2nd
1897/98	18	9	2	7	40	39	20	4th
1898/99	18	12	3	3	63	38	27	2nd
1899/00	18	9	1	8	32	37	19	5th
1900/01	18	5	2	11	22	32	12	8th
1901/02	22	9	3	10	34	38	21	7th
1902/03	22	11	5	6	43	42	27	4th
1903/04	22	8	4	10	42	40	20	7th
1904/05	22	10	4	8	36	26	24	4th
1905/06	22	15	4	3	46	22	34	1st
Not elected to First Division.								
1906/07	22	10	4	8	40	35	24	5th
1907/08	22	8	5	9	41	40	21	7th
1908/09	22	10	3	9	37	33	23	6th
1909/10	22	13	7	2	44	19	33	1st
Not elected to First Division.								
1910/11	22	9	6	7	42	43	24	4th
1911/12	22	9	4	9	31	34	22	7th
1912/13	26	5	8	13	26	47	18	14th
1913/14	22	5	9	8	31	37	19	10th
1914/15	26	15	7	4	54	31	37	2nd

Championship decider between three clubs – placed second.
League suspended due to War.

	P.	W.	D.	L.	F.	A.	Pts.	Pos.
Third Division:								
1924/25	30	13	5	12	48	42	31	6th
1925/26	29†	16	5	8	73	41	37	2nd

† Match versus Galston (away) not played.

	P.	W.	D.	L.	F.	A.	Pts.	Pos.
Second Division:								
1927/28	38	13	9	16	67	71	35	13th
1928/29	36	18	7	11	78	56	43	5th
1929/30	38	23	11	4	92	42	57	1st
Promoted to Division 1:								
1930/31	38	8	11	19	51	85	27	17th
1931/32	38	6	4	28	46	137	16	20th
Relegated to Division 2:								

1932/33	34	10	5	19	43	81	25	16th
1933/34	34	12	8	14	63	60	32	12th
1934/35	34	16	5	13	53	56	37	8th
1935/36	34	15	3	16	67	77	33	9th
1936/37	34	13	5	16	62	65	31	11th
1937/38	34	10	5	13	71	56	37	10th
1938/39	34	10	4	20	57	83	24	16th
1939/40	4	1	0	3	4	7	2	

League suspended due to War.

'C' Division:

1946/47	18	11	3	4	57	33	25	3rd

Promoted to Division 2:

1947/48	30	6	7	17	45	84	19	16th

Relegated to 'C' Division:

1948/49	22	15	3	4	76	29	33	2nd

'C' Division South East Region:

1949/50	30	8	8	14	55	73	24	13th

'C' Division North East Region:

1950/51	30	6	5	19	43	73	17	14th
1951/52	30	5	7	18	46	88	17	15th
1952/53	28	5	6	17	41	87	16	15th

Resigned from League:

The early days of football in Leith

For dogged determination in the face of rejection and indifference, there can surely have been few clubs that can equal the record of Leith Athletic.

Leith is situated just to the North–east of Edinburgh, and is very much associated with the harbour which is adjacent to the Firth of Forth. The Club through much of its life played South of the town. In the general area of Leith, football first put in an appearance during the mid–1870's, and a dozen or more teams soon sprung up in the port town. Amongst the most successful at this time were Lorne Star, Leith Thistle, Leith Harp, Hawthornvale, Trafalgar and Edina; of these Edina became the top team in the area, and played their home matches at the Royal Gymnasium Ground, which was situated in the centre of Edinburgh, and became synonymous with the St.Bernards Club.

Most of these clubs, and others, came and disappeared over the next few years, not least the first one bearing the name of *Leith Athletic*. This club was formed around 1881, and only lasted for about four years. It wasn't until 1887, that a Leith Athletic appeared again, but the latter team had no connection with the earlier one. In fact the Club was created from an amalgam of players from the Royal Oak and Thistle clubs. Prominent amongst these founder–players were Colin Graham, 'Reddie' Thompson, David Linton, Peter Stevenson and Alexander Aitchison, whilst the new Club's first secretary was George B. Logie. The new team had to compete in the area with the likes of Portobello Thistle (who were still playing in the 1920's) and Port Osborne.

The Club played their first match at the start of the 1887/88 season, when Dumbarton were entertained. The Club played in chocolate and white quarters, but the result of the game, or the team members, does not appear to have been recorded. For a home Ground, Hawkhill was secured. It had previously been used by Leith Caledonian Cricket Club, but they lost their usage, when it was bought by the Hawkhill Recreation Company on the 4th of July 1887. This Company, who do not appear to have had any connection with the football Club despite the similar dates of their formations, had five directors, and the Company seal displayed a hawk and a hill surrounded by the Company name.

6,000 shares were issued at 10 shillings (50p) each. Part of the Ground was subject to compulsory purchase in 1902 – by the Caledonian Railway Company – and the Hawkhill Company was wound up in December 1920.

During this first season for Leith Athletic, their status was relatively low, and very little was recorded with regard to their matches. However, they did enter for the Scottish Cup, and with something of a 'scratch' team lost at Bo'ness by 1–4. Within two years the Club had a large membership, and at this time moved to nearby Bank Park. By now the Club's colours had been changed to black and white stripes, which were retained for the rest of their long life. The Club's status within a few years had risen considerably, and during the 1890/91 season they rose to prominence with their appearance at the sixth round (last eight) stage of the Scottish Cup. Included in the early round victories was a 12–0 demolition of the Adventurers, and the Athletic were fortunate to receive a bye in the fifth round. They met their match in the next, when they narrowly lost to Abercorn with a 2–3 scoreline. They also played several prestigious Friendly matches. Ayr were beaten 4–0 at Bank Park, and there was a large crowd present when Northern became the first 'class' visitors from Glasgow, on the 24th of January.

The most memorable game was staged before a *massive* record attendance, on the 24th of January, for the visit of the renowned English Club, Preston North End. Leith were initially overawed by the reputation of their illustrious opponents, but they soon settled down, and by half–time had taken a shock 2–0 lead. The half–time interval must have become an entertainment in its own right:

> *The Preston North End players had their own little picnic on the pitch. Drummond, the Leith captain, entertained the crowd with turnbar balancing feats, whilst the other players amused themselves by having shies at a bottle* (!)

In the second half, and with the sun behind them, the Athletic continued to play well, and finished as final 3–1 victors. But the scribe of the time was not very complementary about the opposition:

> *All that has been heard of the decadence of the North End was borne out today, although for Leith this was one of their best performances.*

At the end of the season, the Athletic met Hearts at Tynecastle on the 16th of May, on what was to become the Club's last match as a non–League team for some years. Entrance to the game cost 6d (2.5p) – double this for a seat in the Stand – and the Athletic lost a close match by 3–4. The team were accepted into the Scottish League – the second campaign – for the 1891/92 season, whilst other, unsuccessful, Clubs formed the Scottish Alliance. Professionalism was not accepted in Scotland until after it had become legal in England, but the continual drain of the best players to South of the border, resulted in 'under the counter payments' by most top Clubs. The Scottish Football Association called in the books of all 45 Senior Clubs, and no doubt being as guilty as most, if not all, Leith Athletic, escaped without even a reprimand!

Leith Athletic become Limited. 12th July 1893.
(S.R.O. Ref. BT2/2540)

Into the League – for the first time

With only four players retained from the previous season, the Club's first League match produced a somewhat sensational result, when they won by 3–0 at Third Lanark on the 15th of August. By now the Glasgow based Club were not the force they had been, but the Leith victory could have been by a bigger margin, and the defence for their part was solid. McQueen played well, and despite his 'call up' for the national team that season, he was by now at the 'veteran' stage. One week later there was a crowd of several thousand present to see the team's home debut. Bank Park had a new Stand and Press box, although the ridgy surface of the pitch left a lot to be desired. The locals were not disappointed when their favourites took a 2–0 half–time lead over Renton. But the homesters faded in the second half, and ended up on the wrong end of a 3–2 defeat.

But overall a good start was made to the Club's League career, not least the 10–0 thrashing they dealt out to Vale of Leven on the 19th of September, the Athletic's all time record score in the competition, and after eleven games they lay in 4th place. The only black mark against them was a 6–0 thrashing at Dumbarton in September (one week before the Vale of Leven match) – the Champions–elect – as the team continued to maintain a good home record. By early December the Club were holding fifth spot in the table. Celtic were beaten 2–1 at Bank Park on the 18th of April, a defeat which contributed towards the loss of the Championship for the Glasgow team, and at the final count the Athletic finished in a very encouraging fourth place in the table. A measure of the Club's standing during the season can be taken from the inclusion in the Scottish International team of both McQueen and Clements. One year later the record was not too good, for the team could only manage a 6th placing in the 10 strong League. But notable home victories were obtained over Renton (6–2) and St. Mirren by 5–1. The surprising statistic was the record which showed that after two seasons, not one away match had been drawn, and even at home there had been only two occasions when the points had been shared. With professionalism now becoming a way of life in Scottish Football, the Club itself adopted this approach, and in July 1893 they became Incorporated as *'The Leith Athletic Football Club (Limited)',* and took over the lease at Bank Park.

On the field, the 1893/94 season turned out to be worse than the previous campaign, for the team finished second from bottom, but six points above wooden–spoonists Renton. Yet again no matches were drawn on the Club's travels, but it was a poor away record – just one victory from the opening match at Hearts – which denied the team a higher placing. The biggest surprise of the season was on March the 17th, when Celtic – on the way to their second Championship – were thrashed 5–0 at Bank Park. It was the end of the road for Renton, who were relegated, but for Leith and next placed Dundee, a reprieve was given when both Clubs were re–elected into the First Division. The 1894/95 season was little short of disastrous. By now the Club had apparently deserted Bank Park in favour of Beechwood Park, although the evidence points to this ground 'change' being no more than a name change for the same venue. 1,000 shares at £1 each were issued, with the Club's Registered Office being given as 42 Leith Walk, Leith. By early November an encouraging number of 491 shares had been sold – of which George Wright held fifty – but the team's poor showing dampened the enthusiasm, and by the following May only eight more options had been taken up.

1990 – Nothing is left of Bank Park. But the later Railway cutting is apparent. Note the close proximity of the Hibs' Ground. (Photo Dave Twydell)

New venue or not, it did not change the Club's fortune! Only three home matches were won (and one drawn), although in the exciting match against Celtic, the Athletic only lost by the odd goal in eleven. But worse was an away record in which nine games were played, and all were lost.

The worst of the defeats was a 7–1 thrashing by Third Lanark. On the 6th of April the Club entertained Dumbarton, in the last League game of the season, a battle between the two bottom clubs. A grim struggle ensued, and the 1–1 draw gave Dumbarton their only away point of the season. Although the two teams were level on points, it was Leith's better goal average that kept them off the bottom. Despite this final placing, the Club were not re–elected to the First Division (For Dumbarton it was their first re–election bid), and in their place near neighbours Hibernian were promoted.

After promising so much in their first season, the Club – just four years later – embarked on their first season in the lower Division. The season started with a friendly game at St.Bernards, where the Athletic lost 5–6 in an entertaining introduction to the campaign.

Kilmarnock were entertained at Beechwood Park on the 17th of August, and the 3–1 victory was a taste of what was to come. The return match with Kilmarnock was scheduled for the 12th of October, but when the referee failed to show up a Friendly match was played instead! The next week Airdrie were comfortably beaten 4–1 (in what was to become their only home league defeat of the season), but after such an encouraging start, the team were humbled seven days later when they lost 0–4 at home to Renton. But they soon picked themselves up and achieved several high–scoring home victories: 6–1 versus Port Glasgow, 7–0 versus Partick Thistle and 6–1 over Motherwell.

Unfortunately their away record did not match the home one (just one defeat), and at the final tally, they could only finish as runners–up to Abercorn, with four points less than the Champions. Abercorn, in their first season of any note since their earlier days in the First division, were chosen to replace the relegated Dumbarton team, and so Leith were left to face another season of lower division football.

On the financial front things were not particularly bright, and in August 1895 a further 1,000 shares were made available. But there was little enthusiasm, or money available from the supporters, since by the next June, only 506 ordinary and 112 preference shares had been taken up in total. The following year saw no increase in sold shares, and even by the summer of 1900, the total had only reached 634.

During the 1896/97 season the team completed a faultless home record, for all nine matches were won, with a goal difference of 40–10. Although only four matches were lost away from home (plus one drawn game), it was Partick Thistle's excellent season which saw them lose only one match, and ensured that the Athletic would only finish as runners–up.

The last League game of the season required Leith to travel to the Champions, who only required one point to confirm their top spot. It was a disastrous day for the Edinburgh team for they were thrashed by 5–0; their worst defeat for two seasons. When it came to the re-elections, the previous mediocre Partick team were promoted in place of relegated Abercorn, a decision which was to become the first of many when Leith were denied a valid promotion bid.

One year later the team slipped from their normal winning ways, although they maintained an unbeaten home record, and could only finish fourth from top. Fortunately the 'double' had been achieved over Renton, before the resignation of this Club from the League (Hamilton Academicals took over their fixtures), but only another two points were gained on their travels when wooden–spoonists Motherwell were beaten 4–2 in November.

The following season saw the Athletic back into their winning ways once again, but not enough to gain the top spot, for as runners–up to Kilmarnock, they finished five points behind. Yet another season passed by without any home defeats in the League, and the eventual record showed a period from the 30th of August 1895 to the 30th of December 1900 (over five years) when the Athletic maintained an unbeaten record at Beechwood Park. Despite a reasonable run of results on their travels (four victories, two draws and three defeats) it was not sufficient. The most amazing result was a 8–5 thrashing by Port Glasgow in October, although this was compensated when the hapless Abercorn were overcome with a 8–1 scoreline the next month. This was the second Championship season in succession for Kilmarnock, and therefore it came as no surprise when they were elected into the First Division to replace Partick Thistle.

The end of the century came with Leith still in the Second Division, and with only 19 points they finished the season in a disappointing fifth position of ten teams. The new century could have been the start of a new prosperity for the football team, but conversely it was to soon become one of failure and eventual oblivion.

The 1890's had seen the team have some reasonable Scottish Cup runs, and on five occasions they reached the second round, which by now had become the last 16 stage in the competition. In 1892 the Athletic lost surprisingly at non-League Annbank by 2-1. One year later the end came at home, with a 0-2 defeat to St. Mirren, followed by a 2-0 defeat at Rangers in 1894. In an earlier round during the 1893/94 season, the Athletic beat Orion 11-2, this match has special significance, for this club together with Victoria United combined a few years later to become Aberdeen F.C. There was then a three year wait before the team reached the second round again. After an easy 5-1 victory over Dunblane in the previous round, the Edinburgh team were drawn to play fellow Second Division team Dumbarton. The pair fought out two draws (4-4 and 3-3) before Leith finally succumbed by 3-2. Dumbarton went on to become the surprise finalists (eventually losing to Rangers), considering they finished as League wooden-spoonists that season! In 1896 the Athletic were thrashed 6-0 at Third Lanark, and in 1898 by Kilmarnock with a score of 9-2, in a best-forgotten rout!

In 1899, Beechwood Park was vacated, and for one season home matches were played at both Hawkhill and at the New Logie Green Ground. This venue is more associated with St. Bernards who had the Ground as a home base for a number of years, and in fact for the 1899/1900 season the two Clubs 'groundshared'. However in 1900 a move was made to a new venue, Chancelot Park, which was located about half a mile North of New Logie Green. These moves coincided with a fairly poor record on the pitch, for the 1900/01 season saw the team finish at their lowest, up to that time, position in the Second Division. Although there were no really bad results during the season, it was their away record (just one victory and two draws), plus indifferent results at Chancelot Park – four victories and five defeats – which ensured their lowly final third from bottom place in the ten team table.

The Second Division was extended to include twelve teams in 1901, but the end result for the Athletic was only a slight improvement. The League season didn't start until the 14th of September, and on that day Leith were on the end of a humiliating 1–6 defeat at the Ground of 'Champions–to–be' Port Glasgow Athletic. The team made some amends one week later with a single goal victory over East Stirling, and seven days later a three goal success versus Motherwell. But it was the team's away record that was to let them down once again, for only four points were obtained from two victories, and the final result was a disappointing mid–table position.

Financially the Club were in the doldrums, and the Board of Directors – which consisted of only the minimum nine (up to fifteen could be appointed) – found it impossible to make ends meet. The Directors came from all walks of life, including a printer, a warehouseman and a solicitor. By the Summer of 1902, the Club – on paper – folded, and letters addressed to the Club, and sent to the registered office were returned marked – *No longer exists* (!) On the 5th of September the Company (Club) was finally dissolved.

Leith Athletic somehow managed to continue, at least on the pitch, although the final placings were only mediocre – 4th, 7th and 4th – leading up to and including the 1904/05 season. It is probable that the Club were run on non–professional lines during these first few years of the century, but at least they kept going, and after their theoretical folding up, they were re–admitted into the Scottish Football Association in August 1906. After four years occupation, Chancelot Park was vacated, and a move made back to Logie Green, but this time to the new Ground – confusingly named *Old Logie Green*, which virtually adjoined the earlier 'new' Ground.

The 1905/06 season was something of a revelation, for the Club sprung to the fore and captured the Second Division Championship! The season started badly with a single goal defeat at Cowdenbeath, followed one week later with a 2–6 rout at mediocre Ayr. At this time the title must have been far from the fans' thoughts. But amazingly during the rest of the season only one more defeat was suffered – by 1–2 at Raith on the 30th of December. At the final count Leith were placed three points clear of the reigning champions Clyde, and looked forward to their hopeful election back into the First Division, as the higher League was to extend its numbers by two. Quite reasonably Clyde took over one of the vacant spots, yet quite inexplicably, **fourth** placed Hamilton were promoted in favour of Leith. Whereas Hamilton had shown themselves to be a strong Second Division team, the Leith club were snubbed for the second – and not the last – time.

There could have been no valid arguments against the team's elevation based on their lack of organisation, for at the conclusion of this excellent season, they were reformed as a Limited Company once again. On the 5th of May 1906, eight directors were appointed to head the newly named *Leith Football Club Limited.* The 'new' Club took over the assets and liabilities of the old, plus the lease on the Ground, for which an annual rent of £40 was required. The old Leith Athletic had debts totalling £50, but their assets included a Grandstand and other facilities on the Ground.

A 'New' Club is born !
But once again enthusiasm was only lukewarm.
(S.R.O. Ref. BT2/6178)

With the intended expenditure of over £250 to provide more cover for spectators, it was predicted that the Old Logie Green Ground would become one of the best equipped venues in the Country. 4,000 shares at ten shillings (50p) each were issued, but within two months only 381 had been taken up, and as before the numbers soon became a trickle, as the locals showed their reluctance to financially support the Club.

Unfortunately Leith were unable to continue where they left off, and for the next three seasons only mediocre placings in the final table of 5th, 7th and 6th could be achieved. During this period the team were unable to match their generally good home performances, with those on their travels. But as had happened a few years earlier, the team surprised everybody when they once again became the Second Division Champions, this time at the end of the 1909/10 season. It was really a two horse race, with both teams jockeying for the top spot. By February, Leith were second in the table having won eight, drawn four and lost only one match, when Raith were entertained at Old Logie Green on the 5th of that month, There was enormous interest in the game, and the normally poorly supported Leith team, attracted a crowd of 5,000. The contest finished goalless, but it had been an exciting and skilful game. One month later the return fixture was played, and another share of the points was the result. With three games remaining Raith were top, by one point, but two excellent home wins by Leith (3–0 over East Stirling and 4–0 versus Cowdenbeath), reversed the position of the top two.

A special train was laid on for the Leith supporters to travel to the last game, at East Stirling. The homesters turned out to provide surprisingly strong opposition, and in fact led at half–time by 2–0 – although both goals were considered by many to have been offside. But with the wind behind them in the second half, the visitors fought back strongly, and forced a 2–2 draw, through goals by Stewart – from the penalty spot in the 75th minute – and a Lindsay equaliser five minutes later. The final ten minutes saw Leith pushing hard for both points, but as Raith had already completed their fixtures, Leith knew that with a superior goal average, the one point would give them the Championship.

Leith were optimistic about their chances of being voted into the First Division, but as Raith had performed well over three seasons (finishing once as Champions and twice in the runners–up spot), it was they instead of the Edinburgh team that were elevated. Once again Leith were overlooked! The Club did reach the City Cup Final, only to lose 0–3 to Broxburn before 1,500 at Old Logie Green, and in the last game of the season they beat St.Bernards 2–1, to win the Roseberry Charity Cup, which was played before a crowd of 2,000 at Easter Road.

On the 20th of August Leith travelled to newly elected Dundee Hibernians, and beat them 3–2 before an enthusiastic crowd of 3,000. But with several injuries, a weakened team lost the first home match, against Ayr United, with the unlikely scoreline of 4–6, which was watched by 2,000. The team were unable to maintain their high standards of a year earlier, and with a poor home record (three matches were lost and three drawn) – although these were coupled with reasonable results on their travels – the final place in the table of fourth was a big disappointment to the fans. With much competition from other clubs in Edinburgh, finance was tight, and towards the end of the season gates in excess of 1,500 had become but a thing of the past.

In the Scottish Cup the Club had achieved little success over the decade. The most notable season was that of 1903/04, when the team fought through to the third round, the last eight in the competition. The first round produced a 2–1 victory at Port Glasgow Athletic, and the next tie an excellent 3–1 home victory over First Division club Motherwell. But Leith met their match in the next round when again drawn at home they lost 1–3 to struggling Morton, also First Division members. Exclusion through to the first round of the competition was not now automatic, and the Club had to fight their way through the qualifying competition. In the 1905/06 season they became the winners of the Qualifying Cup for the first time – beating Beith 2–0 in the final – but losing by 1–2 to Partick Thistle in the first round proper. The Qualifying Cup was again won during the 1909/10 season (Bathgate were easily overcome by 4–0 in the final), but once again further progression was halted in the first round when the strong Clyde team scored the only goal at Old Logie Green.

The 1910/11 season may have had its disappointments in the League matches, but there was plenty of excitement in the Scottish Cup.

The two qualifying finalists from the previous season met in the first round, and 3,000 were present at Old Logie Green to witness a goalless draw. A special train was laid on for the replay, and the station was besieged by eager Leith fans. Despite the rain, the match was watched by 5,000, and after losing by 1-0, Leith lodged a protest, since two Bathgate players had played in a cup-tie for a factory team during the Summer! The protest was upheld, despite the non-attendance of the referee, whom it was said was too frightened to give evidence! The replayed game ended all square at 1-1. Therefore a second replay was necessary, and this was played at Raith, where a crowd of over 2,000 saw Leith as final victors, by 2-0. In the next round Armadale were easily beaten by 3-0, and the third round was also won. Inverness arrived late in Edinburgh for the 4th round, but may as well not have turned up for they were overcome by a 4-0 scoreline. This run had taken the team through to the semi-final, with Johnstone, which was played at their opponents Newfield Park Ground. Before a crowd of over 3,000 Leith took the lead, but with only 12 minutes to go a heavy fog descended, and the match was abandoned.

In the re-match, Leith lost by 1-2, but again lodged a protest, however before this was heard they withdrew. Having reached this stage, the Club qualified for the first round proper. With finance as a major consideration, Leith waived their home draw and played the match at the Ground of their opponents, Falkirk. Falkirk were strong contenders for the First Division Championship, and therefore the Edinburgh team's 2-2 draw was very creditable. But in the replay Leith were easily overcome with a 1-4 scoreline.

Leith's fortunes slumped further during the next two years, with a final League placing of seventh at the end of the 1911/12 season, and bottom one year later! The latter season was very tight at the foot of the table, for another six points would have seen the team in mid-table. The results were not that bad, for apart from a 0-5 thrashing at Vale of Leven, there were no other heavy defeats. The team's solitary away win came in the opening match of the season when neighbours St. Bernards were beaten 2-1. There was no doubt that the Club's past record would ensure their re-election into the Second Division. But one year later the situation was little better, although with one more point than twelve months earlier, this at least ensured a final position of third from bottom.

Once again it was the away record that let the Club down, for they won only one match, and drew one, and defeats included a 0–5 thrashing at mediocre Arthurlie. It was obvious that something had to be done to restore the Club's fortunes, and whatever it was, it worked, for the Club finished the 1914/15 season as runners–up! By mid–season, Leith were in a strong position to take the top spot, yet once again a degree of bad luck was to be their lot, as three play–off matches were held to decide the final Championship, after a trio of teams had obtained the same number of points. After beating their neighbours – and third placed – St. Bernards 2–1 (after thrashing them in their home League fixture by 5–0), they lost to the eventual Champions Cowdenbeath by the only goal of the game. However, any question of promotion to the First Division was academic, for with the First World War raging in Europe, the composition of the First Division remained unchanged for the 1915/16 season, and the Second Division was suspended.

The financial situation by now was desperate, and the share issue that was made back in 1906, had even now only reached a total sale of 417. The Club had just about made ends meet through gate receipts of £520 (plus only £39 taken in advanced season ticket sales), plus transfer fees received of £44, to balance the outgoings which included £447 in wages.

Faced with wartime non–League football, the Club retained most of its players, and entered the newly formed Eastern League, along with former colleagues St. Bernards, Cowdenbeath, Lochgelly, Dunfermline, East Stirling and Dundee Hibernians, together with the strong non–League teams, Armadale, Broxburn United, Bathgate, East Fife and Kirkcaldy United. By the end of November, Leith had become the only Senior team in Britain to remain undefeated, and the players considered that their efforts should be better rewarded. On November the 27th the 'home' match was played at Easter Road against Armadale, and anticipating a big 'gate' they threatened strike action unless their demands for a £5 match fee (very high by the standards of the day) were met.

Eventually £2 plus £3 for those who lost (work) time was agreed. In the event the attendance was only 3,000, and the anticipated receipts of £100 amounted to £60 in total. The normal players payouts consisted of ten shillings – fifty pence – and sometimes only half this amount.

With the War in Europe escalating, football crowds quickly dwindled, and by the end of the year even first Division Hibernian could only attract 500 to their home matches. With these new low 'gates', the Scottish F.A. ruled that maximum player payments should be limited to £1 per week.

Despite their excellent start to the season, Leith missed out in the honours at the end of the season, and along with the other non–First Division Clubs, ceased playing again until peacetime. But the situation was in fact worse than this, for a letter from the Club's solicitors stated that:

"The Club is insolvent and there are very few assets" .

On the 10th of November 1916, the Club was wound up!

A new start – and back into the League

When the War came to an end, football gradually returned throughout the country. For many clubs it meant a new start, not least for Leith Athletic who were reformed in 1919. The pre–War years had been a time of financial struggle for the Club, but there was still a hardcore of keen supporters, who in effect had to start the Club once again from nothing. There was never any question of an immediate return back to the Scottish League as there was a reluctance by the 'powers that be' to return to the status quo, and initially just one Division was reinstated. In view of the lack of coverage of the Club in the newspapers, it appears that they performed in only Friendly and local Cup competitions during the first two seasons.

At the end of the 1920/21 season they appeared in an East of Scotland Shield match. The game was played at Tynecastle, versus the reserve team of Hearts, before a crowd numbering 2,500.

The Scottish League Division 2 re–appeared for the 1921/22 season, but there was no place in it for the reduced in status Leith, but an entry was made into the Western league which had been formed during the War as a competition for mainly pre–War Second Division Clubs. The Club won no honours during the season, and after just one year moved on to the Scottish Alliance. This competition was formed in 1919 for the reserve teams of eight Scottish League teams, and for the 1922/23 season, apart from Queens Park Strollers, Leith was the only Club who entered their first team in the competition. The team again won no honours but at least was gradually building up its status in the hope that once again they could gain a re–entry into the Scottish League. As a home Ground both Chancelot and Wardie Parks were used during this period. Crowds of around 1,000 were the norm, but for Scottish Cup games interest was at a high. During the 1923/24 season Vale of Leven were entertained at Wardie Park, in a replay, and the crowd numbered around 3,000 for this midweek match (after taking the lead before half–time. Leith finally lost 1–2).

By now serious thoughts were turned towards finding a more suitable Ground, a problem which had seriously hampered further progress during the short reformed lifetime of the Club. The season had seen the formation of the Scottish League Third Division, and the Club realised that although the journeys would be long, and the rewards at the gate at many of the small towns within the competition would be small, this was the only way back into the top level of football. In any event the status of the Alliance was gradually being reduced as more clubs gave notice of pulling out their reserve elevens. By this time the Club were playing at Wardie Park, where crowds varied greatly, e.g. 2,000 for Aberdeen 'A' (reserves), but only 500 for the later season encounter with Kilmarnock's second eleven. The Dundee second eleven were beaten by 2–0 on the 5th of April, Leith's last home match in the competition. A few days later, when several young players were tried out in the team, a visit was made to Third Lanark, where Leith drew with the League Club's reserve team. The last match as a non–League Club was played at Tynecastle before a poor crowd of only 1,500, when they were easily beaten by five unopposed goals by Hearts, in the Roseberry Cup Final. However one honour came Leith's way, when St. Bernards were beaten in the final of the East of Scotland Cup.

The Club Officials called a public meeting to decide whether they should make an application to join the Third Division, and a large an enthusiastic crowd attended. They felt that they could hold their own in this competition, and although aware that it would be a financial struggle realised that this was the only way 'up'.

Having by now settled on their pre–War Ground at Old Logie Green, for the home venue (earlier a possible site at Lochend Estate had not materialised), it was decided to take the plunge. As expected the Club were welcomed into the Division, and the Club set about preparing for their new Scottish League career. A 'shilling' fund was opened to go towards the development of the Club, and 400 contributions were received within a few days, and this number had swelled to 3,000 by August.

There was a most encouraging number of season tickets sold during the Summer, and with a not much changed team – a mixture of youth and experience – the season got underway with a pre–season Friendly game which attracted a crowd of over 1,000. On the 16th of August the team travelled to Sanquhar to play Nithsdale Wanderers in the first League match. By half–time the visitors were 1–3 behind, the Leith goal having been scored by Laidlaw. Leith pressed hard in the second period, and Laidlaw scored his second goal, but the final result ended in a 2–3 defeat. The Leith team consisted of:

McNaughton, Alvey, Ness, Brock, Hadden, Spratt, Cornelius, Malcolm, Laidlaw, Orr and Dow.

One week later the Club made their home debut when Clackmannon were entertained. The home crowd were encouraged with an entertaining display, especially from Laidlaw, and a result of 2–1. But two away defeats followed (at Solway Star and Vale of Leven), and the team soon found that the season was going to be a hard struggle. After six matches they languished third from bottom in the table, but gradually the results improved to lift them to a mid–table position. There were two pre–Christmas setbacks, when defeats were sustained at Mid–Annandale (0–1) and at home to Peebles Rovers (2–3). But fortunately the second half of the season proved to be more rewarding, and at the end, the team finished in a very satisfactory sixth from top. The season ended on a sour note with a surprise five goal thrashing at mediocre Beith on April the 25th. In the Scottish Cup, progress was made through to the first round, when Leith were comfortably beaten 4–1 by Hearts. Earlier, in the 2nd qualifying round, Vale of Leithen were entertained before a gate of well over 2,000, and following the drawn match, the replay (which Leith won) attracted a record attendance.

The Club were reasonably encouraged with the support (with gates normally round 1,000), but they knew that it was going to be financially difficult at this level. On League matches £300 had been lost over the season, but this figure was almost balanced by the £250 profit taken in the Scottish Cup qualifying games. Once again season ticket sales were encouraging, the price of them worked out at approximately 6d. (2.5p) per game. The first League match of the 1925/26 season attracted a crowd of 2,000 to Old Logie Green, and the locals were not disappointed with the 6–1 victory over Montrose. The start of the season overall was only moderate, the only real surprise being a 3–5 home defeat to Galston on the 29th of August. By Christmas the Leith record was nothing exceptional, then they 'took–off', with a six goal victory at Peeble Rovers on January the 1st.

Gradually the team rose up the table – to 3rd having played 25 matches – and found themselves in a Championship chasing position. Mid–Annandale were beaten 4–0 before a 1,500 Logie Green crowd, followed the next week with a 4–1 beating of Johnstone, before a similar attendance. It all came down to the last match, and 300 Leith supporters travelled to Clackmannon, and formed the vast majority of the small crowd! Their lowly opponents were home draw specialists, and the game ended with six goals being shared. Leaders Helensburgh had already completed their fixtures, and Leith were left one point behind them. However, with Galston folding mid–season, having played only 15 matches, the one automatic promotion place was not straight forward.

Helensburgh had completed the double over Galston, therefore if these two games were ignored they would have finished with 34 points. Leith hadn't played the away match at Galston, but having lost at home to them, their points total would have remained at 37. Meanwhile Forfar, with 28 games played, had only drawn at home to Galston, and not played the away fixture, although their home fixture with Beith also remained unplayed. Therefore their points total of 35, could reasonably have been amended to plus two points, and less one, giving a final tally of 36. On paper Leith appeared to be the clear favourites for promotion. But in the circumstances the decision went to a vote, and on the casting vote of the Chairman, it was Forfar who were honoured! Yet again Leith Athletic had been snubbed.

At least there was some consolation, for the Club won the Qualifying Cup Competition, beating Solway Star in the final at Love Street, Paisley, before a crowd of 3,000. In the first round proper the Athletic were drawn away to Civil Service Strollers, but the game was played at the St. Bernards Gymnasium Ground, in preference to the Strollers Stenhouse Mills headquarters.

A crowd of over 2,000 paid £100 in total to see Leith win by 2–0. In the second round the team met their match, when they were easily beaten by 6–1 before a crowd of 3,000 at First Division Third Lanark. But success came by way of the Roseberry Cup, when Hibernian were surprisingly beaten on their own Ground, by 4–1, before a somewhat poor attendance of only 3,000. Doubtless the season had been successful on the playing front, yet financially it had been near disastrous, and the Club came close to folding, yet with the enthusiasm amongst the hardcore of support they managed to pull through.

Leith Athletic, having been unreasonably denied a place in the Second Division, now found themselves back in non–League football once again, since the ill–founded Third Division did not continue. But the fans and committee of the Club were determined to succeed, and with very much the same players as the previous season, set out on the 1926/27 campaign, once again in the Alliance; with the influx of former Third Division teams, the competition was regionalised, and Leith competed in the Northern Section. The first match was played at Hearts, against the First Division club's reserve eleven, but before a gate of 8,000, the Athletic lost by 1–2. Reasonable support was still behind the team, and a crowd of between 1,500 and 2,000 were present at the first home game, when Aberdeen were beaten 3–1. A good start was made to the season, for after six matches, the team lay third from top, and maintained this position after a further six games. The crowd numbered 2,000 for Lochgelly's visit in December, and a 4–2 victory lifted the Athletic into second place.

After the bumpy Old Logie Green pitch, it was a vast improvement to play on the *"spick and span, and beautiful flat green pitch at Powderhall"*. The (New) Powderhall Stadium had been improved for both football use and for Speedway. For the inaugural match at the new venue, on the 15th of January versus Montrose, a crowd of nearly 3,000 was present to see an exciting game finish as a 5–0 victory to the Athletic. The Ground was immediately adjacent to Old Logie Green (which confusingly had been formerly known as (Old) Powderhall!) and in fact some of the high wooden palings were common to both Grounds. By mid–February the team were in third position, and a 3–1 victory before 2,000 at Powderhall boosted their chances of honours. After Dundee reserves were beaten by 4–1 on their own Ground, the team had risen to 2nd, and this place was maintained into early April, at which time they were only 3 points behind the leaders. But at the season's end they were unable to shift the Hearts reserve team from the top position, and the runners–up spot had to suffice.

Although there were no later honours won in the Scottish Cup, the team battled through to an entry into the competition proper. On the 22nd of January Leith were drawn at home in probably their biggest ever match, in the first round proper, to the mighty Rangers. 14,000 paid gate receipts of £470 at the new Powderhall venue, but the giants were too strong for the minnows. Although Leith were worthy opponents and played well, they were 3–1 down at the interval, and the visitors added another goal in the second half. At the end of the season, for the third time, the East of Scotland (City) Cup was won. At last the claims of the Club were recognised, and for the 1927/28 season they achieved their ambition, for they were voted back into the Second Division of the Scottish League.

A new surge of optimism was sweeping through the Club, and on the 9th of September they were reformed into a Limited Company once again, under the name of *Leith Athletic (1927) Ltd.* 2,000 shares at 50p each were issued, and 9 Directors were appointed which in effect were the committee of the 'previous' Club. By mid–November 1,099 shares had been taken up, but – as before – the rate slowed down considerably and only 77 more had been purchased by the following July. Thirteen players were retained from the previous season, and the campaign started well with a 4–1 home victory over Kings Park, on the 13th of August. To mark the occasion, the Newhaven Silver band were in attendance to provide pre–match entertainment, and Reid gave the homesters a 14 minute lead, before a crowd of 3,000. By half–time the score was 1–1, but the Athletic overpowered their opponents in the second half, and romped away with a 4–1 victory.

The Leith team consisted of:
   Steele, Bernard, McAndrews, McNeil, Reid, Anderson, Orr,
   Laidlaw, Young, Rae and Elliot.

The next match finished as a scoreless draw at Albion Rovers, and one week later relegated Morton were entertained. A somewhat disappointing crowd of barely 3,000, saw the Athletic lose by 2–3. However a reasonable start was made to the season, and after seven matches the team lay in a mid–table position. Bathgate's visit on September the 10th produced an attendance of only 1,500, but heavy rain was given as the reason for such low numbers. The rain was to badly effect the playing surface at Powderhall, and the home game with Alloa two weeks later was played at the nearby Gymnasium Ground; the crowd numbered 3,000, and the result finished as a 2–1 home win. The indifferent form continued, a 3–4 home defeat was surrendered to Arthurlie (attendance of 1,500), and after 12 matches the team had slipped to a low mid–table position.

A notable 4–3 win was obtained at East Fife, when much of the match was played with only ten men, but by Christmas, the Athletic languished seventh from bottom. The second half of the campaign produced only marginally better results, but not before some reverses in the New year, which by early March had seen the team slump to the bottom place. By now the crowds had dropped, and there was a crowd of only 1,500 for Arbroath's visit. Promotion challengers Third Lanark drew 3,000 to Powderhall – although there was a large contingent of travelling supporters – who saw the Glasgow team win by 3–2.

Fortunately the end of season run–in produced some improved results, the gates rose back to around 2,000, and by the season's end, the team finished in 13th position (of 20). The results had produced some convincing home victories, including the last League match when runaway Champions Ayr United suffered a 2–1 reverse before a 3,000 crowd. But on their travels the team had obtained only two victories, plus eight draws.

The use of Powderhall became little more than temporary, for after less than two seasons the Club were back on the move again. This time it was to a new venue, at Marine Gardens.

The new Ground was located in Portobello, just South of Leith, not far from the Hawkhill and Bank Park Grounds. The venue was opened by a visit from Dunfermline on the 18th of August (although the Edinburgh City inaugural match – with whom the Athletic shared the Ground – preceded this match ten days earlier). A crowd of close on 4,000 were there to see Nicol score the first Leith goal, before the visitors equalised before half–time, and the same score remained at the end of ninety minutes. Although Alloa had been defeated in the first game of the season, the results were generally poor, including two away defeats in September, but a good home record over the season – which produced four draws and no defeats – lifted the team into a final, and encouraging, 5th place.

The year's wages bill amounted to £1,619, but with the home gates receipts totalling £1,425, and £1,183 received as the share at away games, after other expenses, the Club were in a fairly healthy position, a situation that had always been rare both before and later!

At the A.G.M. on the 22nd of May the Club announced of the great efforts that would be made to get back into the First Division, and this sentiment was also expressed by the Supporters Club, who made a £75 donation to the parent Club.

LEITH ATHLETIC FOOTBALL TEAM.
Back row (left to right)—J. Robertson, assistant trainer, J. M'Neill, A. Mitchell, C. Robinson, P. Steele, J. C. Nicol, J. J. Jamieson, W. MacKenzie, trainer
Front row (left to right)—P. Carruthers, R. C. Marshall, G. M'N. Reid, captain, J. Young, J. G. Johnston.

The success of the 1929/30 season surpassed even the most optimistic of supporters. The campaign started with a 3-2 victory at Dumbarton, followed with a 2-1 home victory over Albion Rovers, and then four goals were shared with Armadale. The Club soon swept to the top of the Division. It wasn't until the 28th of December that the first defeat came – by 1-3 in the return match with Albion Rovers – and after the scoreless draw at home to St. Bernards on New Year's Day, the Athletic were still riding high on top of the League, and three points clear of the second placed club. Ten days later another reversal came – at Queen of the South – and since only four League matches were eventually lost that season (all on the Club's travels), then this period of two defeats and one draw, could have been considered a poor one! On January the 25th the visit of Dunfermline attracted a crowd of 5,000 to Marine Gardens, and although only one point was obtained, the Club from then on maintained their lead at the top.

Amongst several high scoring home victories the highest was a 7-1 demolition of Alloa on March the 1st, which was watched by 2,000 fans. But at the end it became a close fight with East Fife, and the Athletic's case wasn't helped when they lost on April the 5th at home to Arbroath, but significantly the attendance was no less than 5,000. However, two weeks later Stenhousemuir were crushed 5-1 at Marine Gardens, and so – on goal average from East Fife – Leith Athletic were declared the Champions. During the campaign the team had scored 92 goals in League matches alone, and J.Nichol was the top scorer with 37.

The excitement wasn't limited to the League, for the Scottish Cup also produced some thrills. In the first round Falkirk Amateurs were beaten at the Brockville Park Ground of Falkirk F.C. The next round saw the Athletic see off the challenge of Clachnacuddin (2-0 at home), which took the team through to the third round, the last 16. A tough test was presented when it was announced that Leith would have to travel to high-flying Falkirk of the First Division. A grim but exciting struggle finished goalless, and earned the Edinburgh team a home replay.

The replay produced gate receipts of £875, as 18,000 packed into Marine Gardens for the 19th of February match. After extra time it was still a stalemate – this time 1-1 – and so a third replay was necessary. The next match produced gate receipts of £550 at Tynecastle, yet after another 120 minutes, neither side had been beaten, a 1–1 draw was the result. The third replay was also held at Tynecastle, and this time the crowd numbered 11,000 (receipts of £412), and after going down by one goal by half–time, the Second Division team fought hard in the second half. But it was all to no avail, and the gallant underdogs eventually bowed out of the competition. The Club also reached the Roseberry Cup final, but bowed out narrowly to neighbours Hearts by 1–2.

After several big disappointments in the past, at last Leith Athletic were not to be denied their glory, and preparations got underway for their return to the First Division.

The season started in reasonable fashion, with a 2–2 home draw versus Falkirk, but subsequent defeats at Aberdeen (1–2) and at home to Hamilton by the same score showed that the team had a tough fight on their hands. On August the 30th, Hibernian were beaten at Easter Road to give the Athletic their first league win of the season, but after Morton were the Marine Gardens victors on the 20th of September, the team's poor record placed them in a very lowly position; the attendance was 'only' 7,000, a figure that a few seasons earlier would have been unheard of!

To put the Club's financial problems in true perspective, when they visited Hearts on the 18th of October – and lost by 2–5 – the crowd that day was a massive 29,000, and it was obvious that the struggle for First Division survival was not going to be confined to the results on the pitch alone. By midway through the season only eleven points had been won, and the team languished at fourth from bottom in the table. At least the crowds were not totally disillusioned for there were 12,000 present at Marine Gardens on January the 10th for the derby match with Hibernian, which ended with two shared goals.

The following week the Athletic were humbled in the Scottish Cup, when they lost to fellow Leaguers Clyde, by 0–7, before an attendance of 16,000 and gate receipts of £704. Although this result was somewhat humiliating, the goalscorers that day certainly had their shooting boots on, for other results included; Ayr versus Clackmannon, 11–2, Dundee versus Fraserburgh, 10–1, Dundee United thrashed Nithsdale Wanderers 14–0, and Partick Thistle thumped Royal Albert by no less than 16–0!

The situation in the League continued poorly, and after 30 matches the Athletic were fifth from bottom. The home match with high-flying Hearts produced two very welcome points, before a crowd of 12,000, on February the 21st.

Leith's goalkeeper Steele saves. White of Hearts challenges, with Battles looking on (21st February. Leith 2 Hearts 1)

Now deep in the depths of Winter, the Club had to face another problem, that of the exposed nature of the Marine Gardens Ground. It was in a very exposed position, virtually on the seafront where the bitterly cold North-easterly winds blew straight onto the unfortunate spectators, and it had to be hardy souls who could suffer this battering, and the indifferent results of their team! All conquering Rangers were the visitors on the 14th of March, but the attendance was only 8,000. It was a very cold day with slush underfoot, and given better conditions no doubt the crowd would have been considerably higher; a 1–3 Leith defeat didn't help. It was left to the penultimate League match of the season before the Club were assured of First Division safety. On the brink of relegation all season, they beat Dundee by 3–1, before a crowd of only 3,000. The next week they lost by 0–3 at home to Celtic, but with 27 points, they finished fourth from bottom.

The position could hardly be deemed a success, but at least they could look forward to another year of top class football. The poor location of Marine Gardens, with barely any protection for the fans from the weather, was recognised, and before the end of the season they moved back to Powderhall. But this was only a temporary move, for the dubious advantage promised by the introduction of Greyhound racing at Portobello – and the consequent influx of cash to improve the facilities – the Club soon returned to Marine Gardens. There are few groups of people that display greater degrees of optimism than football fans, and this was demonstrated on the 8th of August 1931, when, despite the previous season that had seen attendances drop to around 3,000, a record crowd was attracted to Marine Gardens.

Celtic were the first visitors of the season (having been the last ones of the previous), and the score was repeated, 0–3 to the Glasgow team. The 14,000 present at the kick–off swelled to over 20,000 by half–time, at which time the Athletic were one goal down. One week later the team lost by 0–2 at Third Lanark, but then raised the hopes of the fans with an excellent 4–1 home win over Ayr. After a few more games the position was bad but not too desperate, as home victories were achieved over Hearts and Dundee (attendance 6,000), although on their travels the Athletic were finding it a hard struggle. Just two points were picked up by Christmas, from two draws, and by this time the position had become serious.

Goalkeeper Boyce retrieves the ball, after another Celtic goal.

They never rose above fifth from bottom, after 5 games, and the home crowds started to dwindle, for Hamilton's visit on October the 17th there were barely 3,000 present to see the homesters lose by 1–4. After 18 games, and following the 2–5 Marine Gardens thrashing by Rangers, the team had plunged to one from the bottom; the visit of the League Champions attracted an attendance of only 7,000.

Boyce, the Leith Athletic goalkeeper, saving in the match with Ayr United at the Marine Gardens.

By Christmas the position was even worse, bottom and two points below the next placed team. On Boxing Day – a rare win (2–1 versus Third Lanark) – the attendance was barely 3,000.

Moves for the expected Groundsharing arrangement – in addition to the dual football use of Marine Gardens with Edinburgh City – were announced in the 2nd of January match programme:

" We hear that dog–racing will commence on this ground in May, and that a Grandstand on the sea–side will be erected for the opening of the racing season, this should make the ground sheltered and comfortable."

Welcome news indeed for the freezing fans. The match ended as a 1–2 defeat to Cowdenbeath, the crowd numbered 2,000, and the team remained firmly anchored to the bottom.

A run in the Scottish Cup came to an abrupt halt, for after drawing 1–1 at home to struggling Second Division team Albion Rovers (attendance 2,000, receipts £50), the replay was lost. By now the Club were back in a familiar financial plight, although pleas for more support had some response at the next home game. The leaders Motherwell were the visitors on February the 6th, but brought few fans (perhaps they didn't relish having to freeze!), and 3,000 Leith supporters were present to urge on their team – the result was a 0–5 defeat! High scoring home defeats were rare, but not so on the team's travels, and over the months Leith lost to Morton by 9–1, 8–2 at Airdrie, 7–0 at Hamilton, plus one other match where seven goals were conceded and four when six were let in; by the season's end the goal difference read 46–137 (the all time record number of goals conceded in the Scottish League)! In the home game with Kilmarnock the Athletic led by 3–1 at half–time, but eventually lost 6–3, and the visitors missed two penalties.

The playing record had become so bad, that the first point of the year was not obtained until the penultimate match of the season, when four goals were shared with Dundee. The end of First Division football had already been accepted with the visit of Clyde in the last League game, and was watched by just a few hundred diehards. The 1–4 defeat summed up the season for the team, which finished rock–bottom, with only 16 points, three below the next placed team. It was little consolation for the team, when – after 33 years – the Roseberry Charity Cup was won when Hearts were beaten 2–1.

By the end of July, after a mass clearout, only two players had been signed, but the 1932/33 season got underway with a full team at Queen of the South, and a 2–5 defeat, after an even first period had finished at 2–2.

A new team for the 1932/33 season.

(Back) Robinson, Dobson, Little, Mackenzie, Young, Newman.

(Front) Morrish, M'Girr, Crawford, Macfarlane, Grant.

The first home match in the Second Division, versus Dumbarton, was played (and won by 3–1) on August the 20th – the attendance was less than 1,000! After 7 games, a poor start saw the team in a lowly 7th from bottom position, but at least the crowds had partially returned, for the 1–1 draw with Montrose attracted 2,000 to Marine Gardens. At least some fans could look forward to more comfortable months ahead, for the promised Grandstand had been erected at the Ground. The Club found it difficult to establish a winning combination, and for the October match versus Armadale there were three unnamed players in the line–up!

The Leith Athletic goalkeeper beaten in the match with the Hibernians.

Even so a recovery from the poor opening form displays had resulted in a rise up to 9th when Albion Rovers came to Portobello, but of great concern was the crowd numbers which only totalled 500.

By Christmas the form had plunged, and the team were in a dismal 5th from bottom position. Far from improving in the second half of the season, the bad results became slightly worse, and by the season's end, a lowly third from bottom of the League had to be accepted; although this position was somewhat artificial for Armadale and Bo'ness did not complete their fixtures and their records were expunged. The erection of the Stand at the Ground, although appreciated by the few that could afford to use it, did not lure the hoped for crowds, and its position was far from ideal in view of the distance of the structure from the pitch.

The 1933/34 season showed a slight improvement over the previous year, for the team finished in 12th position (or 7th from bottom), having displayed mediocre records both at home and away. But by now the financial situation had become a severe worry, and with home attendances rarely rising above 1,500, the Club had to thank the efforts that continued to be made by the hardcore of enthusiasts.

Action from the home game with Stenhousemuir.
9th September 1933. Leith lost 1–2.

The first match of the following season attracted 2,000 to Marine Gardens for the visit of Montrose (an exciting 5–4 victory), but a mid-table turn of the year position ensured that the crowds by then had started to drift away. However the final eighth place in the League gave rise to a fair degree of optimism for the supporters. Over the season the team had played some exciting, and high scoring, home games, and therefore when the crowd for the first match of the 1935/36 season only numbered a few hundred for the visit of Kings Park, the Directors must have despaired as to what they could do next.

The pessimism of the Leith football fans was justified, for after six matches the Athletic lay at the foot of the table, and only improved to fifth from bottom by Christmas. Aided by an excellent home record during 1936 – when all six matches were won – the team lifted themselves to a respectable 9th final place.

But of particular embarrassment were some of the results on the team's travels: 2–8 at Dundee United, 0–6 at St. Mirren and 1–5 at Cowdenbeath being the worst.

After eight years occupation of Marine Gardens, the venue was abandoned in favour of the Meadowbank Ground from the start of the 1936/37 season. The campaign was the Club's 'Jubilee Year' (1887–1937), and it was hoped that a change of venue from the bleak and inhospitable Portobello headquarters would also bring about an improvement in the team's abilities, and greater support at the gate. In the case of the former the final record showed two points less than a year earlier and a drop to 11th place! In respect of support, there was an overall small rise.

With a much changed team the season started at Meadowbank with a visit from Dumbarton, and a 2–1 victory. Duncan opened the scoring for the homesters after 14 minutes and the lead was held until half–time. From approximately 1,500 at the kick–off the crowd swelled to an encouraging final 3,000.

But after 12 games the team lay 3rd from bottom, and this position only improved by two places by Christmas. On January the 9th, Champions–elect Ayr United were entertained, and most of the above average crowd of 3,000 celebrated a surprise 3–2 victory, despite being 1–2 down at the break.

Captains (Waugh and Richardson) and the referee at the official opening of Leith Athletic's new ground at Meadowbank.

Leith entertain St. Bernards at Meadowbank.
The home goalkeeper McCormack clears, Richardson looks anxiously on.

The team that started the 1936/37 season:

(Back) Richardson, Peat, Mair, Duncan, Harrison, Meikleham.

(Front) Kerr, Jordan, Williamson, Browning, Walker.

The improved form continued into 1937, to lift the team into their final respectable position. Although the wages bill had been cut to £1,555 (a drop over the previous ten years), the home gate receipts produced less than £1,000, around two-thirds of the takings in the Club's pre-First Division days.

The Directors must have once again despaired when an attendance that numbered only around 1,000 were present for the first game of the 1937/38 season, and the supporters must have been equally discouraged when their team lost by 3–4 to Raith Rovers – but to the team that were to eventually become the Champions. Although by the season's end seven points more than a year earlier had been obtained, the improvement had only produced a final one place higher in the League. There had been few surprises during the season, apart from the shock 6–3 victory at Championship chasing Cowdenbeath in October, and conversely a 5–2 thrashing at mediocre Alloa.

All hopes of a revival during the 1938/39 season were soon dispelled after an indifferent start (two defeats on their travels – which included a 5–1 thrashing at Cowdenbeath – and a home win over Kings Park). Poor form then continued until the New Year, by which time the team lay 3rd from bottom. By mid–February the position remained much the same, and was not helped by the 0–7 defeat at Dundee (attendance 2,000). A poor away record coupled with indifferent home form (which included a 1–7 demolition by Airdrie), doomed the team to an inevitable lowly position.

By the end of the season, and with most minds more concerned with the War that was looming, the last match of the campaign was played at home to Cowdenbeath. The visitors were already confirmed runaway Champions, but they only attracted a crowd that could be numbered in the hundreds. After a scoreless first half, the Athletic finally lost by two unopposed goals. The Leith team consisted of:

McCormack, Barker, McDonnell, Cairns, Ewan, Pratt, Donaldson, 'Junior', Doyle, Lees and Duffy.

The club's only consolation was their capture of the Roseberry Cup, in its 56th season. Hibernian were beaten at Easter Road by 2–1, in front of 2,000, and in the final Hearts were defeated by 2–0 – also at Easter Road – before a crowd of under 2,000.

Leith Athletic achieved few successes in the 1930's in the Scottish Cup, and never reached the second round stage during this period.

The 1939/40 season got underway with a 1–2 home defeat to Dumbarton (attendance 1,500) and was followed by a 3–1 defeat at Kings Park. One week later only 1,000 keen fans turned up at Meadowbank, to see the locals lose 0–2, and finally on the 2nd of September the first (and subsequently only) victory of the severely curtailed season was obtained at Dundee United. After a scoreless first half, the visitors netted twice without reply. The team contained almost the same defence as that at the end of the previous season, but with changed numbers '6' to '11', that consisted of:

Russell, Robertson, Kinnear, Broadley, Lees and O'Rawe.

The team 'finished' the season third from bottom.

After a period of non–competitive football, Leith Athletic re–appeared in the 1941/42 season as members of the War–time North–Eastern League. The venture was little short of disastrous, for always hampered by lowly attendances, the numbers dropped even further. Often there were insufficient funds to pay the visiting clubs their minimum guarantee.

The Meadowbank authorities realised the Club's plight, and cut the rental payments on the Ground, but by the season's end – along with St. Bernards – they were considered 'undesirables' by their opponents, and most clubs breathed a sigh of relief when they resigned at the end of the season.

With few friends, and by now no Ground – Meadowbank was taken over for the War effort – the Club effectively folded, and were not to make another appearance for several years. In 1943 several players were transferred to other clubs, notably Chris Duffy to Charlton Athletic, where he made his mark in football. Around the same time the sad news was announced that the Club Chairman David White had died.

A third new start and a (brief) third time in the League

Leith Athletic had never been blessed with good fortune, and their experiences after the War did not change their luck. After several years of inactivity – they had to virtually reform – and did not gain re–admittance into the Scottish League. The League made a reappearance for the 1945/46 season, but were selective with regard to membership, and the Athletic were not included in the set–up. From 72 pre–war members, the total number of Clubs was reduced to 56, but along with a number of other former Second Division Clubs, Leith were excluded. Edinburgh was particularly hit, for St.Bernards had already all but folded; Edinburgh City – with their dismal record – were inevitably not one of the chosen few, and Leith, despite their moderate pre–war record were never welcomed members due to their poor support.

Practically speaking it was obvious that the City could not support so many League teams, however this sort of action was a slur and an insult to the hardworking members, and they naturally took the decision with a great deal of resentment; in any event all the excluded clubs were assured that the measures taken in reducing the membership was only but a temporary post–War solution!

The Athletic decided to join forces with St. Bernards (but as separate clubs both had entered for the Scottish Cup, although in the final event neither teams played their cup–ties) and under the title of *Leith St.Bernards*, they attended the initial meetings for the formation of a new competition – the Eastern League – which was to contain a number of 'rejected' Second Division clubs, plus the reserve teams of the two Dundee clubs. But before the season got underway, the St.Bernards 'element' withdrew, and it was under the name of plain *Leith Athletic* that the team commenced preparations for the new season. However the major problem of a home venue had to be resolved, for the pre–War headquarters at Meadowbank had been vandalised, and damage caused during its wartime usage, made the Ground unplayable. Approaches were made to Groundshare with Edinburgh City (who had also joined the Eastern League) at City Park, but an agreement couldn't be reached, and in September – before any matches had been played – Leith had to reluctantly resign.

Following this season of inactivity, the Club members were able to proceed with more optimism when it was announced at the A.G.M. in May 1946, that Old Meadowbank had now been released, and compensation for the wartime damage could now be negotiated between the two parties. It was intended, among other things, to increase the size of the pitch and improve the terracing at the South–east corner of the Ground. But until the money was forthcoming there was little that could be done. However, following an arrangement with the Edinburgh Corporation, it was agree that for the coming season, the Athletic would be given the use of the immediate adjacent 'New' Meadowbank Sports Ground. Much to the Club's dismay the 'temporary' arrangements with regard to re–instatement of the pre–War Scottish League prevailed, and they had little choice but to accept the offer of entry into the newly formed 'C' Division of the League. This Division consisted of the former Eastern League teams – plus Leith Athletic – and additional reserve elevens. A 'sop' was offered to the small clubs that if any of their number should become the Champions, then they would be promoted into the 'B' (Second) Division; i.e. they would be 'promoted' back into the Division from which they had never been relegated!

It was going to be a hard economic struggle but the only path open to Leith towards progression. On the field the campaign was reasonably successful, for Leith finished third in the table of ten teams, but it was the Champions Sirling Albion who automatically progressed upwards, having finished five points ahead of the Athletic. Earlier, on the 25th of November 1947, at an extraordinary meeting of the Club which was held at the Masonic Hall, it was agreed to increase the share capital by 50% from £1,000. Following the eventual demise – at least from a playing point of view – of St. Bernards, the Gymnasium Ground Grandstand had been purchased for £2,000, and the 1,200 capacity structure moved to Old Meadowbank. The industry displayed by the Leith enthusiasts can only be admired, for they spent many hours – often during the night – to bring the Ground up to a high level, and it was confidently predicted that they would soon have one of the best Grounds in the Country. At least these enthusiasts had a worthwhile goal, for the Scottish League 'B' Division was extended by two, and along with East Stirling, they were elevated to the higher division – second placed Dundee reserves were ineligible for this second promotion place.

Action from the Scottish Cup quarter–final tie with Aberdeen in 1947.

From the Gymnasium to Old Meadowbank

The St Bernards' grandstand at the Gymnasium has been bought by Leith Athletic, and workmen are now dismantling the stand. It will be taken to Old Meadowbank, re-erected, and improved upon to seat 1200 spectators. Leith paid £2000 for the structure. Stirling Albion and Birmingham City offered more.

LEITH ATHLETIC F.C. (1927) LTD.
REGISTERED OFFICE: 18 CONSTITUTION STREET, LEITH
John Thomson Jun., J.P., Chairman

Souvenir programme

OFFICIAL OPENING
of OLD MEADOWBANK, 1947, on
MONDAY, 15th SEPTEMBER, 1947, by
Councillor A. H. A. MURRAY, C.B.E.

Price 3d.

A general view of the scene last night at Meadowbank, where a crowd of over 10,000 witnessed the game between Leith Athletic and Rangers.

On Monday the 16th of September 1947, a crowd of around 11,000 packed into the newly revamped Old Meadowbank for the re-opening of the Ground. Councillor A.H.A. Murray performed the opening ceremony, and Rangers were the visitors. Despite the auspicious occasion there was some resentment by many of the spectators, since the Glasgow side field a virtual reserve team. It may have been coincidental (or deliberate?), since the Rangers could have felt aggrieved that they were only second choice; The English Cup-winners Charlton Athletic had originally been invited – complete with Wembley goalscorer and former Leith player Duffy! The match ended in a 2-2 draw, with Landles scoring both goals for Leith.

After the glamour of this match the serious work of League football for Leith commenced – with crowds of barely four figures at Old Meadowbank. All hopes of progress were soon dispelled, and the campaign became one of struggle. The opening game, on the 13th of August, was lost by 1-0 at home to East Fife. The next match, two weeks later at Cowdenbeath, finished as a 2-1 victory to the Athletic, and the fans hopes were raised. But these soon disappeared as defeat followed defeat. This was to be only away victory of the season, and other points were only obtained from draws at Alloa and Stenhousemuir. The home record was poor, and with just single wins in September and October, the team were soon struggling at or near the foot of the table. By the season's end only 19 points had been obtained, and by finishing as wooden-spoonists, the Club found themselves relegated back into the 'C' (Third) Division. But ever determined, and despite their probable fate already having been accepted, in January it was announced at the A.G.M. that Robert Baxter was to be appointed as a full time manager.

The drop was a serious blow to the Athletic, with another season of financial struggle in prospect. But improvements continued at the Ground, including more terracing, although with the introduction of Greyhound Racing (which soon became the main attraction at Old Meadowbank), the pitch had to be reduced in size. Further large sums of money were spent on the club's future, which unknowlingly at the time was soon to be curtailed. The 1948/49 season in the 'C' Division was nearly as successful as their previous time in such company, and they finished as runners-up. But with only one team promoted – Champions Forfar – there was no way back up to the higher level.

The Club continued their protests that they should, by right, be in the 'B' Division, but their pleas went unheeded. There was a large influx of reserve teams into the 'C' Division for the next season, and it was split into two regions, with Leith being placed into the 16 team South–east section. Although the competition was strong – being principally the reserve elevens of 'A' Division League teams (plus Brechin and Montrose), the attractions were not good enough to encourage more than several hundred keen fans to Old Meadowbank. A lowly final placing of fourth from bottom was the Athletic's final lot, and the prospect of yet another year in the lower reaches had to be accepted. After little more than a year, manager Baxter resigned.

The Club existed for three more seasons, each one being spent in the 'C' Division, and all in the alternative North–east Section. But support dwindled even further, and with far more attractive matches elsewhere in Edinburgh, notably just up the road at Easter Road, it was a miracle that they had been able to continue this long. The Club were unable to attract sufficient quality players who were prepared to play in what was in effect reserve team football. Further pleas were made to reconsider their claim for 'B' status, but as before their wishes were not even considered. Ironically at the A.G.M. in September 1951, it was announced that the extensive Ground improvements had been finished and Old Meadowbank now had a claimed capacity for 30,000, around 100 times the normal attendances that were attracted to home matches! The 1951/52 season produced total home gate receipts of £1,000, plus £54 in season ticket sales, but the wage bill amounted to £2,193, and a massive loss on the season of £2,284 was announced.

The last years produced some degree of success in the Scottish Cup, with the winning of the Qualifying Cup during the 1948/49 season (when Montrose were beaten in the final, at Alloa), and the following year with a victory over Brechin by 5–2 at Stirling; the end of the run came in the first round on both occasions – first by the only goal at home to Raith Rovers, and secondly from a 7–3 crash at St. Johnstone. The attendance for the Raith match produced a record 11,625 crowd. In the 1947/48 season the Athletic qualified and received a bye in the first round, but were easily beaten in the next when defeated at Rangers by 0–4 – but with the compensation of the share of a good 'gate'.

After finishing third, then second from bottom and finally rock–bottom, the writing was on the wall. When the fixture lists were issued for the 1953/54 season, the Club flatly refused to play, after the League turned down Leith's desperate plea for restructuring. They refused to resign, claiming that they could legally withdraw from the 'C' Division yet retain their League membership! They yet again raised the perpetual argument that as they had never been relegated (pre–war) it was the Scottish League that were the guilty party. But they had little support, and finally instead of playing Falkirk reserves on August the 8th, Leith Athletic were expelled from the League. By coincidence it was the reserves of Falkirk that provided the opposition in what had been the Athletic's last League match, on the 27th of April 1953. Landles became the last Leith goalscorer with his equaliser in the 25th minute, but unfortunately the match was finally lost 1–2.

The team consisted of:

Nolan. Laird, Blackie, Till, McCall, Spence, Dalziel, Landles, Reid, Morrison and Bootland.

The Club were by now all but extinct, yet they had entered for the Scottish Cup, and after a couple of friendly games with a scratch side – made up of amateur players on loan that were assembled with the assistance of John Hughes the Secretary of the Players Union – they participated in the first round tie with Fraserburgh in January 1954. The crowd of 2,181 produced match receipts of £189, but despite the goals scored by Finnie in the first half, plus McKenna, Doig and finally the 84th minute Peat effort – in the second half – the Athletic lost by 4–5. On the 16th of January, one of the friendly matches was played against Dunfermline reserves, which ended as a 4–4 draw.

This was the last home match that Leith were to play at Meadowbank. Although still not officially defunct, in order to retain their Scottish F.A. membership they entered for the Scottish Cup again the next season. The Club drew Selkirk in the first round of the 1954/55 season but the game was never played, and their opponents were given a walkover. At an extraordinary A.G.M. on the 17th of May 1955 the club was wound up. A liquidator was appointed ten days later, and at a meeting on the 2nd of May 1957 the final end came. The Club had left liabilities of nearly £12,000, and the assets only amounted to £7,300.

PRIVATE and CONFIDENTIAL.

Leith Athletic Football Club (1927)
LIMITED.

Directors.
W. DONALD, W. T. PEARCE, G. BOLEYN, P. SIMPSON,
A. J. GRANT, and J. MACKENZIE.

Auditors.
Messrs A. T. NIVEN & Co., C.A.

Secretary and Registered Office,
JAMES MACKENZIE, 28 Constitution Street, Leith.

REPORT OF THE DIRECTORS to be submitted to the Shareholders at the EIGHTEENTH ORDINARY GENERAL MEETING to be held at 28 CONSTITUTION STREET, LEITH, on *Saturday, 29th September*, 1945, at 2 o'clock p.m.

The Directors submit herewith the audited Balance Sheet for the year to 21st May, 1945.

For the season 1945-1946 the Club did not take part in football. It was hoped that the Club would get back to playing this season through a joint Committee of the Club Directors and four representatives from St. Bernard's F.C. Application was made to the new Eastern League on the understanding that Home matches would be played at the ground of Edinburgh City F.C., but as satisfactory terms could not be arranged the Committee had no option but to withdraw from the League. The Directors also decided not to take part in the Qualifying Cub Competition.

The ground at Meadowbank is still under requisition by the Army Authorities and the next matter of importance is the question of getting the ground back into condition, the erection of Grandstand, Dressing Rooms and other offices with accommodation; but this may be a difficult and expensive matter at the present time. The Club was unfortunate in having so much of its property maliciously destroyed during the war.

In the beginning of September negotiations were completed with Charlton Athletic for the transfer of C. Duffy, outside left. Duffy played for Charlton Athletic for two seasons while stationed in the London District.

All the Club players, with the exception of J. McCormack, goalkeeper, are still in the Services and may not be available until the beginning of next season.

The Directors who retire by rotation are Mr A. J. GRANT, Mr P. SIMPSON and Mr J. MACKENZIE. They are eligible for re-election.

The Auditors, Messrs A. T. NIVEN & Co., C.A., offer themselves for re-election.

A. J. Grant Director.
Wm. Donald Director.
James Mackenzie Secretary.

28 CONSTITUTION STREET,
LEITH, *22nd September*, 1945.

BALANCE SHEET.
As at 21st MAY, 1945.

Liabilities.		Assets.	
Share Capital:—		Improvements to Ground:—	
Authorised and Issued		Balance at 21st May, 1944 ...	£126 0 0
2000 Shares of 10s. each fully paid	£1000 0 0	Less Depreciation	26 0 0
The Commercial Bank of Scotland,			£100 0 0
Ltd., Overdraft	222 16 4	Scottish League Deposit ...	5 0 0
Loans for Rent	45 4 0	Payments in Advance ...	1 0 6
Loans for Signing Fees ...	4 0 0	Cash on hand	47 8 2
Sundry Creditors	292 8 7	Profit and Loss Account:—	
		Balance brought forward £1410 9 5	
A. J. GRANT, *Director.*		Less Net Profit for Year 59 4 2	
WM. DONALD, *Director.*			1351 5 3
	£1591 8 11		£1504 8 11

Immediately after the War it was with the greatest difficulty that the Club managed to carry on – as can be seen from the directors report of 1945. (S.R.O. Ref. BT2/14743)

COMPANY LIMITED BY SHARES

EXTRAORDINARY RESOLUTION
(*Pursuant to "The Companies Act, 1948"*)

OF

Leith Athletic Football Club (1927) Limited

Passed 17th May, 1955

AT AN EXTRAORDINARY GENERAL MEETING of the Members of the above-mentioned Company, duly convened, and held in 58 Charlotte Street, Leith, in the County of Midlothian on the Seventeenth day of May, 1955, the subjoined EXTRAORDINARY RESOLUTION was duly passed :—

"That the Company cannot, by reason of its liabilities, continue its "business and that it is advisable to wind up and accordingly that the "Company be wound up voluntarily."

Chairman

The struggle didn't finally end until 1955, when the Club was finally wound-up. (S.R.O. Ref. BT2/14743)

EDINBURGH, *26th May*, 1955.

The Grounds:

1. Hawkhill 1887 – 1890:

The Ground was located within the current large Hawkhill Recreation Ground, which is situated to the South–east of Leith, near the junction of Restalrigg Road and Restalrigg Park. Prior to 1887, it was used by Leith Caledonian Cricket Club until the formation of the Hawkhill Recreation Company in July 1887. There is no evidence to suggest that this Company and the Football Club were connected, despite the formation of both around the same time. At this time it is probable that the Ground consisted of nothing more than a (probable) enclosed field. However within a few years a small Stand or Pavilion was soon erected on the East side, and an oval running track was formed that surrounded the central playing area. A narrow embankment ran along most of the West side and the South end. In later years a long Grandstand extended along the West side. A railway line was built along the North side of the ground and traversed part of the later Bank Park Ground. In 1920, the Hawkhill Company was wound up, and the former Ground gradually disappeared over the years, although there are traces of a grassed embankment in the South–west corner which could well be one and the same as the original one.

2. Bank Park 1890 – 1894:

This venue was a smaller (3.6 acre) enclosed Ground located on the East side of Lochend Road, and opposite the current Hermitage Park Grove. Although no traces of a Ground as such are left, the path of the former railway line can be seen from Lochend Road, which overlaid the Ground; Hibernian's Easter Road Ground is just few hundred metres distant. Two small open Stands were built on opposite sides of the pitch, and a very narrow line of open seating was provided along the East end which extended down both sides to the main Stands.

3. Beechwood Park 1895 – 1899:

It appears that this Ground was one and the same as Bank Park – but renamed 'Beechwood'. By 1909 all traces of the ground had disappeared.

4. Hawkhill and New Logie Green 1899 – 1900:

For details of this (new) venue see the St.Bernards section.

5. Chancelot Park 1900 – 1904:

The Club was at a low ebb at this time, and for these few years their Ground may well have been little more than an enclosed flat area. The Chancelot area is about one kilometre to the East of Leith, and this venue may well have been the later named Chancelot Recreation Park. This site is at the North–east corner of Ferry Road and Craighall Road, and a sports ground currently overlays part of the former park.

6. Old Logie Green 1904 – 1916:

Leith made use of this ground some years before St.Bernards. It had formerly been the Heriot Cricket and Football Ground, a large and probably open area with a pavilion on the West side (previously the ground had been known as 'Old' Powderhall). The development of the ground initially consisted of little more than a small covered Stand on the East side, with the main – and probably only – entrance down a wide path off Logie Green Road. By 1914 narrow embankments were formed around the South end, the West side, plus the East side to the Stand. (See also the St.Bernards section)

7. Chancelot and Wardie Parks 1919 –1924:

Once again the Club were at a low ebb, and during this period Chancelot Park was used again and later Wardie Park. Wardie Park was located about one kilometre West along Ferry Road, and like Chancelot was probably completely undeveloped as a football ground, and possibly not even enclosed. It later became known as Ferryfield Recreation Ground, and is located near to the former Edinburgh City's City Park – at the North–west corner of Boswall Drive and Ferry Road.

8. Old Logie Green 1924 –1926:

A return was made to this venue for two years, after St.Bernards' four year occupation.

9. (New) Powderhall 1926 –1928:

Once again this was a Ground that St.Bernards had previously used, albeit briefly (see also St.Bernards section). By now a deep concrete terrace had been built around the west end which narrowed and continued along the North side. A very narrow band continued around the East end where it carried on until marrying up with the main seated and covered Stand that stretched along much of the South side. On the opposite (North) side and at the West end there were other Stands. There is no doubt that with its flat and well grassed playing area, plus good spectator facilities, this could have been an excellent Ground. But it was, and still is, located very close to the Water of the Leith, and at times of heavy rain the pitch became waterlogged. In addition its other uses also included Greyhound Racing, and the dog track around the perimeter restricted the playing area to less than an ideal width.

10. Marine Gardens 1928 – 1936:

This was a virtually purpose built Football Ground, from former wasteland, and was located immediately adjacent to the shoreline of the Firth of Forth, to the South–east of Leith, and in the Portobello district. The site was owned by a Mr.G.Youll, as was the adjacent Ballroom. This could have undoubtably have been a large and fine Ground, had it not for its location.

On the exposed East coast of the estuary, the bitter winds blew off the sea and onto the spectators, particularly those that stood on the high terraced West side. It was cheerless, cold, and a barely developed Ground, and with the Athletic's generally indifferent form during these years it could have only enticed the keenest of supporters out on a freezing Winters day! Apart from the wide West terrace there was eventually built a small covered and seated Stand opposite – comfort for only the minority – with a thin band of terracing each side which extended around the South end. The Ballroom was used as dressing–rooms.   Dirt Track (later named Speedway) Racing was staged at Marine Gardens for a few years, followed by a two year period of Greyhound Racing. The inhospitable nature of the Ground and the distance from the action ensured that it was as equally unpopular for the dog fanciers as it was for the football men! The Ground was eventually taken over by the Corporation, and initially used as a vehicle test area. It is now a large bus depot, at the North–east corner where Seafield road and Kings Road meet; nothing remains of the Ground. Contrary to an often repeated error, the site was **not** the open air swimming pool that was built south of Kings Road.

11. Meadowbank 1936 – 1942:
A move was made inland and further South of Leith, to a Ground that had been used by the respected Leith Amateurs Club. Initially the more hospitable nature of the Ground attracted slightly higher attendances, but the Club's generally poor form at this time, coupled with the coming war, gave them little time to develop the enclosure. Meadow-bank consisted of a five acre site with a wide oval track around the playing area, but which guaranteed only a distant view of the matches. The Club built nothing more than a few wooden buildings, probably dressing rooms, club offices and rudimentary shelter for spectators. Meadowbank was used by the Army as a motor transport depot during the 2nd World War, and this (plus vandalism) resulted in an unplayable Ground at the time of the Club's reformation in 1945.

12. Old Meadowbank 1946 – 1947:
For a short while the adjacent Corporation owned Recreation Ground, which was commonly referred to as Old Meadowbank was used. This Ground had previously been a velodrome (cycle track).   There were few facilities for spectators around the oval shaped pitch and surrounding track, other than a narrow embankment along the South side and West end. Elsewhere there was only flat standing areas and a Pavilion, which also probably incorporated a small covered Stand, at the East end.

13. New Meadowbank 1947 – 1953:
Meadowbank became known as *New* Meadowbank after the Club members superhuman efforts at rebuilding their old Ground.

Concrete terracing was eventually provided all around the oval track – which was later used for Speedway Racing (Edinburgh Monarchs) – and the Grandstand from the former Gymnasium Ground of St.Bernards was re–erected on the South side. The pitch was enlarged to give a 115 x 75 yard playing area, with a 9 foot wide grass verge and a 15 foot track. The final capacity was variously claimed between 24,500 and 30,000. Despite the Club's problems in attaining a higher standard and attracting better crowds, the hardworking supporters continued improving the Ground virtually to the end, and a cover for 2,000 spectators was added to the North (railway) side. The main entrance was off Clockmill Road, and adjacent to both 'Old' and 'New' Meadowbanks was a large car park, a rare (and not so necessary at this time) commodity. For a period after Leith's demise the Ground was used by Murrayfield Amateurs, before they went the same way as the previous occupants! Both New and Old Meadowbank became the site of the modern and current Meadowbank Stadium that is used by Meadowbank Thistle F.C.

PANORAMIC VIEW OF EDINBURGH'S NEW FOOTBALL GROUND.

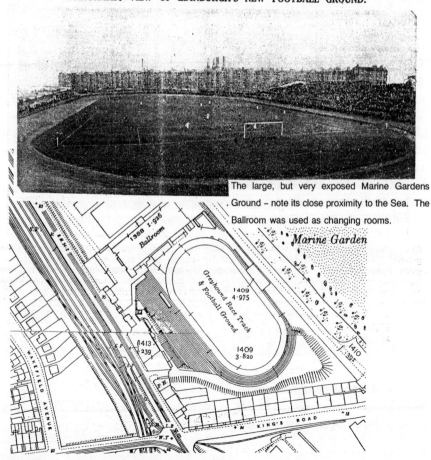

The large, but very exposed Marine Gardens Ground – note its close proximity to the Sea. The Ballroom was used as changing rooms.

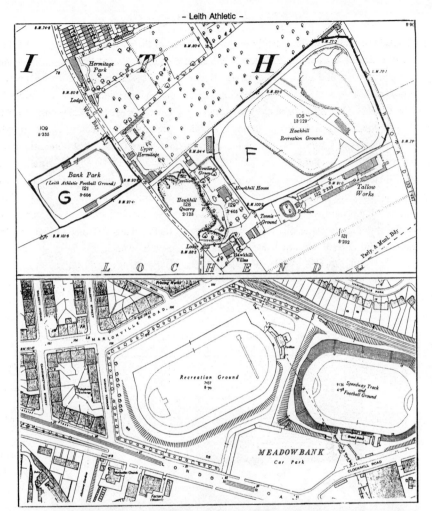

(Top) The two earlier Grounds at Hawkhill and Bank Park. (Hawkhill still exists as an open recreation ground. Bank Park was demolished for a railway line, and the cutting is still evident)
(Above) The *'Speedway Track and Football Ground'*, was the original 'Meadowbank' Ground, and later (post–war) 'Old Meadowbank'. Between times (1946–47) the *'Recreation Ground'* was used and known as 'New Medowbank'. The current Meadowbank Ground incorporates both of these former Grounds.

ST. BERNARDS.

August 1936 – Team Lineup
(Back) Russell, Philip, Fitzsimmons, Cunningham, Rogers, Strathie.
(Front) L.Paterson, Flucker, Weir, Noble, Brooks.

Back Row (left to right)—JOSEPH ALLAN, JOHN KERR, T. G. SMITH, JAMES PHILIP, PETER M'PHERSON, and EDWARD WEIR.
Front—GEORGE GRANT, JAMES JOHNSTON, PETER FLUCKER, JOSEPH DAWSON, and JAMES PINKERTON.

September 1937 – Team Lineup

ST. BERNARDS.

Founded 1878 – Defunct 1946.

League Career:

1878 – 1890:	Friendly and Cup matches.
1890/91 –	Inactive (Banned).
1891/92 – 1892/93:	Scottish Alliance
1893/94 – 1899/00:	**Scottish League Division 1.**
1900/01 – 1914/15:	**Scottish League Division 2.**
1915/16 –	East League.
1916/17 – 1918/19:	Inactive.
1919/20 – 19 1920/21:	Central League.
1921/22 – 1939/40:	**Scottish League Division 2. ***
1939/40 –	Regional League North and East.
1940/41 –	Inactive.
1941/42 –	North–Eastern League.
1942/43 – 1946.	Inactive.

* 1939/40 season, Scottish League fixtures ceased after four matches.

....

Grounds:

1878 – 1880:	Stockbridge Public Park.
1880 – 1889:	Royal Patent Gymnasium.
1889 (part)	(Old) Powderhall (later renamed Old Logie Green).
1889 (part)	(New) Powderhall.
1889 – 1901:	New Logie Green.
1901 –	New Powderhall.
1901 – 1916:	Royal Gymnasium.
1919 – 1923:	Old Logie Green.
1923 – 1924:	Tynecastle.
1924 – 1942:	Royal Gymnasium.

Colours:

To 1889:	Red and White.
1889 – 1920:	Royal Blue.
1920 – :	Blue and White hoops.

Members of the Scottish F.A.
1880 to April 1947.

Major Honours and Achievements:

Scottish League Division 1 – 3rd:	1893/94.
Scottish League Division 2 Champions:	1900/01. 1906/07.
	(Runners–up 1914/15).

Scottish Cup Winners:	1894/95.
Semi–finals:	1892/93. 1895/96. 1937/38 (2 Replays).
5th Round:	1883/84 (last 11). 1886/87 1887/88. (last 16).
4th Round:	1888/89 (last 16). 1923/24 (last 8)
3rd Round:	1884/85. 1893/94 1896/97 (last 8).
	1919/20 1930/31 (last 16). 1931/32 (last 12).

Qualifying Cup Winners: 1907/08. 1914/15.
East of Scotland Challenge Shield Winners: 1896/97.
King Cup Winners: 1896/97.
East of Scotland (City) Cup Winners: 1908/09. 1911/12. 1919/20. 1920/21. 1924/25.
1925/26. 1934/35. 1937/38.

International Players:
(Scotland): W.U. Baird (1897). R.Foyers (1893 and 1894). J.Hutton (1897) J.Lowe (1887). D.McLean (1896 and 1897). J.McMillan (1897). J.Oswald (1895). D.Paton (1896).

Record Victory: *(Scottish Cup) 1883/84, (Home) 13-1 v. Dunfermline.*
                                     (League) 1933/34, (Home) 10-1 v. Morton.
                                     (Away) 10-1 v. Cowdenbeath.

Biggest defeat: *(Scottish Cup) 1925/26, (Away) v. Aberdeen 0-8.*
                                     (League) 1927/28, (Away) 2-9 v. Forfar and 1-8 v. Kings Park.

Most Goals in a match: J.Johnston, 1938/39 v. Forfar - 6.

Record Attendance:
1st January 1932. 27,000 versus Hibernian (League).

St. Bernards Well (Photo Dave Twydell 1990)

Scottish League record:

	P.	W.	D.	L.	F.	A.	Pts.	Pos.
1st Division:								
1893/94	18	11	1	6	53	39	23	3rd
1894/95	18	8	1	9	37	40	17	6th
1895/96	18	7	1	10	36	53	15	7th
1896/97	18	7	0	11	32	40	14	7th
1897/98	18	4	1	13	35	67	9	9th
1898/99	18	4	4	10	30	37	12	7th
1899/00	18	4	4	10	29	47	12	9th
Relegated to Second Division.								
1900/01	18	11	5	3	42	26	27	1st
1901/02	22	10	2	10	30	31	22	6th
1902/03	22	12	2	8	45	42	26	5th
1903/04	22	9	2	11	31	43	20	8th
1904/05	22	3	5	14	23	53	11	12th
1905/06	22	9	4	9	42	44	22	5th
1906/07	22	14	4	4	41	24	32	1st
1907/08	22	8	5	9	31	32	21	8th
1908/09	22	9	3	10	34	37	21	8th
1909/10	22	12	3	7	43	31	27	3rd
1910/11	22	10	2	10	36	41	22	6th
1911/12	22	9	5	8	38	36	23	6th
1912/13	26	12	3	11	39	34	27	7th
1913/14	22	8	6	8	39	31	22	7th
1914/15	26	18	1	7	66	34	37	3rd
League suspended due to War.								
1921/22	38	15	8	15	50	49	38	9th
1922/23	38	8	15	15	39	50	29*	18th
1923/24	38	11	10	17	49	54	32	18th
1924/25	38	14	4	20	52	70	32	17th
1925/26	38	15	5	18	86	82	35	14th
1926/27	38	14	6	18	70	77	34	13th
1927/28	38	15	5	18	75	103	35	17th
1928/29	36	16	9	11	77	55	41	6th
1929/30	38	13	6	19	65	65	32	14th
1930/31	38	14	9	15	85	66	37	11th
1931/32	38	19	7	12	81	62	45	5th
1932/33	34	13	6	15	67	64	32	12th
1933/34	34	15	4	15	75	56	34	10th
1934/35	34	20	7	7	103	47	47	3rd
1935/36	34	18	4	12	106	78	40	5th
1936/37	34	22	4	8	102	51	48	3rd
1937/38	34	20	5	9	75	49	45	4th
1938/39	34	15	6	13	79	79	36	7th

* 2 points deducted for playing an ineligible player.

The Saints are 'Well-founded'.

Although St. Bernards were 'only' founded in 1878, the true formation of the Club probably goes back even earlier. The 3rd Edinburgh Rifle Volunteers partook of a variety of sports, including football, in order to offer suitable diversions to prospective recruits. Such organisations are peculiar to Scotland in as far as their promotion of football is concerned, the most famous of such volunteers being the 3rd Lanarkshire Rifle Volunteers who were the direct descendants of the Third Lanark Football Club. The 3rd E.R.F. were one of the earliest of football Clubs in Edinburgh – they entered the Scottish Cup Competition in 1874, one year after its inauguration. The Volunteers played their home matches in Stockbridge Park, which is now part of the Comely Bank District of the City. With the Volunteers in occupation, it became obvious to the locals of the Stockbridge area that finding suitable sporting opponents would be made easier if they changed from the rugby code to the round ball version. George Heathcote and James Dunn were supposedly the leaders of this new body, and together with several other men who lived in the district, St. Bernards F.C. came into being. The rules of the Club were strict for there were fines for swearing and for non–attendance at matches, whilst a residential qualification required that all Club members lived in the nearby area. With an annual membership fee of one shilling (5p) and a halfpenny weekly sub., the Club were able to purchase a football.

In common with many football clubs in Scotland, the Club's name did not relate to its location. A spring was discovered beside the Water of the Leith in the mid–18th century and was soon acclaimed for its curative properties. A popular legend has it that St.Bernard visited the Scottish Court in Edinburgh, but was not welcomed and had to seek refuge in a cave to the North of the City, and it was from this Saint that the name of the nearby well – St.Bernards – was chosen. When the land was purchased by Lord Gardenstone in 1788, a classical Italian style rotunda was built over the well, and a keeper was installed to regulate those who wished to 'take the waters'. The use of the well gradually diminished and the structure fell into a poor state of repair, until in 1887 – by which time the St. Bernards Football Club had become well established – a believer in the curative properties of the waters, William Nelson, organised suitable renovations at his own expense, including a new statue of Hygeia (the Goddess of health) which was installed to replace the original one. Although no longer a functioning Well, the structure still exists in good repair today, and is located between Saunders Street and Dean Village.

Apart from their choice of name, there is no evidence to suggest that the members of the football club derived any benefit from the Well, but they honoured their namesake in the choice of their first playing kit. This consisted of a white jersey with a red horizontal stripe, and a badge on the left breast which depicted the well. The Club's Ground was located in the Northwest corner of Stockbridge Park, and in their first two seasons they remained undefeated. Much of this success was due no doubt to the claimed poaching of players from other, and older, Clubs in the district – Brunswick, Edina, Norton Park and Hanover! Under the Captaincy of George Heathcote, the Saints soon became the top team of the area, and their first match of note was played in unusual circumstances.

– The original St.Bernards team of 1878 –
(Rear) W.Waugh, W.Robertson(Sec.), J.Baillie, S.Robertson.
(Middle) D.McKinnon, J.Wilson, G.Heathcote, R.Bryce, R.Charlton, J.Dunn.
(Front) G.McBeth and A.Andrew.

The two leading Edinburgh Clubs, Hearts and Hibs., were due to play an Edinburgh Cup–tie at the home of the latter, Mayfield Park. The Hibs. (a Club formed from an Irish background) had a suspicion that their opponents would not show up, and arranged for the St. Bernards team to be at the Ground in order to deputise for the Hearts, should they not appear.

Ignorant of these clandestine arrangements, a large attendance was present for the clash of the Edinburgh giants, and when the Hearts team did not appear, the crowd were incensed when they found that the Hibs. were about to engage the relatively unknown little Club from Stockbridge. Fortunately the Saints put on a worthy show, and so grateful were the Hibs. Officials that £5 was given to them, to share amongst the players. Although this action was not condemned at the time, it is somewhat ironic that St.Bernards should be involved in similar dealings, which led to their suspension, albeit ten years later!

Although this prestigious match was lost, the Saints display did not go unnoticed, and invitations were made, and accepted, to play matches much further afield. Arbroath was one of the Club's first visits, and even invitations were extended by the big Glasgow Clubs. A second appearance, at Glasgow Rangers, was little short of a disaster, for the Saints were heavily defeated, and the Glasgow Officials refused to pay the Club's £3 guarantee and expenses! By the end of this, the Club's second season, they had played 15 games, of which two were drawn, and only three had ended in defeat.

The rapid rise to success led to the Club having to seek a new home Ground for the 1880/81 season, since the support that they could now command justified an enclosure rather than the large open spaces within Stockbridge Park.

First time at the Gymnasium.

William Lapsley, a former Hanover player, had become the Saints' Honorary President on their formation, and became a good friend and benefactor of the Club. Although his occupation was initially as a representative for a London tea company, he later diversified his interests and became involved in the managements of Sports Grounds. His first project was to take over the lease of the Royal Patent Gymnasium Ground in July 1879. This open–air Pleasure Ground, that had been built fourteen years earlier by a local philanthropist, was considered as one of the wonders of the Victorian Age, and rivalled the Crystal Palace (in London) for it's diversions and entertainment value.

Contained within the Grounds were a variety of amusements that were created by the ingenuity of the Victorians, and included a rotary boat that could accommodate 600 passengers and a giant see-saw. Over the years, the facilities were extended, and for an entrance price of 6d (2.5p) – half price for children – the public could enjoy a wide diversity of recreational pursuits, including skating in the winter months. But the novelty waned, and by 1880, the Hanover Football Club had become the principal occupant of the grounds, due to the football pitch that had been incorporated within. With Mr. Lapsley's interest in St.Bernards, and their requirements for a more suitable Ground, the Club became the obvious new tenants.

The Saints were accepted into the Scottish Football Association at this time, and with this higher status, and the better facilities on offer, the Club's rise continued. Their most notable success of the 1880/81 season was their progression through to the final of the Edinburgh Cup – after some emphatic victories in the earlier rounds – where they met the redoubtable Hibs. A sensation was on the cards, for with only 20 minutes remaining, the Saints led by four goals, but a collapse in the closing period led to a draw, and the Hibs. went on to narrowly win the replay.

The Club first made an entry into the Scottish Cup the following season, when they surprised everybody with their 2-1 victory over Hearts, but lost in the second round – by the same scoreline – to Hibs. By now three teams were run by the Saints, and their impressive record for the season produced 40 victories, 5 draws and only 16 defeats.

But the Club rapidly became victim of their own success, and news of its successes reached far a field. Many of the Club's leading players received tempting offers from South of the Border, and amongst the deserters were Bob Bryce to Accrington, plus Purdy Robertson, George Drummond and Jimmy Ross who all met with success at Preston North End.

In order to maintain their ideals as a top Club it became necessary to rescind the 'residential rule' that the Club had made at it's foundation, and this opened the way to the likes of Jimmy Lowe, who later became the first Saints player to be capped for his country.

The fortunes of the Saints somewhat stagnated during the major part of the 1880's as they strove to keep pace with the continuous loss of their most promising players. However, notable successes were achieved in the Scottish Cup, and during this period they reached the fifth round on three occasions, and victories included a 13–1 crushing of Dunfermline in 1883.

The Club could still compete with the 'other' two clubs in Edinburgh, and although they claimed a number of notable victories over Hearts, the greens of Hibernian remained a stubborn obstacle. By 1889, with support at a low ebb, it was decided to make another venue move, and Old Powderhall was chosen, a Ground that could offer more space than the rather cramped Gymnasium Ground.

More space would hardly appear to have been a prerequisite at this time, however perhaps it was an ambitious move that was motivated by the thoughts that better facilities would attract larger crowds, and hence encourage more success on the field.

Brief stays at the 'Old' and 'New' Powderhalls.

Mr.Lapsley again obliged by making the necessary arrangements for the move to (Old) Powderhall – which was later developed into the Old Logie Green Ground – but only for a very short stay. (New) Powderhall – which was immediately adjacent to (Old) Powderhall – had meanwhile been developed into a quarter mile track enclosure, and St.Bernards moved in.

But the Club's occupation was very brief, as the interference with their fixtures, caused by other occupants of the enclosure, proved unacceptable. Therefore the start of the 1889/90 season saw the Club move the very short distance to New Logie Green, which was leased, and was rapidly turned into a worthy Football Ground. Facilities at this new arena included a Grandstand, and the Third Lanark Club became the first visitors – and first victors – at the start of the 1889/90 season. The change in venue brought about a change in colours – to Royal Blue – and also a change of fortune on the football field. But having put their house in order, the Club were about to be disrupted to such a degree that their very future was to hang in the balance.

Trouble came about by virtue of a breach of the Scottish F.A. Rules. The match in question was that between the Saints and the Adventurers in a Scottish Cup–tie, which the Saints duly won. The Adventurers, true to the spirit of teams suffering a cup defeat at that time, protested on the basis of a claim of professionalism, a claim that was upheld, and for their transgression, the Saints were severely punished.

A suspension of six weeks was handed out to the Club, but this punishment was to become, in effect, far more severe. In an effort to find a way around the ban, the Club claimed that they had reformed – under the name of 'Edinburgh Saints' – and under this title played a match against Renton. However, the F.A. were not convinced, and an enquiry resulted in the Saints being adjudged as the 'two' Clubs being one and the same. For this second demeanour the Saints, together with the relatively innocent – it would appears – Renton Club being both banned for one year! But the effects of this ban for the two Clubs was more severe than it would appear, for Renton had just prior to the incident, invited a number of Clubs to discuss the possibility of forming a Scottish League (the counterpart in England had commenced two years earlier).

Effectively St.Bernards were unable to take part in either further meetings, or in the outcome, i.e. the first season of League competition. Renton however were elected to become one of the members, although after only five league games they were charged with professionalism – which stemmed from the earlier Saints match – and were duly expelled from the new competition. But Renton refused to be intimidated by the S.F.A., and sought judgement in the Courts, which found in their, and St. Bernards' favour. This judgement came nearly a year later, and so the two Clubs had had to remain inactive for the 1890/91 season. Two years later, the success of League football resulted in professionalism being permitted in Scottish football! This period of inactivity could have spelt the death knell of the Club, but they weathered the storm, and for the 1891/92 season became the founder–members of the Scottish Alliance, the alternative to the Scottish League. The Saints more than held their own in this competition for the next two years, and with their past misdemeanours forgotten, were sensibly voted into the Scottish League First Division for the 1893/94 season.

Saints Heydays.

During the late 1880's and early 1890's the Club met with varying success in the Scottish Cup. The 1886/87 season saw them play in the 5th round (amongst the last sixteen teams) but were soundly beaten by Port Glasgow Athletic, and one year later repeated this run. However, on the latter occasion they were somewhat fortunate since they only won their 2nd round game – against Broxburn Shamrock – by way of a replay, received a walkover in the next, and a bye in the 4th round! In the 5th round they came down to earth with a 'bump', when they were thrashed with a 0–9 scoreline by Abercorn. In 1889, their run was cut short by Celtic.

There then followed three seasons where no progress was made beyond the 1st round. But the 1892/93 season was the first of four years which could probably be considered as the Club's most successful period in their entire history. The Cup produced early round victories over Queen of the South Wanderers (5–1), Royal Albert and notably Rangers by the odd goal in five.

This took the Club through to the semi-finals of the competition, but any major shock was soon thwarted by Celtic who ran out as comfortable five goals to nil winners. But even more successful days were on the horizon!

No major shock was produced in the Scottish Cup in the 1893/94 season, in fact the Saints were humiliated with a 3rd round defeat by Celtic, and a 8–1 scoreline.

This Cup game however was a unique event, since it was played under floodlights. Friendly games, played under artificial lighting, had become commonplace in England, but this Scottish Cup fixture was without doubt the most prestigious to be competed for in such conditions. The lights were mounted on fifty foot high poles, but the wiring to them stretched across the pitch and provided a hazard for the flight of the ball. In fact on this principle, the Saints protested, but their complaints were turned down, for it was believed that the ball had only been impeded on two occasions.

However, in the Scottish League, the Club more than held their own. The Saints became the First division's third Edinburgh team (alongside Leith Athletic and Hearts – meanwhile Hibernians were about to dominate the newly formed Second division), and helped to make up the total of ten Clubs in the competition. They got off to an indifferent start, on the 19th of August, when they lost at Third Lanark by 3–5, and followed this defeat with a scoreless draw at home to Rangers. An excellent victory at Dumbarton (by 5–1) was then obtained before St. Mirren were beaten at their own Ground. As the season progressed, the Club showed that their inclusion with the elite of Scottish Football was more than justified, and by the season's end they finished third from top; with 23 points they were six short of Champions Celtic total. Amongst other matches against English teams, the Saints first competed with the renowned Corinthians team on the 4th of January 1889, and five further matches followed (with only one victory to the Scots), before they scored a resounding 4–0 win on the 2nd of January 1894.

The following season was not so successful in terms of the League for the team could only finish in a modest mid–table position, but pride came by way of the Scottish Cup. After duly beating Airdrie in the 1st round, the Club overcame Kilmarnock by 3–1 at Old Logie Green before a crowd of 2,000.

That season the cup was marred by a particularly high number of protests, and St.Bernards were inevitably involved. At the quarter final stage (the 3rd round), they overcame Clyde at Borrowfield Park with a 2–1 scoreline, but the defeated team protested on the basis of ineligible players used by their visitors.

The protest was somewhat pathetic since Crossan was shown to have played for Glasgow Fish Market against Glasgow and South Western Street Station Club, in an obvious very minor match, whilst Oswald had turned out for Tradeston Gas Works in a five–a–side competition. The objections were overruled, particularly since the incidents had occurred during the previous season! Not to be outdone, the Saints then lodged their own protest against the Clyde Club with regard to the attack they had suffered from irate supporters, a charge that was denied by the referee. No further action was taken, but the attitudes of both Clubs, hardly did anything to the raise the prestige of either.

For the semi-final match the Saints opposed Hearts, in a local derby game at Tynecastle on the 9th of March. The game produced a scoreless draw, but the replay – at the same venue four days later – aroused great interest, and a new ground record was set when 15,000 packed into the enclosure. So packed was the Ground, that some fencing gave way causing many spectators to spill onto the track surrounding the pitch, but there were no injuries. Despite illness, George Murdoch played – against Doctor's order – and became the hero of the day when he scored the only goal for the Saints. Predictably the Hearts Club protested, but their objections against three of the Saints players were quashed.

Old foes, Renton, became the other unfashionable Club to reach the final, which was played at Ibrox Park, Glasgow. With no direct Glasgow involvement, the attendance only amounted to 12,000, including around 1,000 from Edinburgh. The Saints team consisted of:
Sneddon, Foyers, Hall, Murdoch, Robertson, McManus,
Laing, Paton, Oswald, Crossan and Cleland.
George Murdoch was the worthy captain, for despite a spell at Third Lanark he became a Saints player for ten years, and appeared in the Final despite being not fully fit.

St Bernard's Team—Winners of Scottish Cup in 1894-95.
Back Row—T. Robertson (the famous referee who died last Saturday), Jas. Oswald, B. Crossan, and Jas. Sneddon. Middle Row—J. Wilson (trainer), R. Laing, P. M'Manus, G. Murdoch (capt.), C. Hall, R. Foyer, and W. Baird. Front—D. Paton and Jas. Cleland.

The Edinburgh team were favourites to win the game, although they played a cautious game, with the attack well led by Cleland and Paton. Within three minutes of each other, and from the same spot, Cleland scored twice, and the Saints went on to win a sporting game by 2–1. It was a very proud President, Lapsley, who received the cup on behalf of the team. Despite a preference for the more local Renton team, the Glasgow public who formed the majority of the crowd, sung the praises of the Edinburgh Club, and the team were carried shoulder high to their transport that was to take them back to their City.

In addition to their cup–winners medals the team also received gold replicas of the Cup that were presented by the local merchants in the North of Edinburgh, and a few months later when the team travelled to London to play the Corinthians, their new found prestige was recognised by a large attendance that was present for the Friendly encounter.

One year later, there was the presence of the three top Edinburgh Clubs in the Cup semi–finals, but the Cup–holders were defeated by Hearts, and it was they and Hibernians who were left to settle the final issue. However, St.Bernards did have an indirect involvement in the Cup Final, for their Ground at Logie Green was chosen as the venue, the only time that the Final has been held outside of Glasgow.

The 1896 Scottish Cup Final
(The only time the game has been staged outside of Glasgow)

Relegation – and no return.

After such heady days, the Saints fortunes declined, and five indifferent seasons followed, which ultimately led to their relegation to the Second division of the League. During those years the highest that the Club was able to finish was seventh (of ten), on three occasions, and in 1898 only just managed to hang onto its status when it finished second from bottom in the League, following just four wins, and a total of only nine points. With professionalism well established in the country, many players were lured away to the wealthier English Clubs, including Danny Paton who moved on to Aston Villa, but between times had become one of the few Saints players to have won an International Cap (versus Wales in March 1896) whilst playing for the Club.

After their successive Final and Semi–final appearances, they were never to repeat these performances, and in the years leading upto the end of the century they never reached further than the 2nd round. It was only in local competitions that any real success came, for in 1897 they won both the King Cup and the Edinburgh and District Challenge Shield, surprisingly the only times that these trophies were captured by the Saints.

Dens Park, the home of Dundee, was opened in August 1899, when St.Bernards were the visitors for a friendly match in which two goals were shared. With a crowd of approximately 10,000 the gate takings amounted to over £217. Despite the lean years, the only really bad season was that of 1897/98.

As well as being crushed by non–League Queens Park in the Scottish Cup, by five unopposed goals, there were some heavy defeats in League matches. Only one point was obtained on the team's travels, from a goalless draw at Dundee, and the 'best' defeat was the 2–4 reverse at Hearts. Elsewhere heavy losses included a 1–8 drubbing at Rangers plus 0–6 at Third Lanark and by 2–7 to St. Mirren. To redress the balance, Partick Thistle were beaten 9–1 at Old Logie Green, these goals accounting for over half of those credited at home! It took a play–off match to decide the fate, and relegation, of the Club in 1900. They finished joint second from bottom with St.Mirren, and to determine the final outcome a deciding match was played.

The Saints lost by 1–2, but it was only the voting of the other First Division Clubs that decided St.Bernards demotion. Along with wooden–spoonists, Clyde, they were voted out, and they were never to regain their premier status. The decision was a severe body blow to the Club's Officials, and there was even doubts on whether it was worth continuing as a Football Club. But the final outcome was an application for membership of the Second division, entry was not automatic, but the Club were voted in.

With a few notable exceptions, the Saints found the going hard during the next few seasons at this lower level. Things turned out well in the first season, for after beating Port Glasgow in the opening encounter they scarcely looked back. By the season's end they had become the Division's Champions, finishing three points clear of runners–up Airdrie, but this success was not sufficient for them to be voted back into the First division. The three following seasons however were disappointing, for the Saints could only manage mid–table final placings in their League. During this time there were no surprising results, and despite this moderately poor record, the only really bad blow was a 0–5 defeat at Champions–elect, Port Glasgow Athletic during the 1901/02 season, and a four goal defeat on the 26th of September 1903 on the Ground of fellow mediocre Albion Rovers. The home record was generally good, with a memorable 8–3 victory over Falkirk in October 1902.

The lease on the Old Logie Green Ground expired, and coincided with their drop down to the Second division in 1900, and once again William Lapsley became their saviour when he arranged for the Club to use the (New) Powderhall Stadium. But this proved to be a short, and unhappy occupation, for as in the case of a decade earlier, a clash of fixtures with the other occupants (Professional Athletics) proved the joint use to be unworkable. With the Royal Gymnasium becoming vacant once again, and despite the Club's earlier reservations with regard to its size, they were happy, in the circumstances, to be allowed to move back there. Financial pressures resulted in the Club losing the services of a number of promising players, including Bell and Houston to Hearts, Annan to Sunderland and Turner to London, and the Woolwich Arsenal Club.
In 1903, the Club's great friend and financial adviser, William Lapsley died, and such a personality, who had guided the Club from its early days, could never be replaced.

The problems were compounded for the Club by the end of the 1904/05 season, when they reached their lowest ebb, by finishing bottom of the League. The season started badly with two away defeats in August, at Falkirk and Hamilton. Only one League match was played in September, when a rare point was obtained on the Saints' travels, and apart from a moderately successful October, it was all downhill from then on. With only eleven points (and only three victories in twenty-two matches), the Club finished six points behind the next placed, Abercorn, team.

Until the First World War caused the cessation of matches, the Club plodded through the years in a general state of mediocrity. Although the disastrous season of 1904/05 was never repeated, they generally finished around mid-table, except on three occasions. After finishing in a satisfactory fifth in the League in the 1905/06 season, they managed to fight their way to the top once again, and one year later had claimed the Championship. Once again it was a case of steady performances rather than sensations, although the 1-5 defeat at Arthurlie in January must have caused some ripples within the Club! In view of their previous performances it cannot have come as a surprise when re-election back with the elite was again denied the Club.

The Club were in a lamentable state financially by 1908, and on the 1st of September, a Limited Company was formed, with 12 directors, that took over the assets and liabilities of the 'former' club. 1,000 shares at £1 each were put up for sale, although after one year only 300 had been taken up - and most of these by the directors!

The exceptional season did nothing to spur the Club on, and apart from third placings in 1910 and 1915 (only play-offs deciding the final positions of the top three Clubs in the latter year), there was little evidence to suggest that the Club would regain their former glories. In fact by 1911 so bad were the finances, that it was only the personal money of four directors that kept the Club's head above water.

From 1904, the Club were required to fight their way in the Scottish Cup through from the qualifying rounds, and for a team that had so comparatively recently won this prestigious competition, their efforts were little short of dismal!

On most occasions they did not even reach the first round proper, and on the four occasions when this stage was reached, they never managed to progress through to the second. The Club's only other successes during this pre–war period was its capture of the East of Scotland (City) Cup, on two occasions, and two appearances in the Consolation Cup Final, one of which was won. Promising players were a rarity, although Reid's performances led to him being transferred to Sunderland in the early part of this period, and Graham, who had been signed from a Junior Club, moved on to Hearts in 1914. One notable character was Hossack, who was very selfconscious of his bald head, and in order to hide his deficiency, insisted on wearing a cap whilst playing!

Travelling problems and availability of players brought about the end of the Second Division at the end of the 1914/15 season, and although the club managed to carry on for one more year, when they played in the (Wartime) East League. During this one season they were able to call upon the services of several players from other Clubs, notably Warnie Cresswell from South Shields, but when the Military Authorities took over the Royal Gymnasium Ground at the end of 1916, the Club had little choice but to close down for the rest of the War.

No League place in Post–war Scotland.

By 1919, a degree of normality had returned to Britain, and St.Bernards, along with the other pre–war Second Division Clubs were ready to recommence league battles. But these Clubs were stunned when the Scottish League, in their debateable wisdom, decided to continue with only the single First Division (that had remained during the 1915 –1919 period), leaving the lesser teams to determine their own fate. With a post–war public anxious to be entertained, there was no lack of support, and therefore these 'second class' Clubs set about forming their own leagues.

Three new Leagues were created – the Eastern, Central and Western – with additional pre–war non–League teams, and a number of Reserve elevens from the Scottish League, being recruited to form competitions of ten, sixteen and twelve members respectively. Although the Clubs within these new competitions were still members of the Scottish F.A., they were of course, completely independant of the Scottish League, and therefore not bound by the latter's rules.

With finance generally more available due to the upsurge in interest in the game, the lesser Clubs were able to pay to players, whatever wages they could afford, and were not bound by the transfer rules of either the Scottish League, or by the 'sister' Football League from over the border. This resulted in many leading players opting for higher wages that were now available with the 'non–Leaguers'!

This somewhat ludicrous situation was allowed to continue for two seasons, during which time the Saints played in the Central League, without distinction. Early in 1921 the acrimony between the different League organisations brought about a change of heart by the Scottish League, and was acceptable to those Clubs outside of this organisation. It was agreed that the Central League should form the basis of a revised, and extended, Second Division; for a few Clubs, they would continue to be non–League teams despite their higher pre–war status – although this situation was resolved in part, two years later, with the addition of the Third Division (from those Clubs playing in the Western League). In addition, automatic promotion and relegation would operate between the two divisions (a situation that had already been in force for many years in England). In return, the Clubs involved, agreed to return to the more senior Clubs the players who had been enticed away from them. Honour was seen to be done, and the Saints along with their contemporaries were allowed to continue their Scottish League careers.

March 1924 Team Group: (Back) Taylor, Penmann, Murray. (Middle) Sorbie (Trainer) Henderson, Law, M'Alpine, Dunsmuir, M'Leod, Lauder. (Front) Leitch, Ross, Paterson, 'Wilson', Penman

Although the Club's problems had been resolved with regard to a suitable League, they were experiencing difficulties with regard to an acceptable arena. The Authorities war–time use of the Royal Gymnasium, had rendered the Football Ground unsuitable due to the heavy lorries and tractors that had been parked, stored and repaired on it; the playing surface had been severely damaged and the drainage system destroyed. The Saints managed to obtain the use of (New) Logie Green immediately after the War, which was situated adjacent to New Powderhall, and had been previously used by Leith Athletic – a Club that did not re–appear until 1924. The Saints tenancy ended with the completion of the 1923/24 season – by which time they were Ground–sharing with the Edinburgh City Police F.C.

Meanwhile a small band of St.Bernards enthusiasts managed to purchase the Royal Gymnasium Ground late in 1922, with compensation money that had been received. with only 600 of the original shares sold, the Company was wound up, but as a Club they continued. On the 27th of october the 'new' Club was formed, under the name of *St.Bernards Football Club Grandstand Company Ltd* ! The immediate objective was to aquire the Gymnasium Ground again, and 4,400 preferance shares at £1, plus 100 ordinary shares were issued.

Until sufficient money could be raised and extensive work undertaken, an agreement was once again made for the Club to occupy New Powderhall. After two unsuccessful, and shortlived tenancies, this third attempt fell through, and for a short period the Club arranged to Groundshare with Hearts at Tynecastle. Ironically with Hibernians carrying out work at Easter Road, they too needed a temporary alternative venue for matches, but were forestalled by the Saints!

Back 'Home' at last.

On the 15th of November 1924, the extensive refurbishment, including the re–orientation of the football pitch, rendered the Ground ready for the Club, who at last could return to its true 'home'. The opening ceremony was conducted by Patrick Ford M.P., but unfortunately the match ended in a 0–1 defeat to Arthurlie, and watched by a crowd of around 3,000.

The St Bernards' new stand in course of construction.

The Gymnasium, the St Bernards' F.C. ground.

In the interim three years, the Saints had hardly set the football world alight, as they first finished in a mid-table position (in a League now containing 20 Clubs), and then twice in a lowly third from bottom slot. But at least the post-war boon in football ensured that the Club was able to feel financially secure, and their low standing in the League was in part compensated by a good Scottish Cup run in the 1923/24 season.

They won through to the fourth round (four years earlier they reached the third round, the last sixteen), the quarter-finals, and along the way had won by the only goal of the game at the high-flying First Division, and much fancied, Raith Rovers. But they could not emulate this performance in the fourth round, at Aberdeen, where they lost by three unopposed goals. The only other point of merit in the immediate post-war years, was the Club's winning of the East of Scotland (City) Cup again, in 1919 and 1920.

By now there was always the threat of the ultimate degradation, relegation to the Third Division, and in their first season back at the Royal Gymnasium, they only just avoided this, when they finished fourth from bottom, just four and five points respectively ahead of the hapless Johnstone and Forfar. The rest of the 1920's passed by, with the Club not only struggling on the field – apart from finishing sixth from top in the 1928/29 season, their familiar finales placed them well in the bottom half – they also had to contend with ever increasing financial problems. The novelty of, and post-war interest, in the game had by now waned, and coupled with the General Strike in 1926, the smaller Clubs (including the complete abandoning of the Third Division) were finding it a struggle to make ends meet.

Fortunately for the Saints they were assisted by a well run Supporters Club – which was started in 1925 – and their support and financial donations (over £100 in its first year), led to the Football Club voting onto the Board of Directors a representative from the supporters, a very rare occurrence, considering that most Clubs, in a somewhat aloof manner, would only tolerate such Supporters Associations, despite their valuable financial contributions!

But the Saints did not always conform to the norm, for in the 1924/25 season, they appointed a Manager (Mr. Heatlie), such an appointment that was normally reserved for only the bigger Clubs.
Heatlie, although well liked by the Players, was a very nervous man, and could not bare to watch a St.Bernards game. He could be seen walking outside the Ground during a match, but on his last excursion he never came back – for he left hurriedly after accusations relating to the destination of certain gate moneys!

```
                    [DUPLICATE FOR THE FILE.]

No 13341


Certificate  under s. 87 (2) of the Companies (Consolidation) Act,
1908 (8 Edw. VII. c. 69), that a Company is entitled to commence business.


                            I hereby Certify, That

        "The Saint Bernard's Football Club Grand Stand Company, Limited"



which was Incorporated under the Companies Acts, 1908 to 1918, on the ——Seventh——
day of ——October——19 24—; and which has this day filed a statutory declaration in the
prescribed form that the conditions of s. 87 1 (a) and (b) of the Companies (Consolidation) Act, 1908,
have been complied with, is entitled to commence business.

        GIVEN under my hand at Edinburgh, this ——Third——day of——January——
One Thousand Nine Hundred and Twenty-five.


                                        Registrar of Joint-Stock Companies.
```

The *'St.Bernards Football Club and Grand Stand Company Limited'*, becomes incorporated.
(S.R.O. Ref. BT2/13341)

Fortunately the occasional 'find' could always be sold to the more prosperous clubs, the most notable during the 1920's being the outside right – Jimmy Boyd – who was transferred to Newcastle United for the enormous sum of £2,000, after the Club had refused an offer of £250 from Hearts.

Following the Club's Jubilee in 1928, the supporters hoped that soon, and within the next fifty years, the Club could return to its former glories. But such hopes were never achieved, and, except for the latter half of the 1930's, such an uplift in the Club's fortunes appeared to be distinctly unlikely. Until the 1934/35 season, the highest position that the Club could reach was fifth in the League, but there then followed a few years that gave optimism to the fans. In 1935, the team finished third, just three points behind Arbroath in the promotional second slot.

During the season the Saints had achieved some memorable high-scoring results, including 7–0, 5–0, 6–1 and 6–2 (twice). Their eight successes on foreign soil included a surprise 5–2 victory at Arbroath and 6–2 at Edinburgh City. Hopes of a big promotion push the next season were dashed when the Club dropped two places in the final League table, although the third position was attained again at the completion of the 1936/37 season. On this latter occasion they only missed promotion by three points again. One year later the same points difference prevented an elevation, for this time they were fourth in the table, with 45 points, but only two behind Aidrie, and three short of second placed Albion Rovers.

A well attended Edinburgh Shield match at the Gymnasium Ground in 1931.
St.Bernards put pressure on the Hibernian defence.

It was not until 1931, that another team Manager was appointed – a gap of four years, during which time team selections were made from an essentially young group of Players, by the Directors. Soon after this first appointment, Bob Innes took on the role, and his term of Office lasted until 1939. The economic situation worsened during the years leading up to the second World War, and various methods had to be devised, in order to ensure the continued suvival of the Club.

The, potentially, most profitable innovation was the introduction of Greyhound Racing to the Royal Gymnasium in 1934. But this failed after only 18 months, during which time crowds of over 200 were rare, and although this would have been a means of financial salvation, such usage never received the approval of the Football Authorities, due to the Ground alterations that often had to be made, and the risk of attracting 'undesirables' to the venues! The hiring of the Ground was also taken up by several Junior and Amateur sporting organisations, for important matches, but after one notorious summer when this near continuous use left the pitch hardly playable for football, this wholesale usage was stopped.

THE GYMNASIUM SAINTS

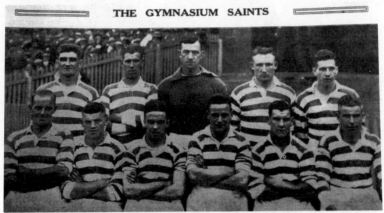

August 1931 Team Group: (Back) Marley, King, Keenan, Robertson and Dunn (Front) Brown, Walls, Davidson, Drummond, Duff and Eadie.

A flying clearance by the St Bernards goalkeeper against Albion Rovers.

The Saints get the 1932/33 season off to a fine start with a 4–1 home win, over Albion Rovers, on the 13th August.

This 'top of the table' clash was won by the Saints 3–2.

– **Team Group** – April 1935 –

St Bernards F.C.
Back Row—(left to right)—Fitzimmons, Allan, Cunningham, Igoe, Marley, Weir.
Front Row—Laidlaw, Russell, Eadie, Noble and Hay.

The Edinburgh City defence under pressure from the Saints
in this 1936 Gymnasium Ground derby match

Late Thirties revival.

EDINBURGH SAINTS' BID FOR PROMOTION

Back Row—Allan, Kerr, T. C. Smith, Philip, Russell, Aird, and Mr Tait, a director.
Front Row—Flucker, Johnston, "Newman," Dawson, and Kemp.

After so many years of near obscurity, the 1937/38 season thrust the Club to the forefront, which many thought would be the signal for a more permanent revival.   Although the Club's exploits had been somewhat frustrating, with their near promotion to the First Division, it was to the Scottish Cup that their glory came. After their noted passage through to the 4th round in 1924, several years followed during which time the Club never progressed further than the 2nd round, and were often despatched from the Cup in a no uncertain manner; 2–5 to Hamilton Academicals in the 1924/25 season, 1–8 at Aberdeen a year later and by 1–5 in a local derby at Hearts Ground the following season. In the latter campaign they did achieve a good victory by overcoming Third Lanark by 5–3, but fell to the Tynecastle Club in a second round replay.

The 1930/31 campaign saw the Club through to the third round for the first time in seven years, but after beating Stranraer and Kings Park, they were defeated by First division Cowdenbeath by three unopposed goals in the next Cup encounter. Mediocre performances followed once again – apart from another Third round appearance in 1932 – but the Club's excellent performances during the 1937/38 season must have come as a surprise to even their most ardent followers.

With the Club contending for promotion, their victory over the non–League Vale of Leithen Club in the First round was expected, but it was only achieved by a single goal. The Saints hardly impressed in the next round, for after sharing two goals with Kings Park, at the Gymnasium Ground, they only won through by the narrowest of margins in the replay, with a disputed goal, to give them a 4–3 victory. Luck was with the Club for they received a bye in the Third round, and therefore reached through to the quarter–finals – their furthest progress since 1924. The respected First division Motherwell Club came to the Gymnasium Ground on the 19th of March for this fourth round match. What should have been a 'bumper' payday for the Saints turned sour, for in their efforts to swell the coffers, they doubled the admission price to two shillings (10p), and were 'rewarded' with a very poor turnout of only 3,600, and match receipts of £304.

The visitors were a great disappointment, but, against the run of play took the lead after 15 minutes. The Saints deservedly equalised just one minute later, and the score remained so until half–time. The crowd increased to around 5,000 for the second half (the gates were opened after the break!), but the earlier drizzle had by now turned to heavy rain. After Motherwell had wasted many opportunities, the homesters right–winger, Grant, scored a controversial goal, following Flucker's charge on the goalkeeper, but an action that the Motherwell team considered was not by virtue of a fair shoulder to shoulder encounter! St. Bernards sealed their victory with their third goal, just five minutes from the end, after an earlier effort had been disallowed for offside.

This victory ensured the Club a place in the semi–finals, their first since 1896. With the chance of drawing Kilmarnock or Rangers, the Club's luck appeared to hold, when they were pitted against their fellow Second division rivals, East Fife. The team for the match at Tynecastle on the 2nd of April 1938 consisted of; T.G.Smith, Allan, Kerr, Aird, Russell, Kemp, Grant, Johnston, Flucker, Dawson and Pinkerton. Near the end of a sporting and evenly matched first half, Johnston opened the scoring from the edge of the penalty box, only for East Fife to storm back and equalise almost immediately. During the second half the Saints had the edge, but the deadlock was not broken, and so a replay, at the same venue, was set for the following Wednesday.

Despite the status of the two competing teams, the first match captured the imagination of the fans, and the attendance was in excess of 36,000. But despite the game being a 'home' match for the Saints, their football standing in Edinburgh was demonstrated by the poor vocal support that they were able to command. In the replay, the Saints dominated the play, and after hitting the woodwork on eight occasions, on the ninth occasion, the Referee awarded a goal. But fierce protests from the East Fife players resulted in a consultation with the linesman, and a reversal of the decision.

This judgment lifted the visiting team, and they proceeded to twice get the ball in the net, but to no avail as both efforts were disallowed. After 90 minutes there was no score, but in extra time East Fife took the lead, and in a fluctuating encounter, the Saints equalised, to produce another deadlock. Of particular satisfaction was the attendance of 30,185, and the receipts of £1,054.

The venue for the second replay favoured the Saints with the match on the 13th of April being played at Tynecastle once again. Despite it being a Wednesday game, football followers turned out en–masse yet again and the crowd numbered 35,264 and takings of over £1,200 were realised. Another even contest ensued, and although the St.Bernards defence played well, the forwards were generally disappointing. No goals were scored until 16 minutes from the end, when Miller gave East Fife the lead. With the likelihood of the Fifers increasing their tally, Kerr equalised for the Saints from the penalty spot. Extra time was looming, when McKerrell scored the winner for East Fife, and so it was they, and not St. Bernards, who went on to meet – and beat – Kilmarnock in the Final, the first time that a Second Division team had won the coveted trophy.

But the composition of the East Fife team in their St.Bernards matches was not without criticism. The match–winner McKerrell had been taken on loan from Falkirk just a few days earlier (and replaced the team's weakest player from the earlier two games). On loan Herd, from Hearts, was injured in the first Cup game, but the Edinburgh Club obliged East Fife by providing the services of Harvey for the next two matches. St Bernards reasonable protests after the event led to changes in the rules with regard to the playing of on–loan players.

Flucker's shot hits the post in the 1938 Scottish Cup semi-final.

After the Club's challenge for promotion and near ultimate Scottish Cup success, the only silverware to come to the Gymnasium Ground during the 1937/38 season was the consolation of the Roseberry Charity Cup. In the Final they beat Leith Athletic, and the attendance at Tynecastle – by now the Saints second home (!) – was 2,886, a far cry from the earlier packed Stands and terraces during their Cup marathon.

The near successes, and the gratefully received additional revenue, put St.Bernards in an optimistic frame of mind at the start of the 1938/39 season. Now with a bigger playing staff, the Club got off to a good start when Leith Athletic were beaten in the first League game of the season. Four goals were then shared at Forfar – although the team nearly came away with both points – and in the third game of the campaign, with new goalkeeper Libberton between the posts, Brechin City were thrashed 7–1 at the Gymnasium Ground. The supporters were hardly prepared for the shock that awaited their team at East Stirling, when the struggling homesters registered a shock 5–2 victory on September the 3rd. But this defeat was only a temporary hiccup – at least for a while – for the Saints went on to record a winning run of five matches, by early October. Later that month, the newly demoted Morton team were unceremoniously thrashed by five unopposed goals at the Gymnasium –Dawson recording a hat–trick – to put the team well in contention for promotion. They now lay fourth in the League, just three points behind table–toppers Cowdenbeath. This team were the next visitors to Edinburgh, following only one earlier defeat, they triumphed by 2–1.

Although further victories came their way up to the New Year, the Saints promotion push started to falter, and a 1–6 crash – on an ice covered pitch – at Alloa, began to seriously sow the seeds of doubt.

1939 started with further indifferent results, and an early Scottish Cup exit at Dundee, and the 1–4 defeat at Dunfermline in late January, virtually condemned the team to further Second division football.

Russell and Johnston, of St Bernards, hard at work.

On February the 18th, Forfar visited Edinburgh, and were beaten 6–2, but of particular note was the performance of J. Johnston who deputising for regular centre–forward Tams, scored all six St. Bernards' goals! The Club's 'up and down' form continued to the end, and after suffering a single goal defeat to Airdrie on the 15th of April – the Saints last home Scottish League game – they shared two goals with Leith, four days later. By finishing in a moderate 7th place in the League, the season, although perhaps disappointing – was hardly a disaster, and with a view to developing their own youth players, the Club were reasonably happy with regard to their future prospects. But they had not reckoned with Hitler, and the Second World War!

On the 12th of August 1939, the Saints opened their League programme with a scoreless draw at Brechin City, and followed this up with a morale boosting 6–2 home victory over Forfar Athletic. But once again the Saints only flattered to deceive, for seven days later they crashed by 5–1 at Methil, the home of East Fife. The Club's fourth, and last ever, Scottish League encounter came on the 2nd of September when the amateurs of Queens Park were entertained. The Glasgow team were a much respected Club, and having just been relegated, and making a determined bid for promotion, the crowd at the Gymnasium Ground, was the biggest for many years. A disappointing tussle ensued and ended up goalless. The Team for this last League encounter was composed of:

McKay, Dick, Gilchrist, Philp, Flucker, Aird, S.Johnston, J.Johnston, Walker, Dawson and Kemp.

In the earlier defeat at East Fife, J. Johnston was to become the last scorer of a Scottish League goal for the Club.

The declaration of War brought about a cessation of football activities, although by mid–October, following meetings of the Scottish League, a regionalised War–time programme was created. Six League Clubs initially declined to continue – notably including the two other Edinburgh teams of 'City' and Leith Athletic (for which the future for both was also to be short) – and for those left, two competitions were devised. St. Bernards were placed in the East and North League, along with fifteen other Clubs of varying abilities. With a vastly changed team they lost their first encounter at Cowdenbeath, with a 0–4 scoreline. In the somewhat unreal atmosphere of guest player usage, the Saints acquitted themselves well, and although amongst a number of former First division teams managed to maintain a mid–table position by the turn of the year.

Much of their success was down to Jimmy Logie, a temporarily returned Saints player (he had signed for Arsenal in June 1939 and in post–war years became a key player for the Gunners), but his second departure coincided with a turn in the Club's fortunes and by the end of the season they had slipped to 14th. For a short while it appeared that the Scottish League would return to its pre–War composition, but with a greater involvement in the War required by Britain, this plan was nipped in the bud.

The Saints last ever Scottish League game.

The end in sight.

The East and North League ceased to exist for the 1940/41 season, and for one year the Club, along with several others went into hibernation. But the next campaign got underway with the Saints playing in the newly formed North–eastern League, but with only seven other teams. St.Bernards who had always found things a financial struggle, by now were suffering on the field, and after finishing 5th in the first series League, they completed the second series, and finished bottom of the table. It came as no surprise when the Club were refused League entry for the 1942/43 season, since their opponents guaranteed share (20%) of gate money at the Gymnasium Ground, rarely covered their travelling costs. Examples of the lamentable returns included match receipts of £12–50 for the visit of Dundee United and a pathetic £7 when Dunfermline came to Edinburgh.

The last match played by St Bernards F.C. occurred on Saturday the 16th of May 1942, when a virtual 'scratch' team, consisted of –
Matthews, Newman, James Duffy, Gillies, Murphy, Gilbert,
Dougall, Dingwall, Moodie, Junior and John Duffy.
In a lack–lustre match, with the Saints playing with only ten men for much of the second half, they succumbed to a 2–3 home defeat to East Fife, with Dougall, in the 75th minute, becoming the last player to score a goal for the Club. The attendance was around 1,000, which could be considered good for the period, but was no more than the number that had bothered to watch the Club in the far more successful days.

The Directors, and the few remaining supporters, could not have envisaged that the Club were never to play again, when they made the sensible decision to discontinue in 1942. The death during the War of Director Cooper led to the executors of his Will clawing back the maximum assets that he had ploughed into the Club over the years. On the 9th of February 1944, there was a voluntay winding up of the Club, at the extraordinary meeting that was held at 25 Rutland Square. One month later a liquidator was appointed. The sale of the Club's assets fetched a total of £3,196, and all creditors were paid their proportional debts on the 1st of March 1945. The Club came close to amalgamating with fellow–strugglers from Edinburgh, Leith, but eventually the Athletic battled on, on their own, for a few more years.

In a very optimistic frame of mind the name of *St. Bernards* was re-registered with the Scottish F.A., and they were even drawn against Duns for a qualifying Cup match, in July 1946, but a ball was never again kicked by a Saints team. A poignant footnote to this longlived Club, is the Supporters Club that lived on – at least in name – for many years, despite the fact that lack of support was probably one of the biggest factors in the Club's demise!

Stockbridge to Gymnasium – The Grounds.

It is fitting that a particular physical memory of this well respected Club still exists, not by virtue of a former Ground, but by way of St. Bernards Well, from which the Club took it's name, and perhaps gained the advantage of long life that the waters were supposed to provide, but not immortality!

The sites of the Clubs former Grounds, bar one, have all but disappeared. Stockbridge Public Park, was located just to the North-west of the City centre and was no more than it's description suggests. This area has now been well developed over the last century or so, with Inverleithen Park being a prominent, formally laid out recreation area. St. Bernards, from their formation, played in the North–west corner of Stockbridge Park, and probably located within the more modern park. In 1880, they moved around half a mile East to the quaintly named Royal Patent Gymnasium grounds.

The only remains of the Gymnasium Ground. The Iron gates that led to the 'bridge' and directly into the Stand. (Photo DaveTwydell)

The grounds were first used for sporting pursuits when Mr. Bauchope was allowed to run foot–racing on a built up track within, in April 1865. The Club chose wisely when they made Mr. Lapsley the Honorary President, for after taking over the lease of the grounds in the summer of 1879, he gave the Saints permission to use the small football Ground that had by now been created within the Gymnasium enclosure. Football was probably played along the East side of the grounds, but offered little, if anything in the way of facilities for spectators, and the Club's gradual rise in stature resulted in them moving away in 1889.

Mr Lapsley's lease on (Old) Powderhall enabled the Club to relocate, just a few hundred yards North. By the mid 1890's, this site became known as the Heriot Cricket and Football Ground, and was later developed into the Old Logie Green (Football) Ground. Old Powderhall was until the 1889 New Year used for racing. The Club's stay on this field was shortlived, for plans by the City of Edinburgh to form a large Park encompassing the area, required the termination of Mr. Lapsley's lease (and the one for the Gymnasium grounds). This left the Club with no Ground, but when the Authorities abandoned their development plans, Mr Lapsley was not only allowed to renew his lease on Old Powderhall, but also to take another on the adjacent site immediately to the East, which soon became known as New Powderhall. This latest sporting area was rapidly turned into a comparitively well developed arena. The elongated oval, with a quarter mile running track, contained open seated Stands on the South side, with a pavilion at the West end. Mr. Lapsley again came to the rescue, and allowed the Football Club to share the facilities of New Powderhall, but it was an unhappy relationship as the Saints were unable to contend with fixture clashes, and within a few months had moved yet again.

The 'New' Logie Green Ground site – scene of the 1896 Scottish Cup Final.
The road runs down the length of the former pitch.

They managed to obtain a lease on a Ground which became known as New Logie Green, and was situated adjacent to, and South-west of, the former Old Powderhall site. At last the Club were able to enjoy a degree of permanence, and for eleven years enjoyed good facilities that were soon provided at Old Logie Green Ground. The Ground was enclosed, and contained some part-natural embankments, with additional open Stands that were built on the West side, together with a large seated and covered Stand. So highly was the Ground regarded that in 1896, it was used for the Final of the Scottish Cup, when a Ground record attendance of 16,034 (match receipts of approximately £1,000) was present.

The lease of the Ground expired in 1901, and with the Club's fortunes at a low ebb, they were bailed out again by Mr. Lapsley. Very soon after the Club's departure from (New) Logie Green, the site was developed, with a new road, 'Logie Green Road', running down the centre of the former football pitch. Mr Lapsley allowed the use, again, of (New) Powderhall, which was still very much as it was a decade or so earlier. But, as before, this proved to be only a stopgap solution, due to fixture clashes with the foot-racing residents, and within a few months the Club were on the move once again. Powderhall is the only former Ground of the Club that remains today, although it has been substantially developed over the years. The Saints chose to return to the, by now, near derelict Royal Gymnasium grounds, and over the ensuing years developed the Ground into a well established arena.

City development had already enveloped the Western portion (in the vicinity of the current Eyre Terrace), but within the remains of the grounds a long, but low, covered and seated Stand (with cramped Club offices, etc. below) was erected on the East side with a paddock in front, and off Eyre Place a new main entrance was created. Following it's Wartime use the Ground became all but uninhabitable, and the Club had to once again seek pastures new, on their reformation in 1919.

They chose the now well developed (Old) Logie Green Ground, that they had briefly inhabited in 1889. By now it embraced embankments around most of the perimeter of the pitch, plus a small covered and seated Stand along the centre of the East side. So close to New Powderhall was it, that only a fence separated the Ground from New

Powderhall! By the early 1930's the site had ceased to become a 'Ground' and greyhound kennels (for nearby Powderhall) were built over half of the pitch. No traces remain today, and much of the site is occupied by a Supermarket.

Old Logie Green was only regarded as a temporary refuge, and when the Club received repayment for the damage caused during the War, to the Gymnasium Ground, they set about planning for the future. Between times, the local Council had roughly levelled and grassed the pitch area, but all the facilities – the Stand, Dressing rooms etc. – had been demolished, and this (by now) very sub-standard ground was used by local minor teams. Over a period of about eighteen months, the Ground was re-built. The pitch was realigned to lie East to West, and new entrances were created off Logan Street (which branched off Eyre Place), Eyre Place, and along the Southern perimeter off Royal Crescent. The main entrance, opposite Dundonald Street was of particular note, since it was at a high level and access to the ground was gained via an iron gate and bridge. Under the bridge lay a pathway to the turnstiles for the other supporters. Near to this latter entrance was situated a house which had previously been used by the groundsman, but then became an equipment store for the Club. Two separate and distanced Dressing-rooms were incorporated, the visitors under the East end of the Stand, and the homesters at the other end, but both teams entered the pitch via the centre of the Stand.

The 1,200 capacity covered and seated Stand complete with a terraced paddock was constructed, which stretched for a third pitch length along the South side. The steel and brick Grandstand cost £4,000 to build, and was designed by Civil and Construction Engineer J.Gilchrist. Extensive embankments were created to supplement the natural ones, giving at least part raised areas all round the pitch, and additionally a thin band of concrete terracing was built along the East end. With the addition of a tea hut on the North embankment, the Club could be proud of their work, which resulted in a Ground with a claimed capacity of 40,000. But such a vast expanse was hardly necessary, and even the record attendance at the Gymnasium Ground only reached 27,000 (a figure many times more than the norm), when Hibernians were League visitors in the 1931/32 season.

With little money to spare, further development, and even reasonable maintenance, was no more than the minimum, and the arrival of greyhound racing required modifications to the end terracing and the pitch itself (at the corners) in order to form an oval arena. After the Club's demise, in 1947, the Grandstand was purchased for £2,000, and moved to Leith Athletic's Ground at Meadowbank.

The remnants of the Ground soon disappeared, to be replaced with King George's Playing Fields (a public park), and more recently these have shrunk considerably in size with virtually nothing left to remind the visitor of it's former history.

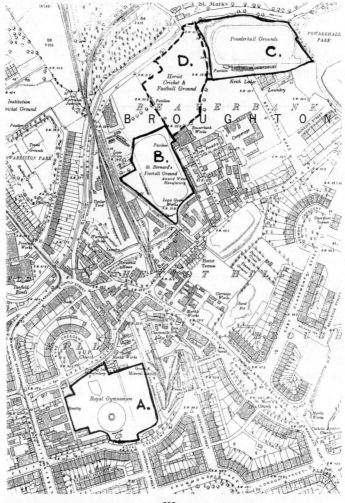

Old Maps of Edinburgh tell the 'story' of four Football Grounds:
(Reading from Left to right)   (See also page 71)

1896: 'A' – The Royal Gymnasium Ground. 'B' – The Old Logie Green Ground (used for the 1896 Scottish Cup Final). 'C' – The later (New) Powderhall Ground. 'D' – The site of (Old) Powderhall, and later named New Logie Green Ground.

1908: The Royal Gymnasium has by now been laid out as a Football Ground. Old Logie Green has been built over, and Old Powderhall has become the developed New Logie Green Football Ground.

1914: Some embankments have been added at New Logie Green, and developments continue at New Powderhall.

1931: The pitch at the Gymnasium Ground has been turned through 90 degrees, New Logie Green has all but disappeared, and substantial terracing has been added to New Powderhall.

St. Bernards:	Leith Athletic:	Edinburgh City:
1878–80: Stockbridge Park	–	–
1880–89: Gymnasium	–	–
	1887–90: Hawkhill	–
1889: (Old) Powderhall		–
1889: (New) Powderhall	1890–94: Bank Park	–
1889: Gymnasium		–
1889–01: New Logie Green	1895–99: Beechwood Park	–
	1899–00: Hawkhill/	–
1901 – (New) Powderhall	New Logie Green	–
	1900–04: Chancelot Park	–
1901–16: Gymnasium	1904–16: Old Logie Green	–
1919–24: Tynecastle	1919–24: Chancelot &	–
	Wardie Parks	–
1924–42: Gymnasium	1924–26: Old Logie Green	–
	1926–28: (New)Powderhall	–
	1928–36: Marine Gardens	1928–31: Marine Gardens
	1936–42: Meadowbank	1931–34: (New) Powderhall
	1946–47: Old Meadowbank	1934–35: Marine Gardens
		1935–54: East Pilton Park
	1947–54: Meadowbank	

N.B. '(New) Powderhall' was built in 1889. 'Old Logie Green', which succeeded 'New Logie Green' was a completely separate Ground ('New Logie Green' was the site of the former 'Old Powderhall'). 'Meadowbank' and 'Old Meadowbank' were adjacent Grounds. 'Bank' and 'Beechwood' Parks are believed to have been one and the same.